Best wishes

LET ME TELL YOU
ABOUT WINE

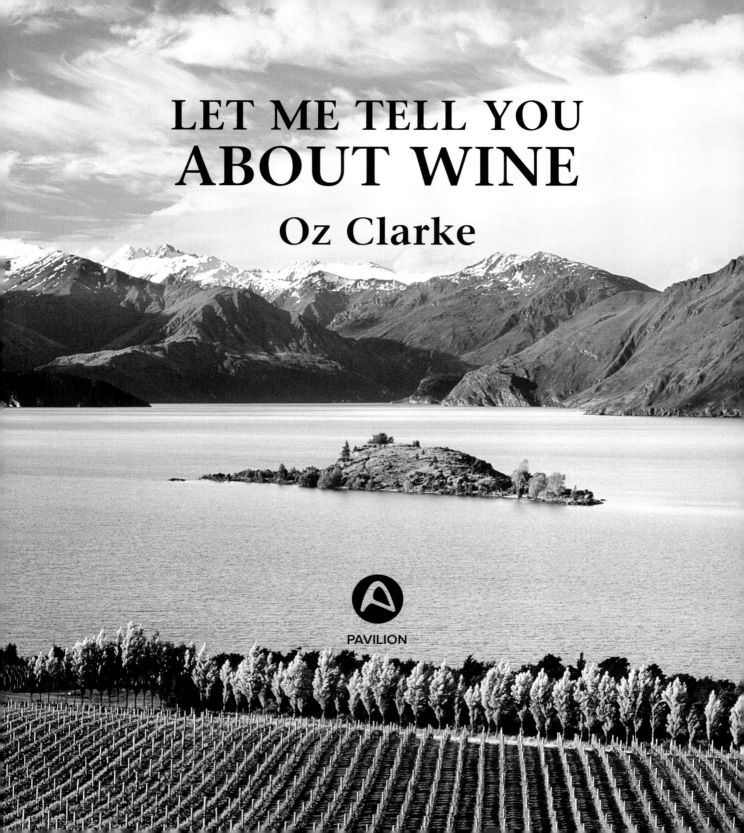

LET ME TELL YOU ABOUT WINE

Oz Clarke

PAVILION

First published in 2009 by Pavilion Books
Reprinted 2011, 2012

An imprint of Anova Books Company Limited
10 Southcombe Street, London W14 0RA

www.anovabooks.com
www.ozclarke.com

A CIP catalogue for this book is available from the British Library

ISBN 978 1 862 05865 1

10 9 8 7 6 5 4

Commissioning editor Fiona Holman
Designers Georgina Hewitt and Isobel Gillan
Editors Maggie Ramsay and Andy Lloyd
Indexer Angie Hipkin
Colour reproduction by Dot Gradations, London
Printed and bound by Times Offset in Malaysia

READER'S NOTE
In **Part One, Discover Grape Varieties** the star symbol ★ next to
a grape heading indicates that the grape has been highlighted by Oz as
a future star

In **Part Three, The World of Wine**, the price bands for the wines
recommended in the *Quick Guide* sections, for example on page 112,
correspond to the following sterling prices for a standard 75cl bottle.
Prices are intended for guidance only and may vary.

➊ under £7   ➋ £7–£12   ➌ £12–£18

➍ £18–£25   ➎ over £25

Pages 2–3 Lake Wanaka in Central Otago in New Zealand's South Island
is for me one of the world's most beautiful wine regions.

PICTURE ACKNOWLEDGMENTS
Front cover Anova Books (Gary Moyes)
Back cover Cephas (Duncan Johnson)
Alamy Pat and Chuck Blackley 167; Michael Busselle 99;
Lordprice Collection 104; Hans-Peter Siffert 129; Westend 61 GmbH/
Holger Spiering 191
Anova Books Stephen Bartholomew 83 (above), 89, 90; Robert Hall 86,
86–87 (below), 95; Gary Moyes 7, 26, 38, 77, 94, 97; Lucinda Symons 1,
10, 18, 23 (left), 56 (left), 65, 82, 83 (below), 84, 85, 145
Cephas Picture Library 57; Jerry Alexander 163; Kevin Argue 171;
Nigel Blythe 27, 68, 109 (left), 124, 153; Karine Bossavy 105;
Hervé Champollion 113; Andy Christodolo 2–3, 34 (left), 48, 132 (left),
156 (right), 173; Jeff Drewitz 184; Fresh Food Images 9 (above),
9 (centre), 22; Dario Fusaro 130, 131; Mark Graham 193 (right); Tom
Hyland 31; Duncan Johnson 60; Kevin Judd 4–5, 34 (right), 41 (right), 49
(background), 49 (below), 50, 52, 53, 176, 179, 180, 187; Pierre Lapin 13,
15 (left), 19 (left), 20, 100; Herbert Lehmann 92, 128, 155, 158; Joris
Luyten 74; Char Abu Mansoor 193 (left); Diana Mewes 146 (left); Jánis
Miglavs 46; R & K Muschenetz 162, 174; David Pearce 15 (right); Neil
Phillips 138; Alain Proust 117, 190; Graeme Robinson 189; Mick Rock 28,
29, 30, 33, 35, 36, 40, 43, 44 (right), 45 (above), 49 (above), 54, 55 (left),
55 (right), 56 (right), 61 (left), 61 (right), 63, 71, 108, 118, 120–121, 122,
126, 132 (right), 134, 136–137, 139, 142, 146, 141, 146 (right), 147, 148,
149, 150, 154, 164, 166, 181; Ian Shaw 58, 59, 62, 67; Ted Stefanski 9
(below), 37 (above), 39; Martin Walls 156 (left); Matt Wilson 32, 177
Bodega y Estancia Colomé Ossian Lindholm 47
Corbis Tom Bean 42; Richard Klune 44 (left); Gunter Marx 170;
Swim Ink 2, LLC, poster by Jean d'Ylen 45 (below);
iStockphoto pages 12, 14, 19 (right), 23 (right), 24, 25
Jánis Miglavs page 165
Tourism Queensland page 185
Visit Missouri/Hermann page 168
Wines from Brazil page 172
Wines of Colorado page 169

Contents

Next time you walk into a wine shop, stop for a moment and have a good look around. Don't head straight for this month's special offer, don't blinker your vision to everything but your trusty favourites, just have a good gawp at the whole range that's on display. If the shop is big and you're anything like me, your head will start to spin and the overwhelming abundance of different wines will leave you dizzy with delight. Imagine it – there's a unique flavour stoppered up in every one of those bottles. So open your mind, pick a bottle, any bottle, and head off on a lifetime's joyous voyage of discovery.

But is it really worth making the effort to know the difference between all those bottles on the shelf? Oh yes! Yes, yes and yes again. Just a little knowledge will double the pleasure you get from a glass of wine and will give you the key to choosing wines that you like. And if a little knowledge can give you that, does a little more knowledge sound attractive? That's why this book is here, to help you look beyond those special offers and trusty favourites – to help you discover for yourself a world of new, exciting and delicious flavours. Are you ready? Then get reading, get shopping and start enjoying yourself!

PART ONE
THE FLAVOURS OF WINE

When you buy wine, buy it for its flavour. Reputation, packaging and price all vie to influence your choice, but they can't titillate your tastebuds. The grape variety used is the most significant factor in determining the taste of a wine, but everything that happens to the grapes and their juice on the long journey from the vine to the glass in your hand contributes to that wine's unique identity. Read on and start getting the flavour you want.

get the flavour you want

Your chances of walking into a wine shop and coming out with a wine that's enjoyable to drink, whatever the price level, are better now than ever before. The last quarter of the 20th century saw a revolution in wine, in terms of both style and quality.

All wines are cleaner and fresher-tasting than they were; reds are juicier, rounder and softer; whites are snappier, zestier, more appetizing. There are more new oak barrels being used in expensive wines, which in terms of taste means vanilla and buttered toast. But this isn't to say that all wines taste alike. Indeed, there's never been a wider choice. It's just that modern winemaking is rapidly eliminating faults – it's not eliminating individuality.

So how do you choose? How do you tell a wine that's just right for summer lunch in the garden from one that would be better suited to a winter evening in front of a log fire? Well, imagine if you could walk into a wine shop and just pick up a bottle from the 'green, tangy white' shelf or go for a 'spicy, warm-hearted red'. That would make things pretty easy, wouldn't it?

You see, all those thousands of different flavours fall into the 18 broad styles shown here and which I describe in detail over the next few pages. So, even if you don't yet know a thing about grape varieties and wine-producing regions, just choose a style that appeals and I'll point you in the right direction. And come back to these pages whenever you fancy something new – I'll do my best to set you off on a whole new flavour adventure.

1 Juicy, fruity reds

Refreshing, approachable and delicious – Chilean Merlot shows what modern red wine is all about

2 Silky, strawberryish reds

Mellow, perfumed wine with red fruit flavours – Pinot Noir is the classic grape for this

3 Intense, blackcurranty reds

Reds from Cabernet Sauvignon are most likely to give you this traditionalist's thrill

4 Spicy, warm-hearted reds

Gloriously rich flavours of berries, black pepper and chocolate – Aussie Shiraz can't be beaten

5 Mouthwatering, herby reds

Intriguing wines with a rasping herby bite and sweet-sour red fruit flavours – Italian reds do this better than any others

6 Earthy, savoury reds

The classic food wines of Europe, led by France's Bordeaux and Italy's Chianti

7 Delicate rosés

Fragrant, refreshing and dry – an elegant summer apéritif. Bordeaux and southern France hit the spot

8 Gutsy rosés

More colour, more fruit flavour, more texture to roll around your mouth. Spain, Chile, Australia and New Zealand do best

9 Sweet rosés

Blush is the usual name, and most of it comes from California as Zinfandel. Anjou Rosé is France's version

10 Bone-dry, neutral whites

Crisp, refreshing wines like Muscadet and Pinot Grigio

11 Green, tangy whites

Sharp, gooseberryish Sauvignon Blanc from New Zealand, South Africa and Chile lead the way

12 Intense, nutty whites

Dry yet succulent, subtle and powerful – white Burgundy sets the style

13 Ripe, toasty whites

Upfront flavours of peaches, apricots and tropical fruits with toasty richness – the traditional flavour of Aussie and Chilean Chardonnay

14 Aromatic whites

Perfumy wines with exotic and floral fragrances – Gewürztraminer gets my vote for scent, Viognier and Muscat for exotic fruit

15 Sparkling

Bubbles to make you happy and delicious flavours, too. Smile, you're drinking fun, not just wine

16 Rich, sweet whites

Luscious mouthfuls with intense flavours of peach, pineapple and honey, such as Sauternes

17 Warming, fortified

Sweet fortified wines with rich flavours – ports, madeiras and sweet brown sherries

18 Tangy, fortified

Bone dry with startling sour and nutty flavours – this is real sherry, and I love it

1 Juicy, fruity reds

Lots of fruit flavour makes for tasty, refreshing reds ideal for gulping down with or without food. This is the definitive modern style for the best cheap and not-quite-so-cheap red wines, emphasizing bright fruit flavours and minimizing the gum-drying toughness of tannin.

Chilean Merlot is bursting with blackberry, blackcurrant and plum flavours

This style had its birth in the New World – you'll find it in wines from **Australia**, **California**, **Washington State**, **New Zealand**, **South America** and **South Africa** – but it has spread right through Europe, overturning any lingering ideas that red wine must be aged. You don't age these wines. You buy them and you drink them. And then you buy some more. For juicy, fruity flavours, don't even look at a wine that's more than about two years old.

Chilean Merlot is the benchmark for this worldwide phenomenon: young, well-balanced, and bursting with blackberry, blackcurrant and plum flavours.

Spain produces lots of inexpensive soft, supple reds in the same mould. Anything from **La Mancha**, **Jumilla**, **Navarra**, **Campo de Borja** or **Calatayud** is worth a try, as are young **Valpolicella** and **Teroldego** from Italy and unoaked reds from Portugal's **Douro** region. **California** does a nice line in young Merlots and Zinfandels and **Argentina** has smooth Tempranillo, ultra-fruity Bonarda and juicy Malbec.

If you want French wine, **Beaujolais** is famous for this style, sometimes so fruity you think you're sucking fruit gums. **Loire Valley** reds have sharper, but very refreshing fruit and **Pays d'Oc Merlot** can be good.

2 Silky, strawberryish reds

Mellow, perfumed reds with a gentle strawberry, raspberry or cherry fruit fragrance and flavour. Good ones feel silky in your mouth.

Pinot Noir is the grape that produces the supreme examples of this style. Great Pinot Noir has a silkiness of texture no other grape can emulate. Only a few regions make it well and the good stuff is expensive.

Pinot Noir's home territory, and the place where it achieves greatness, is **Burgundy** in France (**Bourgogne** in French). Virtually all red Burgundy is made from Pinot Noir. The best wines mature to develop aromas of truffles, game and decaying autumn leaves – sounds horrible, I know, but just one taste is enough to get some people hooked for life.

Beyond Burgundy the best Pinot Noir comes from **California** – particularly **Carneros**, **Sonoma Coast**, **Russian River** and **Santa Barbara** – from **Oregon**, **Chile**, **New Zealand** and, occasionally, **Australia**. **Germany** can nowadays hit the spot, too, with fine Pinot Noir, locally called Spätburgunder.

Cheap Pinot Noir is rarely good, but **Chile**'s usually have loads of vibrant jellied fruit flavour. **Somontano** in Spain has some tasty budget examples, too.

Red **Rioja** and **Navarra**, also from Spain but made from different grapes, principally Tempranillo, are soft and smooth with a fragrant strawberryish quality. This also appears in the lightest **Côtes du Rhône-Villages** from France. None of these wines, however, has the silkiness of Pinot Noir.

Red Rioja and Navarra
are soft and smooth
with a fragrant
strawberryish quality

3 Intense, blackcurranty reds

Full-flavoured red wines with a distinctive blackcurrant flavour and those slightly bitter tannins from the grape skins that dry your mouth but make it water at the same time. They're made from Cabernet Sauvignon alone or blended with Merlot and other grapes to enrich the fruit flavours and soften the texture.

Cabernet Sauvignon is the grape to look for here. The Cabernet-based red wines of **Bordeaux** in France are the original blackcurranty wines with, at their best, a fragrance of cigar boxes and lead pencils. **New World Cabernets** have more blackcurrant, but also a vanilla-y flavour and sometimes mint. It's hard to know who's ahead on quality at the top. At the less expensive end it's perfectly obvious: the New World wins almost every time. The cheapest red Bordeaux can be joyless stuff.

Nevertheless, Cabernet Sauvignon is one of the most reliable wines you can get. It retains its characteristic flavours wherever it's from, and at every price level – and that's rare in wine. Expensive ones should be ripe and rich with layers of intense flavour; cheaper ones have simpler flavours that are more earthy, more jammy, or more green-pepper lean.

For budget Cabernets, check out **Argentina, Chile, Australia, South Africa** and France's **Pays d'Oc**. If you want to pay a bit more, try **Penedès** in Spain, **South Africa, New Zealand** and **Chile** again, and, cautiously, Bordeaux or its better-value neighbour, **Bergerac. Australia** and **California** at the higher price level is outstanding. You'll also find these blackcurrant flavours in Spain's **Ribera del Duero**, from the Tempranillo grape, and a number of grapes, especially Touriga Nacional, give black fruit flavours in **Portugal**.

4   Spicy, warm-hearted reds

Dense, heartwarming, gloriously rich flavours of blackberry and loganberry, black pepper and chocolate, and mainly found in Syrah/Shiraz.

Australian Shiraz is the wine to try: often dense, rich and chocolaty, sometimes fresher, with peppery, blackberry fruit, sometimes with a whiff of smoke or a slap of leather. You can get good examples at all price levels. In France's **Rhône Valley** the same grape is called Syrah, and, of course, it was grown here long before the Aussies got their hands on it. Rhône Syrah tends to be a little more austere in style, and smoky-minerally to Australia's rich spice, but the best have lush blackberry fruit. Look for the label **Crozes-Hermitage** or **St-Joseph**.

For good value from France try **Pays d'Oc Syrah**, **Fitou**, **Minervois** or heavier styles of **Côtes du Rhône-Villages** (lighter ones are more in the silky, strawberryish style). **Portugal** offers good value with a whole host of indigenous grape varieties found nowhere else. In Spain, try the weighty plums and vanilla flavours of **Toro** and the more expensive **Montsant** and **Priorat**.

California Zinfandel and **Petite Sirah** are powerful, spicy and rich. **Argentina**'s heart-warming **Malbecs** and **Chile**'s great big spicy-savoury mouthfuls of **Carmenère** are excellent value. Take a look at **South Africa**'s smoky **Pinotage**, too.

5   Mouthwatering, herby reds

Intriguing wines with sweet-sour cherry and plum fruit flavours and a rasping herby bite. These wines almost all hail from Italy and have a character that's distinctly different from the international mob.

Sicilian reds are rich and mouthfilling

It must be something to do with the Italian attitude to drinking wine. With food. Always. There's a rasp of sourness in these reds that's intended to cut through steak or pasta sauce, not be sipped as an apéritif. You'll find that same irresistible sour-cherries edge on wines made from all sorts of grapes – **Dolcetto**, **Sangiovese**, **Barbera** – in wines from **Chianti**, and in the rare but lip-smacking **Teroldego**, **Lagrein** and **Refosco**. Some may have a delicious raisiny taste, too. Even light, low-tannin **Valpolicella** – at its best – has this flavour.

Up in Piedmont, tough, tannic wines from **Barolo** and **Barbaresco**, made from the stern **Nebbiolo** grape, have a fascinating tar-and-roses flavour. Good Barolo is frighteningly expensive these days, but a decent **Langhe** will give you the flavour for less money. Down in the South, there's a whole raft of reds, made from grapes like **Negroamaro** and **Primitivo**, which add round, pruny flavours to the sour-cherry bite. **Sicilian** reds, especially **Nero d'Avola**, are rich and mouthfilling.

California and **Australia** are starting to get to grips with Sangiovese, Barbera and Nebbiolo.

Argentina's Bonarda and Teroldego from **Brazil** can have a refreshing acid streak.

6 Earthy, savoury reds

These are the classic food wines of Europe, the kind where fruit flavours often take a back seat to compatibility with food and the ability to cleanse the palate and stimulate the appetite.

France, especially **Bordeaux**, is the leader in this style. I'm not necessarily talking about the glitzy, expensive Bordeaux wines, rare, difficult to obtain and costing increasingly silly amounts of money, but most Bordeaux reds do keep an earthy quality underpinning their richness. Even **St-Émilion** and **Pomerol** generally blend attractive savouriness with lush fruit. Below the top level are **Haut-Médoc**, **Médoc**, **Pessac-Léognan** and **Graves**, whose strong or earthy flavours are usually excellent. **Côtes de Bourg**, **Blaye** and basic **Bordeaux** and **Bordeaux Supérieur** are usually marked by earthy, savoury qualities. You can find these flavours all over **South-West France**.

Italy's main earthy, savoury type is **Chianti**, though the top levels move up into something altogether richer. Basic **Sangiovese** and **Montepulciano** wines throughout Italy often share this trait, as will whatever nameless carafe of red you pour with your pasta in a thousand villages nationwide. Of the Eastern European reds, **Croatian** and **Hungarian** Merlot are refreshingly earthy, **Greek** reds almost stony, and the more basic reds of northern **Portugal** and **Spain** follow this line, but generally it is cool-climate wines that are most likely to taste like this.

In the New World fruit is riper and generally too rich for many of these styles to thrive, but some Cabernets and Merlots from places like **Canada**, **New York**, **Washington State**, **New Zealand**, **South Africa** and even **China** may fit the bill.

Red wine wheel

Here's another way to get the flavour you want. I've arranged the world's red wines according to their intensity and the broad type of flavour. The wines at the outer edge have layer upon layer of flavour; those near the centre are light and simple.

Black fruits Blackcurrant, blackberry, dark plum, damson and black cherry flavours.

Red fruits The soft flavours of strawberries and raspberries and sharper hints of cranberries and red cherries.

Herbs/spices The wild flavours of herbs or dried herbs; peppery and aromatic spices; often mixed with tastes such as chocolate or liquorice.

KEY

The styles I have described in this chapter fit the zones of the wheel like this:

Juicy, fruity reds RED FRUITS or BLACK FRUITS, with light to medium intensity

Silky, strawberryish reds RED FRUITS, though the most intense have a shade of BLACK FRUITS, too.

Intense, blackcurranty reds BLACK FRUITS, maybe with a touch of RED FRUITS or HERBS/SPICES.

Spicy, warm-hearted reds HERBS/SPICES, but many combine this with RED FRUITS or BLACK FRUITS.

Mouthwatering, sweet-sour reds RED FRUITS and HERBS/SPICES.

Earthy, savoury reds BLACK FRUITS or RED FRUITS and HERBS/SPICES.

BLACK FRUITS

top Californian Cabernet Sauvignon

top Australian Cabernet Sauvignon

top Washington Cabernet and Merlot

top Bordeaux from St-Émilion and Pomerol

top Bordeaux from the Médoc

top Pessac-Léognan

top Chilean and South African Cabernet Sauvignon

Ribera del Duero

BLACK AND RED FRUITS

BLACK FRUITS AND HERBS/SPICES

top Argentine Malbec

top Chilean Merlot

mid-priced Australian Cabernet Sauvignon

New Zealand Merlot

top Loire reds (Chinon, Bourgueil, Saumur-Champigny)

top Australian Shiraz

Douro

mid-priced Californian Cabernet Sauvignon

Navarra

mid-priced South African Cabernet Sauvignon

big Zinfandel

southern Portuguese reds

New Zealand Cabernet Sauvignon

hefty Pinotage

mid-priced Argentine Malbec

mid-priced Bordeaux (crus bourgeois)

Bulgarian Cabernet Sauvignon

South African Shiraz

light Australian Shiraz

Hungarian reds

Côte-Rôtie

Priorat

California Syrah and Mourvèdre

cheap Chilean Cabernet and Merlot

Loire reds (Chinon, Bourgueil, Saumur-Champigny)

Hermitage

Toro

North Italian Merlot

Valdepeñas and La Mancha

Premier and Grand Cru Burgundy

Mexican Petite Sirah

Coteaux du Languedoc and Côtes du Roussillon

Penedès

LIGHT AND SIMPLE

LIGHT AND SIMPLE

LIGHT AND SIMPLE

LIGHT AND SIMPLE

simple Burgundy and light Beaujolais

light Rioja

Australian Pinot Noir

Chilean and South African Pinot Noir

Minervois

Austrian reds

cheap German reds

Beaujolais crus

New York Pinot Noir

Cornas

Fitou

cheap Bordeaux

cheap Italian reds

cheap Argentine reds

Argentine Tempranillo and Bonarda

Côtes du Rhône

New Zealand Reserva and Gran Reserva

Crozes-Hermitage and St-Joseph

Cahors

Chianti Classico

light Chianti

Provence reds (e.g. Bandol)

basic French Cabernet and Merlot

Costières de Nîmes

light Pinotage

Oregon Pinot Noir

good Burgundy

HERBS/SPICES

Dão and Bairrada

Valpolicella Classico

mid-priced Zinfandel

top Rioja Reserva and Gran Reserva

Barbera

southern Italian reds

Corbières

Dolcetto

RED FRUITS

Brunello di Montalcino

Barolo

Barbaresco

Chianti Classico Riserva and Vino Nobile di Montepulciano

Côtes du Rhône-Villages

Gigondas and Vacqueyras

Australian old vines Grenache

RED FRUITS AND HERBS/SPICES

Châteauneuf-du-Pape

7   Delicate rosés

Good rosé should be fragrant and refreshing, and deliciously dry – not sickly and sweet.

France is a good hunting ground for this style of wine. Attractive, slightly leafy-tasting **Bordeaux Rosé** is usually based on Merlot. **Bordeaux Clairet** is a lightish red, virtually rosé but with more substance. **Cabernet d'Anjou** from the Loire Valley is a bit sweeter but tasty. Better still is **Rosé de Loire**, a lovely dry wine. Elegant Pinot Noir rosés come from **Sancerre** in the upper Loire and **Marsannay** in northern Burgundy. In the south of France and southern Rhône Valley (**Coteaux d'Aix-en-Provence**, **Lubéron** and **Ventoux**) produce plenty of dry but fruity rosés. **Costières de Nîmes** produces light, slightly scented styles. **Côtes de Provence** is dry, beguilingly smooth but often expensive. **Bandol** and **Bellet** are pricier still from specific coastal regions of Provence.

Northern Italy produces light, fresh pale rosé called *chiaretto*, from **Bardolino** and **Riviera del Garda Bresciano** on the shores of Lake Garda and from the same grapes as neighbouring red Valpolicella, and **Lagrein** from high in the Dolomites. Finally, another wine to try is tasty Garnacha rosado from **Navarra** and **Rioja** in northern Spain. And **English** pinks are coming on nicely.

8   Gutsy rosés

Dry, fruity rosé can be wonderful, with flavours of strawberries and maybe raspberries and rosehips, cherries, apples and herbs, too.

Most countries make a dry rosé, and any red grape will do. Look for wines made from sturdy grapes like Cabernet, Syrah or Merlot, or go for Grenache/Garnacha or Tempranillo from Spain's **La Mancha**, **Campo de Borja** and **Jumilla**. **Puglia** and **Sicily** in southern Italy make mouthfilling rosés, too. In the southern Rhône Valley big, strong, dry rosés from **Tavel** and **Lirac** go well with food. Drink them young at only a year or so old if you want a refreshing wine.

South America is a good bet for flavoursome, fruit-forward pink wine – try robust **Shiraz** and **Cabernet** from **Chile** or **Malbec** from **Argentina**. Other wines to try include dry, fairly full rosé from **California**, often from **Syrah** (not to be confused with the sweeter 'blush' Californian rosés, often labelled as White Zinfandel), fruity Australian **Grenache** from the **Barossa Valley**, or **New Zealand** pinks.

9   Sweet rosés

The original examples are Rosé d'Anjou (from the Loire) and Mateus and Lancers rosé (from Portugal).

Zinfandel from California, which is white with just a hint of pink and often described as 'blush', is fairly sweet, but OK as a chilled-down drink. Other sweetish rosés are **Rosé d'Anjou** from the Loire Valley, usually sweetish without much flavour, and Portuguese rosés such as **Mateus** and **Lancers**.

10 Bone-dry, neutral whites

Crisp, refreshing whites whose flavours won't set the world alight – but chill them down and set them next to a plate of shellfish and you've got the perfect combination.

These wines may not sound very enticing, but there are plenty of occasions when you just don't want to be hit over the palate with oak and tropical fruit.

In France, **Muscadet** from the Loire Valley is the most neutral of the lot. Unoaked **Chablis** from Burgundy is the adaptable Chardonnay grape in a dry, minerally style.

Italy specializes in this sort of wine, because Italians don't really like their white wines to be aromatic. So **Frascati**, most **Soave**, **Orvieto**, **Verdicchio**, **Lugana**, **Pinot Grigio**, **Pinot Bianco** and **Chardonnay** from the north all fit the bill. **Greek** whites are usually pretty neutral, but often brushed with minerality.

You won't often find this style in the New World – winemakers there don't want neutrality in their wines. Even when they grow the same vines (and mostly they don't), they make fuller, more flavoursome wines from them – even from Pinot Grigio. **Chenin Blanc** from **South Africa** at the lower price levels gets close.

11 Green, tangy whites

Sharp, zesty, love-them-or-hate-them wines, often with the smell and taste of gooseberries.

Sauvignon Blanc from **New Zealand** – especially from **Marlborough** – has tangy, mouthwatering flavours by the bucketful. **Chile** makes similar, slightly softer wines, **South African** versions can have real bite and Spain blends Sauvignon with Verdejo to give **Rueda** some extra zip.

Sancerre and **Pouilly-Fumé** from the Loire Valley in France are crisp and refreshing with lighter fruit flavours and a minerally or even a smoky edge. **Sauvignon de Touraine** offers similar flavours at lower prices.

The biggest bargain in Sauvignon Blanc is dry white **Bordeaux**. It's generally labelled as **Bordeaux Sauvignon Blanc** or maybe **Bordeaux Blanc**, and standards have risen out of sight in recent years. It's always softer than Loire or New Zealand versions.

The Loire also produces sharp-edged wines from **Chenin Blanc**, such as **Vouvray** and **white Anjou**. Loire Chenin has a minerally acid bite when young, but becomes rich and honeyed with age.

Riesling is the other grape to look out for here. Rieslings can be peachy, minerally or smoky when young, with a streak of green apple and some high-tensile acidity. With a few years' bottle age those flavours mingle and mellow to a wonderful honeyed, petrolly flavour – sounds disgusting, tastes heavenly. The leanest, often with a touch of scented sweetness to balance the acidity, come from Germany's **Mosel Valley**; slightly richer ones come from the **Rhine**; drier, weightier ones from **Austria** and **Alsace**. **Australian Rieslings**, particularly from the **Clare** and **Eden Valleys**, start bone dry and age to an irresistible limes-and-toast flavour.

12 Intense, nutty whites

Dry yet succulent whites with subtle nut and oatmeal flavours. These wines are generally oak-aged and have a soft edge with a backbone of absolute dryness.

If you like this style, you've got a taste for French classics, because the best expression of it is oak-aged Chardonnay in the form of white **Burgundy**. This is the wine that earned Chardonnay its renown in the first place and the style is sometimes matched in the best examples from **California, New York State, New Zealand, Australia** and **South Africa**. Not any old examples, mind you – just the best. Italian producers in **Tuscany** are having a go, too.

Top-quality oak-aged **Graves** and **Pessac-Léognan** from Bordeaux are Sémillon blended with Sauvignon Blanc, giving a creamy, nutty wine with a hint of nectarines. Unoaked **Australian Semillon** (note the 'unoaked' – it means it hasn't been aged in oak barrels) from the **Hunter** and **Barossa Valleys** matures to become waxy and rich. The best white **Rioja** from Spain, too, becomes nutty and lush with time.

None of these wines comes cheap and they all need time to show their best. Less costly alternatives which give an idea of the style are Spanish Chardonnays from **Navarra** and **Somontano**.

White wine wheel

This wheel of dry white wine styles works in the same way as the red wine wheel on pages 16–17. The wines at the outer edge have layers of intense flavour; those near the centre are light and simple.

Fruity Peachy, tropical fruit or honeyish flavours without the buttery overlay of oak.

Crisp Fresh, clean flavours with a bite, like lime, gooseberry or green apples.

Aromatic Wines with intense floral or exotic fragrances such as lychees and rose petals.

Oaky Wines with the toasty vanilla flavours that come from oak barrels.

Wine flavours

Increasing intensity

KEY

The styles I have described in this chapter fit the zones of the wheel like this:

Bone dry, neutral whites The lightest wines in the CRISP zone.

Green, tangy whites CRISP wines, but shading into FRUITY and into AROMATIC styles.

Intense, nutty whites These are OAKY wines; the best are intense but subtle.

Ripe, toasty whites Wines full of OAKY and FRUITY flavours.

Aromatics They have the AROMATIC zone to themselves, but some are OAKY too.

OAKY AND FRUITY

OAKY

Grand Cru Burgundy

top Californian, Australian, NZ, South African and Italian Chardonnay

Graves and Pessac-Léognan

Australian oaked Semillon

Australian Chardonnay/Semillon

top NZ and South African Riesling

FRUITY

good Burgundy

oaked Rioja

mid-priced Chardonnay from Australia, California, Washington and Chile

Alsace Pinot Gris

oaked South African Chenin Blanc

Australian and NZ Semillon/Sauvignon

cool-climate Chardonnay from the USA, Canada and NZ

mid-priced Chardonnay from South Africa and southern France

Hungarian Chardonnay

Viognier from southern France

AROMATIC AND OAKY

Viognier from the northern Rhône (Condrieu and Château-Grillet)

Viognier from Australia and California

NZ Sauvignon Blanc (North Island)

Californian Fumé Blanc

Bulgarian Chardonnay

Australian Chenin Blanc and Verdelho

basic French Sauvignon Blanc

Colombard

Chilean Sauvignon Blanc

South African Sauvignon Blanc

NZ Sauvignon Blanc (South Island)

CRISP AND FRUITY

top NZ Sauvignon Blanc

good Rhône whites from Marsanne and Roussanne

SIMPLE

LIGHT AND

LIGHT AND

SIMPLE

Trebbiano

cheap South African Chenin Blanc

Soave

Verdicchio

Vinho Verde

North Italian Chardonnay

Entre-Deux-Mers and Bordeaux Blanc

Vouvray and Saumur

Sancerre and Pouilly-Fumé

Australian Riesling

Müller-Thurgau

Liebfraumilch

Alsace Pinot Blanc

unoaked Chablis and basic Burgundy

NE Italian Pinot Grigio and Pinot Bianco

Savennières

Rueda

Oregon Pinot Gris

Hungarian (Irsai Olivér)

dry Muscat

Italian and southern French

Argentine Torrontés

Alto Adige Gewürztraminer

Austrian Grüner Veltliner

dry German Riesling (Rhine)

Washington Riesling

Austrian Riesling

Premier and Grand Cru Chablis

dry white Rioja

AROMATIC AND OAKY

Gewürztraminer from NZ and Chile

Alsace Muscat

off-dry German Riesling (Rhine)

Rias Baixas

New York Riesling

dry German Riesling (Mosel)

off-dry German Riesling (Mosel)

Premier and Grand Cru Chablis (unoaked)

Alsace Riesling

CRISP

AROMATIC

CRISP AND AROMATIC

13 Ripe, toasty whites

Upfront flavours of peaches, apricots and tropical fruits, spiced up by the vanilla, toast and butterscotch richness of new oak barrels. Modern examples are generally showing more restraint.

This is the flavour of the **Chardonnays** that shocked and thrilled the world when **California** and then **Australia** began making them 30 years ago. They changed our view of what was possible in white wine flavour and style. Since then we have begun to back off a little from such lush flavours and the producers have throttled back a good deal. Many current Californian and Australian examples are relatively restrained. But the high-octane Chardies are still around if you hanker for the buzz.

The style was virtually invented in California and Australia, and it has been the hallmark of most Chardonnay in the **US** and **South America**, as well as being common in **South Africa**. Chardonnay from the north-east of **Spain** and many **Italian** versions – particularly those from the south – also fit in here.

Not that the style is confined to Chardonnay. If you ferment **Viognier** in new oak it also gives toasty, exotic results. **Sémillon** in oak becomes mouthfilling and creamy, and barrel-fermented **South African Chenin** can be quite a mouthful. It's not so difficult to give lots of different whites that tropical flavour, and new oak barrels will supply the toast and butterscotch – but Chardonnay was the original and is still the best.

14 Aromatic whites

Perfumy white wines combining exotic fragrances with aromas of spring flowers.

It seems impossible that a wine could smell and taste the way **Gewurztraminer** from **Alsace** does. It's packed solid with roses and lychees, face cream and a whole kitchen spice cupboard. No, it's not subtle, but with spicy food, especially Chinese, it can be wonderful.

Viognier is at its apricots-and-spring flowers best in Condrieu

Nowhere else in the world has the nerve to produce such over-the-top Gewürztraminer. **German** versions are more floral, and the **Italians** prefer to make their Traminer rather more toned down. But **Slovenia**, **Slovakia**, **Croatia** and the **Czech Republic** have a go, and **New Zealand** Gewürztraminer is a delight.

If you want this sort of full-blown aroma from other grapes, then it's back to Alsace. Dry **Muscat** here is floral with a heady, hothouse grape scent. **Southern France** and **Spain** make less scented styles, and you can get delicate floral Muscats in **northern Italy**, sometimes pink and sometimes as scented as tea-rose petals.

You still want more aromatic grapes? **Viognier**, at its apricots-and-spring flowers best in **Condrieu**, in the northern Rhône Valley, is planted in the **south of France**, **California** and **Australia** as well; and **Godello** from north-west Spain is also apricotty, but crisper. **Irsai Olivér** from **Hungary**, **Torrontés** from **Argentina** and **Malagousia** from **Greece** are heady and perfumed. **Müller-Thurgau**, from **Germany**, **Luxembourg** or **England**, can have a light, vaguely floral scent.

15 Sparkling wines

Fizz is there to make you feel brighter and happier – but good bubbly can have delicious flavours as well.

Champagne – the genuine article from the Champagne region of northern France – sets the standard. Good Champagne has a nutty, bready aroma, appley freshness and fine bubbles. Don't buy the cheapest, though: much of it is too acidic to be drinkable, let alone enjoyable.

Good Champagne has an appley freshness

Sparkling wine from **Australia**, **California** and **New Zealand** is made in the same way and it's often just as good and usually cheaper. Much of the best stuff in these countries is made by subsidiaries of French Champagne producers – Roederer, Veuve Clicquot and Moet & Chandon are the most active.

Other good French fizzes are the elegant **Crémant de Bourgogne** from Burgundy and **Crémant d'Alsace**, the rather sharp sparkling **Saumur** from the Loire Valley and the appley **Blanquette de Limoux** from the south.

Italian sparklers made from **Chardonnay** and **Pinot Noir** are in the Champagne style, but light, creamy **Prosecco** and sweet, grapy **Asti** can be more fun. The best **Lambrusco** is red, snappy and refreshingly sharp, but the sweetened stuff is pretty dull. Spanish **Cava** can be a bit earthy, but is good value. German **Sekt** is often pretty poor, but when made from Riesling can be lean, sharp and refreshing.

Australian sparkling red wines are wild things, packed with pepper and blackberry jam. You'll love them or hate them, but you haven't lived until you've given them a try.

16 Rich, sweet whites

Rich, luscious mouthfuls for dessert time or when you're in a contemplative mood, often with intense flavours of peach, pineapple and honey.

In France the sweet wines of Bordeaux are at their gorgeous best in **Sauternes** and **Barsac**. These are rich and syrupy wines with intense flavours of peaches and pineapples, barley sugar, butterscotch and honey, all balanced by acidity, and they can age for 20 years or more. **Monbazillac, Cérons, Loupiac** and **Ste-Croix-du-Mont** are happy hunting grounds for cheaper, lighter versions. **California, New Zealand** and **Australia** have a few intensely rich wines in this style, too.

The Loire Valley produces rather unusual sweet wines that are less rich and often less expensive. They're honey- and quince-flavoured with a firm acid grip and a minerally streak. **Quarts de Chaume, Bonnezeaux, Coteaux du Layon** and **Vouvray** are the wines to look for. Only a few Vouvrays are sweet: they're labelled as *moelleux* or *liquoreux*.

Alsace sweeties are rich and unctuous. **Sélection de Grains Nobles** is sweeter than **Vendange Tardive**, and **Gewurztraminer** versions will be fatter than **Pinot Gris**, which will in turn be fatter than **Riesling**.

The sweet wines of **Germany** have a language all of their own. **Beerenauslese** and **Trockenbeerenauslese** are intensely sweet and extremely expensive; **Auslese** is less sweet and less expensive. All should be very high quality, and the best are made from Riesling: its piercing acidity keeps the sweetness from being overpowering. **Austria**'s sweet wines are similar in style to Germany's, but tend to be weightier.

There's also a rarity called **Eiswein** made from frozen grapes picked in the depths of winter, which manages a thrilling marriage of fierce acidity and unctuous sweetness. Apricotty **Canadian icewine** is made in the same way, and **China** has made some.

Hungary's **Tokaji** has a wonderful sweet-sour smoky flavour and quality is very high. Simple sweet **Muscat** from Spain, such as **Moscatel de Valencia**, is a simple-hearted splash of rich fruit but incredibly good value.

TWO TYPES OF SWEETNESS

Sweet wine is wine that is perceptibly sugary – you can detect the sweetness on your tongue tip. However, an ever-increasing number of modern dry wines emphasize ripe fruit flavours, which I often describe as **sweet fruits** to do them justice. Fruit is at its most delicious when it's ripe, and it's sheer joy to taste those flavours in a wine. But fruit loses much of its character when it overripens: the freshness disappears, the flesh becomes soggy and soft. There is a move towards making dry wines at high alcohol levels from overripe fruit. One expert calls these 'dead fruit wines'. A good term. They are heavy and lifeless and rarely have you angling for a second glass. If I like a wine, I always want a second glass.

17 Warming, fortified wines

Sweet wines tasting of raisins and brown sugar, plum and blackberry syrup, and able to take on board all kinds of other scents or flavours as they age.

Port, the rich red fortified wine of Portugal's Douro Valley, is the classic dark sweet wine and no imitator can match the power or the finesse of the best, though **Australia** and **South Africa** both make exciting port-style wines. The Portuguese island of **Madeira** produces some of the most fascinating warming fortifieds, with rich brown smoky flavours and a startling acid bite: **Bual** and **Malmsey** are the sweet ones to look out for.

Oloroso dulce is a rare and delicious sherry with stunning, concentrated flavours and black-brown **Pedro Ximenez** (or **PX**) is about as sweet a mouthful as the world possesses. Cheap sweetened 'brown' sherry is a weak parody of these styles.

Australian sweet **Muscat** from the **Rutherglen** region is astonishingly rich and dark, even treacly. From the islands off southern Italy, the fortified **Marsala** of Sicily and **Moscato di Pantelleria** are good brown-sugar drinks with a refreshing shiver of acidity.

18 Tangy, fortified wines

Bone-dry wines with startling stark, sour and nutty flavours. It's a taste that takes a bit of getting used to, but which is well worth acquiring.

These are the original sherries from Jerez in Andalucía – check the label to make sure they're bottled where they were made – in southern Spain. **Fino** is pale in colour, very dry with a thrilling tang. **Manzanilla** can seem even drier, even leaner, and has a wonderful sourdough perfume and tingling acidity. **Amontillado** is chestnut-coloured and nutty. Traditionally amontillado is dry, not medium-sweet as we often see it. Dry **oloroso** adds deep, burnt flavours and at its intriguing best is one of the world's greatest wines.

Montilla-Moriles is the neighbouring region to Jerez and produces similar wines, but only the best of these reach the standard of good sherry. The driest style of Madeira, **Sercial**, is tangy, steely and savoury; **Verdelho** is a bit fuller and fatter.

Australia and **South Africa** make excellent sherry-style wines, though without the tang of top-class Spanish *fino* or *manzanilla*.

Manzanilla can seem even drier, even leaner, and has a wonderful sourdough perfume and tingling acidity

discover grape varieties

The simplest way to become familiar with wine flavours is through grape variety. Each grape variety has its own hallmark flavours, so two wines with different names made in places thousands of miles apart will have a fair amount in common if they're made from the same variety.

Not all wines are made from a single grape variety. Red Bordeaux, for example, usually contains at least three, and one of Australia's classic wine styles is a blend of two famous varieties: Cabernet Sauvignon and Shiraz. But once you know the taste of different grapes you'll have a good idea of what to expect from a blend.

Red wine grapes

I'm going to start with the red grapes – some people call them black, but they're deep purple or bluish in reality, so I reckon it's easier to link them to the type of wine they generally make. There's more to red wine than sturdiness, power and 'good with red meats and cheese'. Delicacy, freshness and intriguing perfumes are all within the scope of the world's red grape varieties. It all depends on where you grow the grapes and what style of wine the winemaker wants to achieve. In general, red grapes grown in warm places will give richer, riper styles, and you'll get more delicacy, perfume and restraint from grapes grown in cool places.

WINE TERMS **Noble grapes**

Some grapes have achieved such a level of greatness in a particular region that they have been elevated to the peerage of the grape world and are often referred to as noble grapes. The major examples are: **Cabernet Sauvignon** in Bordeaux, France; **Chardonnay** and **Pinot Noir** in Burgundy, France; **Syrah** in France's Rhône Valley and in South Australia, where it's called **Shiraz**; **Chenin Blanc** in France's Loire Valley; **Sauvignon Blanc** in the Loire Valley and New Zealand; **Nebbiolo** in Piedmont, Italy; **Sangiovese** in Tuscany, Italy; **Riesling** in Germany; and **Zinfandel** in California. You can find out about them in the next few pages.

Cabernet Sauvignon

The epitome of the intense, blackcurrant style of red wine, Cabernet Sauvignon is never among the lightest of reds and it always has some degree of tannic backbone. The best mature slowly to balance sweet blackcurrant flavours with a scent of cedar, cigar boxes and lead pencil shavings. It is often blended with Merlot for a richer flavour.

Where it grows Almost every country where wine is made has a fair bit of Cabernet in its vineyards. Bordeaux is its homeland, but you'll find it in the south of France as well. Italy has some top-class versions; good Spanish ones come mostly from Navarra or Penedès; and it produces inexpensive wine over large tracts of Eastern Europe, notably in Bulgaria.

New World examples are vibrantly fruity, with rich texture, soft tannins and sometimes a touch of mint or eucalyptus. California and Australia have world-class examples; Chile's have piercing fruit and are excellent value; South Africa's are dry and blackcurranty; and New Zealand goes for a style closer to Bordeaux.

Keep it or drink it? Lots of people think of Cabernet Sauvignon as needing to age in bottle after you buy it, but that's only because the best red Bordeaux and top California and Australian Cabernets need age. Most New World Cabernets and less expensive red Bordeaux will age, but can be drunk straight away.

Splashing out Wine from Bordeaux's Haut-Médoc villages, such as Margaux, St-Julien or Pauillac, from Coonawarra and Margaret River in Australia and Napa Valley in California.

Best value Chile and southern France are the places for tasty bargains. Bulgaria is, well, cheap.

Cabernet with food Modern Cabernet is an all-purpose red, but it's best with simply cooked red meats.

Not to be confused with Cabernet Franc, a related variety, or the white grape Sauvignon Blanc.

The Bordeaux region is renowned for its many stunning châteaux. This is Château Pichon-Longueville in Pauillac.

Merlot

Juicy, fruity wine that is lower in tannic bitterness and higher in alcohol than Cabernet Sauvignon, with which it is often blended. Blackcurrant, black cherry and mint are the hallmark flavours.

Where it grows Merlot started out as Cabernet Sauvignon's support act in Bordeaux, but has risen to worldwide popularity because of its softness. The great wines of Pomerol and St-Émilion in Bordeaux are based on Merlot, with Cabernet in the blend. These wines show Merlot at its sturdiest and most intense, but they're still fruitier and juicier than Bordeaux's top Cabernet-based wines.

Chile is Merlot heaven, at best producing gorgeous garnet-red wines of unbelievably crunchy fruit richness that just beg to be drunk. California and Washington State have more serious aspirations for the grape, but the soft, juicy quality still shines through. Australia and South Africa are only just catching on, but Merlot already makes some of New Zealand's best reds.

Merlot has become the wine drinker's darling because of its soft juicy fruit. These vines are in California, one of its success stories.

Italy uses Merlot to produce a light quaffing wine in the Veneto region, and offers more flavoursome examples from Friuli, Alto Adige and Tuscany. Hungary and Croatia are making rapid progress with the grape. In the hot South of France Merlot tends to lack distinctive character but produces a fair bit of gently juicy red.

Keep it or drink it? In general, drink it young, especially Chilean and Eastern European examples. Top Bordeaux Merlots, however, can last for up to 20 years.

Splashing out Château Pétrus and Château le Pin from the Pomerol region of Bordeaux are the two most expensive wines in the world. Other Pomerols and St-Émilions are less expensive lush mouthfuls.

Best value When it's good, you can't beat young Merlot from Chile.

Merlot with food Merlot is a great all-rounder – barbecue red, cassserole red, picnic red – but savoury foods with a hint of sweetness, such as honey-roast ham, particularly suit the soft fruitiness.

WINE TERMS **Varietals and blends**

A wine made solely or principally from a single grape variety is known as a **varietal**. These wines are often named after the relevant grape. This is the simple, modern way to label wine and I am all in favour, because it is the grape variety that contributes most strongly to the flavour. The law in the country or the region of production specifies the minimum percentage of the grape that the wine must contain to be given a varietal name. Very few stipulate 100%. A **blend** made from two or more varieties does not signify an inferior wine: on the contrary, many grapes need to have their weaknesses balanced by complementary varieties. The famous Châteauneuf-du-Pape red wine can have 13 different grape varieties, and rarely has less than four. Almost all the famous Bordeaux whites and reds are blends of two or more varieties.

Pinot Noir

At its best Pinot Noir is hauntingly beautiful with a seductive silky texture; at worst it is heavy and jammy or insipid and thin. Good young Pinot has a sweet summer-fruit fragrance and taste. The best mature to achieve unlikely and complex aromas of truffles, game and decaying leaves – and fruit, of course.

Where it grows Pretty widely these days, since winemakers tend to fall in love with it. Its home is in Burgundy, and the aim of all those acolytes worldwide is to make a wine that tastes like great red Burgundies such as Volnay or Vosne-Romanée. Outside Burgundy the most successful Pinots are from regions that have developed their own style – like Carneros and Sonoma Coast in California, and Wairarapa, Marlborough and Central Otago in New Zealand. Not very obliging, it obstinately refuses to taste as it should unless you treat it precisely as it likes. The best wines from California, Oregon and New Zealand show that winemakers there have cracked it and there are some good ones from Victoria and Tasmania in Australia and Overberg in South Africa. Chile's cooler vineyards can produce lovely delicate styles. Northern Italy produces an attractive, fragrant style and Germany more serious stuff. Other versions can be less convincing.

Keep it or drink it? Drink it, on the whole. Only the best ones repay keeping – and then not for as long as you'd keep the equivalent quality of Cabernet Sauvignon.

Splashing out Grand Cru Burgundies in the Côte d'Or are the pinnacle of Pinot Noir. Premier Cru Burgundy should still seduce you, but for a fraction of the price. (For more on Burgundy's Grands and Premiers Crus see page 114.)

The Romanée-Conti vineyard in the Côte d'Or region of Burgundy is said to be the most valuable vineyard land in the world.

Best value Chile makes some reasonably priced examples, as does Marlborough in New Zealand. For a taste of true Burgundy, try a basic Bourgogne Rouge from a leading Burgundy grower.

Pinot with food This is food-friendly wine. It suits both plain and complex meat and poultry dishes. It also goes well with substantial fish, such as fresh salmon.

Also known as Spätburgunder in Germany, Pinot Nero in Italy and Blauburgunder in Austria.

Not to be confused with the white grapes Pinot Blanc and Pinot Gris, or the related red grape Pinot Meunier.

Fizz fact Pinot Noir is a major component in much white Champagne, even though it is a red grape.

Syrah/Shiraz

Intense is the word for Syrah/Shiraz wines. Intensely rich, intensely spicy, intensely ripe-fruited, or even all three at once. The most powerful begin life dark, dense and tannic but mature to combine sweet blackberry and raspberry flavours with a velvety texture. Others are gorgeous right from the word go.

Where it grows Most famously in France's Rhône Valley and Australia – and unusually, the two styles are running neck and neck in terms of quality. French Syrah is more smoky, herby and austere; Australian Shiraz is richer, softer, more chocolaty, sometimes with a leathery quality. But Australia is a big place, and styles vary across the country. Victoria Shiraz can be scented and peppery, Barossa Valley Shiraz leathery and chocolaty. Old vines Shiraz, wherever it's from, should be gratifyingly intense. There's some in South Africa, lots in southern France, a bit in Italy and Switzerland. California, New Zealand, Argentina and Chile make good stuff in their cooler regions.

Keep it or drink it? Cheaper Syrah/Shiraz is immediately drinkable, but will age. Top wines will last over ten years, and a great Hermitage might peak at 15.

Splashing out Hermitage or Côte-Rôtie from the northern Rhône; Hill of Grace or Grange from Australia (it's no coincidence that this wine was known for years as Grange Hermitage).

Best value Gluggers from southern France or Chile.

Syrah/Shiraz with food This is a wine that can stand up to powerful flavours. I love it with peppered salami and tangy cheese – and, obviously, barbecues.

Why two names? It's Syrah in France; Shiraz in Australia. Other regions use either name.

Not to be confused with Petite Sirah, a grape grown in California and Mexico.

Baskets of luscious-looking Syrah grapes grown by top producer Guigal in the Côte-Rôtie vineyards, northern Rhône.

Other red wine grapes

There are literally hundreds, if not thousands, of different grape varieties grown around the world, but most of them have only a very local reputation at best. And many have no discernible character. But there's a second division of grape varieties with loads of character. Some of these grow in only a few specific places at the moment, but all have the potential to make good to excellent wine elsewhere in future.

Barbera

This is a high-quality, characterful grape, yet without a single world-famous wine style to its name. Its base is in north-west Italy, in Piedmont, where it makes wines so Italian-tasting that you find yourself instantly craving a plate of pasta. It's that herby, sour-cherries bite that does it: Barbera is the epitome of the mouthwatering, sweet-sour style I talked about earlier. But that rasping acidity is matched by plum and raisin fruit, and it's low in gum-puckering tannin.

It appears in umpteen guises all over Piedmont, but Barbera d'Alba and Barbera d'Asti are the best versions to go for. California uses Barbera for its simplest wines, but there's good stuff from Argentina.

Not to be confused with *Barbaresco, a powerful, tannic wine from the same region of north-west Italy.*

Cabernet Franc ★

A relative of Cabernet Sauvignon, which makes earthy, blackcurranty wines. Used in red Bordeaux blends and on its own in the Loire Valley and north-east Italy. Starting to make its mark in Chile, Brazil, Argentina, Australia, Virginia, New York State and Ontario.

Carignan

Widely grown red grape in southern France, used for rough everyday wines – but wine from old vines can be deliciously spicy or sturdy. There's lots in Spain, California and some gems in Chile.

Barbera is one of north-west Italy's best grapes and is excellent with food. Roberto Voerzio is one of the leading new-wave producers in the Alba region of Piedmont, making outstanding Barbera d'Alba and world-famous Barolo wines.

Collecting crates of harvested Carmenère grapes in Lapostolle's Clos Apalta vineyard in Chile's Colchagua region. Carmenère has become a Chilean success story, producing some excellent wines with rich black fruit flavours and unmistakable savoury scent.

Carmenère ★

Red grape from Chile making delicious spicy wines. It was originally a Bordeaux grape thought to be extinct. It reappeared in Chile under the umbrella title of Merlot and is now proudly labelled under its own name. Makes marvellously rich, spicy, savoury reds. Some of the Cabernet in north-east Italy is now reckoned to be Carmenère.

Cinsaut

Red grape used in southern French blends, also grown in South Africa and Lebanon. Produces light, fresh wines.

Corvina

The major grape of Italy's Valpolicella, a cherryish and bitter-sweet red, with a gentle, easy-going texture. Some in Argentina.

Dolcetto

Vibrant, purplish-red wine from Italy, full of fruit flavour with a bitter-cherry twist. Drink it young.

Gamay

Gamay, to all intents and purposes, equals Beaujolais. It's one of those freaks of wine that this grape happens to flourish on an expanse of granite hills in the south of Burgundy, and effectively nowhere else. The Ardèche region of southern France has some, as does the Loire Valley in the west. But that's about it.

Gamay is rarely a grape to take too seriously. With a few top Beaujolais exceptions, it makes refreshing wines with sharp, candy-like cherry and raspberry flavours. Drink lightly chilled on hot days.

Grenache

The most widely planted red grape in the world. Most of its plantings are in Spain and the south of France where it makes wines high in alcohol with sweet and peppery flavours. It's most often used in blends – mainly with the more scented and powerful Syrah/Shiraz, the pallid Cinsaut or the rough and ready Mourvèdre. If you ever come across a heady, juicy rosé, there's a good chance that it's made from 100 per cent Grenache.

It's actually a Spanish grape, and its original name is Garnacha Tinta. It beefs up the blend of some red Riojas, makes juicy, herby reds in Campo de Borja and Calatayud, makes Rioja and Navarra *rosado* (the Spanish for rosé) in increasingly good light styles and contributes to extremely concentrated, usually expensive, rich, full-bodied reds in Priorat and Monsant. Old vine Grenache makes some gorgeous sexy fruit bombs in South Australia, often from century-old vines. California, South Africa and North Africa have some.

But Grenache is, as I said, at its best in good company, and it finds it in France's southern Rhône Valley. Grenache is the most important of no fewer than 13 permitted grape varieties in this region's most famous wine, Châteauneuf-du-Pape – a complex, sweet-fruited super-rich red splashed with the scent of hillside herbs. The raspberry/strawberry character of this grape shines alongside a hint of hot, dusty earth in the softest Côtes du Rhône and Côtes du Rhône-Villages. Grenache from the neighbouring Ardèche region is light, fruity and good value. A lot of the juiciest, headiest rosés and *rosados* around the Mediterranean come from Grenache.

Also known as *Garnacha in Spain and Cannonau in Sardinia.*

Grenache vines enjoying the heat in Châteauneuf-du-Pape, southern Rhône. The distinctive round pebbles, called galets, *soak up the fierce heat during the day and release it slowly at night-time.*

The high region of Luján de Cujo in Mendoza, Argentina, is making a name for its Malbec wines from magnificent old vines.

Malbec ★

The best red grape in Argentina, making smooth, rich reds at all price levels. It's also the major grape of Cahors in South-West France, which can be juicy and plummy at best. Chile, Australia, New Zealand, California and South Africa also have some Malbec. Expect to hear more of this variety as Argentina's reds become more famous.

Also known as *Côt or Auxerrois.*

Mourvèdre

Red grape that gives backbone and grunt to southern Rhône wines, also grown throughout southern France, Spain, Australia, California and South Africa. Can be hard and earthy, but develops smoky, leathery flavours as it ages.

Also known as *Monastrell or Mataro.*

Nebbiolo

If you taste it too young, Nebbiolo could well be the most fiercely aggressive red you will ever encounter. It takes a few years for the staggering levels of tannin and acid to relax their grip and release the remarkable flavours of tar and roses, backed up by chocolate, cherries, raisins and prunes, and an austere perfume of tobacco and herbs. It's the severest incarnation of the sweet-sour style of Italian reds, always at its best with sturdy food.

Nebbiolo is virtually exclusive to the Piedmont region of north-west Italy. The classic wines are the frequently forbidding Nebbiolos from Barolo and Barbaresco. Modern styles mature in five years rather than the traditional 20, which is a relief for today's wine drinkers. Softer, plummier wines come from elsewhere in Piedmont – Nebbiolo d'Alba, Langhe, Gattinara, Ghemme and Carema.

A few committed Italophiles in California are pretty much the only other producers, though a few Australians are starting to look at it seriously and Argentina has some vines.

Also known as *Spanna.*

Pinotage

Conceived to meet the demands of the South African soil and climate, this grape produces both rough-textured damsony wines and smoother, fruity styles with flavours of plums, bananas, redcurrants and toasted marshmallows. Either way, it's a wine to love or hate. And it's not only drinkers who are divided: some producers adore it, others won't touch it. Spicy, warm-hearted reds are the best wines. Pinotage has not ventured far afield from South Africa, but that may be set to change. New Zealand has a few vines, and Chile, California and Australia are now experimenting with the grape.

Sangiovese

The name of the grape might not be familiar, but it's the principal variety behind Chianti, Italy's most famous red wine. It's responsible for Chianti's tea-like bitter twist and cherry-and-plum fruit. So it's one of those mouthwatering sweet-sour grapes, Italian down to its toes.

And it's not just grown for Chianti. You'll find wines made from Sangiovese in most of Italy, though not the very north, and some will be a bit dilute and thin and acidic, but a lot will be light, attractive everyday red with herby fruit and a rasping finish – just the thing with the lunchtime pasta.

In the best parts of Tuscany, however, it is taken very seriously indeed. Big, heavyweight wines like Brunello di Montalcino and Vino Nobile di Montepulciano are made entirely from Sangiovese. These are world-class wines that need aging, as do the best Chiantis, but most Sangiovese is best drunk young and fresh.

Sangiovese is the most planted red grape variety in Italy and reaches its greatest heights in central Tuscany. These vines are in the Chianti Rufina area east of Florence.

You'll find some Sangiovese in California, Australia and Argentina, as well, and they're starting to do interesting things with it; but for the moment there is nothing to equal the best Italian wines.

Also known as *Brunello and Prugnolo.*

Tannat

Sturdy, spicy red grape from Madiran in South-West France. It also does well in Uruguay. Results in Argentina and Brazil are promising.

Tempranillo ★

Spain's maid-of-all-work crops up all over the country, producing wines of all shapes and sizes. There are grand, prestigious wines in Ribera del Duero, mellow but ageworthy reds in Rioja and Catalunya, powerful beasts in Toro and young, juicy, unoaked styles in Valdepeñas, La Mancha, Somontano and many other regions. Its flavour is good but not always instantly recognizable the way that Cabernet Sauvignon or Pinot Noir is: Tempranillo's most distinctive feature is its good whack of strawberry fruit, but in the biggest, weightiest wines this tends to go plummy and blackberryish and spicy, overlaid with vanilla oak. Only the finest wines need aging – and the simplest really must be drunk young and fresh.

In northern Portugal Tempranillo is called Tinta Roriz and it is an important grape for port, the classic fortified wine, as well as appearing

The Ribera del Duero region in Castilla y León, Spain, produces mouthfilling reds from Tempranillo.

WHITE WINE FROM RED GRAPES

The juice inside a grape is clear, whatever the colour of the skin. So if you separate the juice from the skins before fermentation, hey presto, you'll end up with white wine.

The French call this style Blanc de Noirs and it works well with Pinot Noir in Champagne. A less edifying example of the white-from-red conjuring act is white or 'blush' Zinfandel. The problem is that you lose all the berry-fruit character that makes Zinfandel exciting.

However, making white wine from black grapes is not, apart from these two examples, all that common. In Champagne the purpose of using Pinot Noir like this is to give weight and body to the blend, and in California the original purpose of white Zinfandel was to use up a grape that was temporarily out of fashion. Demand for red wine is just too high now for red grapes to be denuded of their colour without very good reason.

And another thing. Pretty much all the flavour and perfume of a red grape variety is also held in the skins. When you macerate the juice and skins together to extract colour, you also release all the grape's personality, too.

in reds from both Dão and Douro. Under the alias Aragonez it's responsible for some juicy numbers from Alentejo in the south.

Argentina grows it for its vivacious fruitiness and Australia, California, Oregon and the south of France are experimenting with it.

Also known as *Ready for this? Cencibel, Tinto del País, Tinto del Toro, Tinto Fino, Tinto de Madrid or Ull de Llebre in Spain; Tinta Roriz or Aragonez in Portugal. And that's the abbreviated list.*

Touriga Nacional ★

Red grape with plenty of colour, perfume and fruit used in port and modern Portuguese dry wines. Worldwide interest is increasing.

Zinfandel

California's speciality grape can be all things to all people. The best Zinfandel and the type I'm interested in is spicy, heart-warming dry red wine. Other styles range from off-white, sweetish and insipid 'blush' wines to high-intensity sweet port-style reds. All red California Zinfandel shares a ripe-berries fruitiness, but the intensity varies dramatically from light to blockbustingly powerful.

Cheap examples are usually lightweight juicy, fruity reds. The top-quality Zinfandels are at the sturdier end of the scale and they're expensive. Mendocino County produces strapping Zin full of blackberry fruit, spice and tannin. It's rich, ripe, dark and chunky in Napa, rounder and spicier in Sonoma and wild and wonderful from old vineyards in the Sierra Foothills. The full-throated, brawny flavours of these big Zins will wash down anything from barbecue ribs to the richest Pacific Rim cooking.

Zinfandel from regions outside the US, which place a lower value on the grape, are an economical alternative. It's grown in one or two outposts in Australia, South Africa, Brazil and Chile and not much money will buy you a sumptuous, rich, almost overripe mouthful. India is having a go.

Researchers have shown that Zinfandel is the same variety as the southern Italian grape Primitivo, and if you're looking for good value, Primitivo gives you the most bang for your bucks.

Also known as *Primitivo in Italy and is the same as Croatia's Crljenak Kastelanski, too.*

California Zin can be anything from strapping rich wines from old vines to light, sweetish wines often called White Zinfandel.

White wine grapes

Green, yellow, pinkish or even brown on the vine, these are the grapes that promise refreshment. But that's not all: white wines range from the breathtakingly sharp to the most luscious and exotic flavours you will ever encounter.

CLASSIC BLENDS

The modern approach of labelling wines by the name of the grape variety has led to the great popularity of single-varietal wines. Cabernet Sauvignon, Merlot, Sauvignon Blanc and Chardonnay have all swept to fame on their own merits. But many of the classic flavours of France and other European wine nations are based on blends of two or more grape varieties.

Cabernet Sauvignon may be the most famous grape of red Bordeaux, but if the wines were made solely from Cabernet, most would be unbearably austere. Merlot and other grapes in the blend soften the wine and add exciting layers of flavour at the same time.

It's the same story with Bordeaux whites. Sémillon and Sauvignon Blanc are often better together than alone, and a grape called Muscadelle adds fatness to both dry and sweet wines. Champagne, Rioja, Chianti and port are all (for the most part) blended wines, and a bottle of Châteauneuf-du-Pape can include the juice of as many as 13 different grape varieties.

European blends are often emulated in the newer wine-producing nations, but new partnerships have become established too. Australia, in particular, has made modern classics of Chardonnay blended with Semillon and Cabernet Sauvignon with Shiraz.

Chardonnay

The world's most famous white grape variety can make anyone fall in love with wine, because it's so generous with its easy-to-relish buttery, lemony flavours. Chardonnay has an affinity for oak-aging and styles divide into unoaked which is lean, minerally and restrained; lightly oaked, when it can be nutty and oatmealy; and heavily oaked, which is where butteriness, tropical fruits and butterscotch come in.

Where it grows Chardonnay is everywhere. I'd be hard pushed to name a wine-producing country that doesn't grow it. It originates from the French region of Burgundy, where it produces stylish, succulent wines with a nutty richness from time spent in oak barrels yet still with bone-dry clarity. However, in the north of Burgundy is Chablis, where Chardonnay has a sharp, minerally acidity that may or may not be countered by the richness of oak – I prefer it all in its naked, unoaked glory.

The modern style has its origins in Australia and California: upfront, pineappley, oaky and sumptuous, but nowadays becoming a lot more restrained.

New Zealand versions are either fruity or surprisingly nutty. Chilean versions are on the fruity side. South African ones are mixed in styles, but very good at their best. In Europe, modern styles come from southern France, Italy, Portugal, Greece and Spain.

Keep it or drink it? Most Chardonnay is ready the moment you buy it, but top wines from France, Australia and California will improve for five years or so.

Splashing out Of all Burgundy's mercilessly expensive Grands Crus, Le Montrachet is finest of the fine. Top Californian and Australian Chardonnays are also pricey.

Best value Chilean, Australian or southern French.

Chardonnay with food The whole point of modern Chardonnay is that it will go pretty well with almost anything. It is wonderful with all fish, whether lightly grilled or drowned in a rich, buttery sauce. The richer the sauce, the oakier the wine can be.

Golden yellow Chardonnay grapes growing in California's sunshine.

Riesling

It's not a grape that everyone takes an instant liking to, Riesling, but it has undeniable finesse. Piercing acidity is the most startling and recognizable feature in styles ranging from thrillingly dry to richly sweet, with flavours that range from apple and lime zing to pebbles and slate to peaches and honey.

Dispel any confusion lurking in your mind between Riesling and Liebfraumilch, that simple, sweetish, first step in wine drinking invented in Germany which rarely contains any Riesling at all.

Where it grows Riesling is the grape of Germany's greatest wines. In the Mosel region it produces mostly light, floral wines with a slaty edge. Rheingau Rieslings are generally richer, fruitier and spicy. Both are surprisingly low in alcohol. They need a few years to mature before the flavours are at their best.

Across the border into France, Alsace makes a more alcoholic, dry, spicy Riesling. In Austria it's minerally and dry with a good, weighty slap of alcohol. Australian Riesling is different again – with an invigorating lime aroma that goes toasty with age. New Zealand, Chile, South Africa and the US have some decent wines, but Germany, Alsace and Australia have defined the key styles.

Keep it or drink it? Some German Rieslings can age almost indefinitely, but the simpler everyday ones can be drunk at 1–2 years old. As Riesling ages it often develops a petrolly aroma (nicer than it sounds). Top Australian wines will keep for 10 years or more.

Splashing out The great sweet German Rieslings. Alsace, Austria and Australia make superb dry versions.

Best value Mosel and Rhein Kabinetts from Germany and surprisingly good, big-brand Australians.

Riesling with food Good dry Rieslings, such as those from Austria and Australia, are excellent with spicy cuisine. Sweet Rieslings are best enjoyed for their own lusciousness but can also partner light, fruit desserts.

Also known as Johannisberger Riesling, Rhine Riesling or White Riesling – and Riesling Renano in Italy.

Not to be confused with Laski Rizling, Olasz Rizling, Riesling Italico or Welschriesling.

The steep slopes overlooking the Mosel river, here at Piesport, are home to some of Germany's top Riesling vineyards.

Sauvignon Blanc

This is the epitome of the green, tangy style: an unrestrained wine with aromas and flavours of green leaves, nettles, gooseberries and lime zest.

Where it grows New Zealand, particularly the Marlborough region, produces what has become the classic style, all pungent gooseberries and nettles. Australia seldom matches New Zealand for lean pungency. Chile delivers lean, fairly punchy flavours from cooler regions such as Casablanca and Leyda. South Africa is becoming increasingly exciting for Sauvignon Blanc, particularly from the cold west coast. California is a little warm for Sauvignon, but is now producing some good lean examples as well as fuller styles aged in oak barrels.

The grape's European home is in France's Loire Valley. The wines are milder and less pungent than New Zealand versions. Sancerre and Pouilly-Fumé are the Loire's famous wines; Menetou-Salon and Sauvignon de Touraine offer more green flavour for less money.

Sauvignon is also an important grape in Bordeaux. Elsewhere in Europe there are full-flavoured Sauvignons in Spain, especially in Rueda, neutral ones in the north of Italy and light ones in Austria. Eastern European versions vary, but tend to lack pungency, except from Hungary and Slovenia.

Keep it or drink it? Apart from a few top wines, Sauvignon Blanc is for drinking

Sauvignon Blanc from New Zealand's Marlborough region became an overnight bestseller in the 1970s.

as soon as you can get the bottle home and the cork out.

Splashing out Cloudy Bay from New Zealand is a cult wine that sells out as soon as it hits the shops. Its Marlborough neighbours are just as good at around half the price.

Best value Entre-Deux-Mers in Bordeaux – and Bordeaux Blanc in general – is pumping out bargains with a good tangy flavour.

Sauvignon with food New World Sauvignon is a favourite match for the sweet-sour, hot-cool, spicy flavours of Chinese and South-East Asian foods; it goes well with some Indian cuisine and with tomato-based dishes in general. It's also a fine drink on its own.

Also known as Fumé Blanc in California and Australia.

Other white wine grapes

Traditionally the world's leading white grapes have come from the cooler areas of France and Germany. But there's been an exhilarating re-invention of white winemaking in warm countries like Spain and Italy, and we'll see a lot more of their varieties in the future.

Albariño makes trendy white wines in the rolling hills of Galicia, Spain's rainy, green, north-west corner.

Albariño ★

Characterful, refreshing white from Spain tasting of lime zest and grapefruit, but with a soft, yeasty texture. It's trendy, so it's expensive. Also used in Vinho Verde in Portugal and starting to appear in places like California.

Aligoté

Grown in Burgundy and Eastern Europe to produce simple sharp wines. The Burgundy village of Bouzeron does it best: dry yet mouthfilling.

Chenin Blanc

What an extraordinary flavour – a striking contrast of rich honey, guava and quince with steely, minerally flavours and whiplash acidity. Chenin can produce gum-numbing dry wines, sparkling wines, medium-sweet styles or super-sweet wonders from noble rot-affected grapes. That's Chenin in France's Loire Valley. Chenin in South Africa might taste as pale as water. Let's deal with France first.

Chenin accounts for the white wines from the Loire's heartland – Vouvray, Savennières, Saumur and others. It can have a problem ripening here but global warming has recently provided a series of excellent vintages. Simple dry Chenin has a flavour of apple peel and honey but a good Vouvray has a streak of minerally flavour. The best sweet Loire Chenin comes from Bonnezeaux, Quarts de Chaume and Coteaux du Layon. These wines need to mature for years to attain their full quince and honey richness.

Chenin is South Africa's most widely planted grape. It generally makes rather hollow stuff but an increasing number of winemakers realize it could make South Africa's best whites if treated seriously. New Zealand, Australia, California and Argentina produce small amounts. It makes India's best white.

Colombard

Reliable everyday white: fruity and crisp, occasionally with tropical fruits aromas. Widely grown in southern France, Australia, California and South Africa.

Falanghina ★

Once a fairly obscure white from Campania near Naples – if you've ever been to Capri and tried its white it was probably made from Falanghina. But the new wave of Italian winemakers has realized it can make really interesting, minty, apple-blossom-scented whites, and so it's spreading across southern Italy. Next stop, the New World.

Fiano ★

When I tasted a peachy, mint-scented Fiano from Adelaide Hills in South Australia, I realized this grape was no longer a south Italian secret. But most of it is grown from around Naples in Campania right down to Sicily and it's making some of Italy's most interesting new-wave whites.

Gewürztraminer

A fragrant blast of lychee and rose petals followed up by a luxurious, honeyed, oil-thick texture, a whiff of Nivea hand cream, a twist of fresh black pepper – dry or sweet, it's the most intensely aromatic wine in the world. 'Gewürz' translates as spice, although it's difficult to think of a single spice that exactly resembles Gewürztraminer. Great with Asian food, it's also wonderful to sip by itself.

Alsace is the place to go for Gewurztraminer (they take the accent off the 'u' here). Even the most basic wines have a swirl of aromatic spice, while great vintages can produce super-intense wines in styles from dry to richly sweet.

You have to keep your nerve to make Gewürz (its short nickname) work. If you don't like its perfume, why grow it? But the rise in popularity of Asian cuisine has seen producers become more confident. Germany, northern Italy (where the grape originates) and New Zealand all now produce a few deliciously indulgent examples. Croatian Traminač can be rich and succulent.

Also known as *Traminer, Traminač.*

These Gewurztraminer grapes come from Alsace, where the sunshine can continue well into November. If you leave the grapes on the vine this long the wines will be luscious and perfumed.

Malvasia

Widely grown in Italy and found in many guises, both white and red. It produces fragrant dry whites, rich, apricotty sweet whites and frothing light reds. Also grown in Croatian Istria, Spain and Portugal, it's the grape of the sweet fortified Madeira wine called Malmsey.

Marsanne

Originally from the Rhône Valley where it can make rich and honeysuckle-scented wines. It is also used in southern French blends. In Victoria, Australia it makes big, broad, honeyed wines.

Muscadet

The grape of Muscadet, the simple but refreshing white wine from the mouth of the Loire Valley around Nantes. It doesn't have much flavour itself, but the better wines are left in contact with their yeast lees in the vat, resulting in a very pleasant, prickly, creamy white which is perfect as a summer aperitif or accompanying the local seafood. Look for the words *sur lie* on the label.

Below left: Muscadet is just the perfect refreshing white wine to accompany a plate of local Breton seafood.
Below right: This is the leftover yeast at the bottom of the vat that helps make the most interesting Muscadet wines.

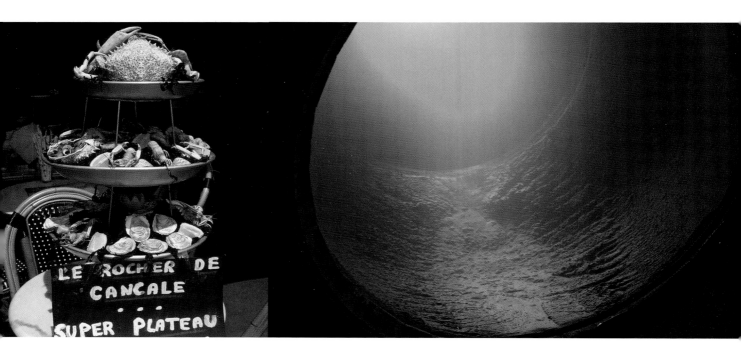

Muscat

The only grape to make delicious wine that actually smells of the grape itself comes in a multitude of styles. Rich, sweet and fortified, floral and dry or exuberantly frothy, Muscat wines all share a seductive grapy aroma. Intensely sweet Muscats often add an orange-peel and tea rose fragrance.

To start with the darkest and sweetest, Rutherglen in north-eastern Victoria, Australia, is a sticky heaven for those who crave its raisiny, perfumed fortified Muscats. Golden, sweet Muscats, again fortified, come from the south of France (from Beaumes-de-Venise, Frontignan, Rivesaltes and other villages) and Portugal, and have lighter, but sensuous, delicate orange-and-grape aromas with a touch of rose petals. Spain's Moscatel de Valencia is cheaper, more foursquare, but a good rich mouthful all the same.

Alsace is the place for dry Muscat – irresistibly scented, thrillingly dry – though Italy, Spain, Portugal and Australia all have a go. And if you're in a bubbly sort of mood, Muscat makes delightful grape- and blossom-scented sparklers in Italy (Asti is the most famous) and Brazil.

Also known as *Muscat Blanc à Petits Grains (its full name), Muscat de Frontignan or, in Australia, Brown Muscat. The Italians call it Moscato. The less thrilling Muscat of Alexandria (Spain's Moscatel) and Muscat Ottonel are related grapes. Orange Muscat does smell of oranges, and the rare pink Muscat (Moscato Rosa) does make divine wine smelling of tea roses. Black Muscat – well, I like it; we used to grow it in a greenhouse when I was little.*

Not to be confused with *Muscadet, the bone-dry white wine from the Loire Valley in France.*

Palomino and Pedro Ximénez (PX)

The white grapes behind sherry and Montilla-Moriles: Palomino for dry styles, PX for sweet ones.

Pinot Blanc

A light quaffer. At best it makes creamy, floral, appley wine in Alsace; good in northern Italy too.

Muscat can be used for both delicious, dark sticky wines from Victoria, Australia and light, frothy Asti sparklers from Italy.

Pinot Gris

Intensity is a key issue with Pinot Gris. Whether you like your white wine bone dry and neutral or rich and spicy, or anything in between, the right Pinot Gris for you is out there somewhere. A hint of honey (sometimes admittedly very faint) is the linking theme that connects the grape's different incarnations.

Rich, smoky and honeyed dry whites from Alsace in France show Pinot Gris at its most pungent and impressive. The US has had success with lighter, crisper, spicy versions from Oregon, while New Zealand is producing a fair number of soft, pear-scented examples. Eastern Europe produces outstanding dry or off-dry and spicy wines.

Germany takes the grape into sweet-wine territory and sometimes calls it Ruländer. Dry German Grauburgunders aged in oak are fat and smokily honeyed. Fairly neutral wines, and plenty of them, labelled as Pinot Grigio, come from Italy. But really good Italian Pinot Grigio is floral and honeyed.

Also known as *Pinot Grigio in Italy, Ruländer (usually sweet) or Grauburgunder (usually dry) in Germany, Malvoisie in Switzerland.*

Not to be confused with *the other Pinots: Pinot Noir, Pinot Blanc and Pinot Meunier (one of the official Champagne grapes).*

Roussanne

A white Rhône grape – a more aromatic and elegant cousin of Marsanne, with which it is frequently and successfully blended.

Semillon

Semillon comes into its own in two key areas, France's Bordeaux and Australia, and it comes in two totally different styles: dry and sweet. By the way, the French put an accent on the 'é'. Either way, it can produce wonderful quality.

It pops up in various parts of Australia for dry wine, but Hunter Valley Semillon is the most famous. The traditional style here is unoaked. When young, unoaked Hunter Semillon tastes neutral, even raw, with just a bit of lemony fruit. But unoaked Hunter Semillon should not be drunk young. It needs up to a decade in bottle – and then it will amaze you with its waxy, lanoliny, custardy fruit. Oaked Australian Semillon, often from the Barossa or Clare

Oregon's Willamette Valley is becoming renowned for crisp styles of Pinot Gris.

Valleys, is different. Dry, toasty, waxy and lemony, it's good young but the best can age for a few years, too. Riverina makes light, waxy Semillon, much of which is blended with Chardonnay.

In Bordeaux Sémillon is usually blended with Sauvignon Blanc, which adds a refreshing streak of sharp acidity. The best dry versions come from Graves and Pessac-Léognan: oaked, with flavours of cream and nectarines, they improve for several years in bottle.

Sweet wines are another story. Here Sauternes is the star: this Bordeaux appellation produces extraordinarily concentrated wines from grapes affected by noble rot, with flavours of barley sugar and peaches. This golden, sweet style is imitated, in small amounts, in California, Australia and New Zealand. Hand-picking the noble rotted grapes, sometimes berry by berry, means these wines can never be cheap; but the flavour is so special it's worth the money.

The Bodega Colomé estate, high in the Calchaquí Valley in north-west Argentina, has some very old plantings of Torrontes, Argentina's number one white grape variety. This is some of the highest vineyard land in the world and the high altitudes and very dry climate mean the grapes produce intense flavours.
PS There is also a gorgeous hotel here – the drive here is so tough, you'll need some pampering and a stopover.

Torrontés ★

The star white grape of Argentina, producing highly aromatic wines, especially from high-altitude vineyards in the north.

Verdejo

Increasingly popular grape variety from Rueda in northern Spain, where its sharp acidity and greengage fruit is prized.

Verdelho

Originally a grape grown for the fortified wine of Madeira, but it also produces full-bodied, leather- and lime-scented dry whites in Australia.

Verdicchio

One of Italy's non-aromatic white grapes, now gaining some respect for its ability to impart a richness like baked cream and a haughty, dried herb scent to its wine. Best known for the wine of the same name from eastern Italy – Verdicchio.

Vermentino

Light, perfumed dry white from Sardinia, or green-apple fresh from the Tuscan coast. As Rolle it is Provence's best white grape. Australia makes it bone dry, with a herby, licorice perfume.

Vernaccia

White grape that makes an Italian equivalent to sherry in Sardinia and a tasty golden dry white in Tuscany.

Viognier

Heady, hedonistic, with a rich scent of apricots and breeze-blown spring flowers, Viognier is an aromatic dry wine so luxurious that it seems almost sweet.

It used to be confined to a few small areas of the northern Rhône Valley in France, but fashion is a powerful force. Suddenly Viognier is appearing all over the south of France – never in large quantities, to be sure, but at prices that give a taste of the grape to those of us who can't fork out the premium-plus rates for classic top-quality Condrieu and Château-Grillet from the northern Rhône.

California, Australia and South America are trying their hands at it, too. Results vary, but are distinctly promising to very good. Viognier should be drunk young and fresh – the ravishing scent fades rapidly after a year or two.

Viura

The main white grape of Spain's Rioja, light and apple-fresh in its simplest form, but full, custardy and orange-scented when fermented in oak barrels. It is most commonly used in blends.

Also known as *Macabeo in Spain and as Macabeu in Languedoc-Roussillon.*

The Condrieu vineyards high above the river Rhône are the original home of the Viognier grape.

INSTANT RECALL: RED GRAPES

Barbera A snappy, refreshing Italian red

Cabernet Sauvignon The blackcurranty red par excellence

Carmenère Dark, blackcurrant- and pepper-flavoured Chilean red

Gamay The juicy red grape of Beaujolais

Grenache Ripe strawberry and spice, often in a blend

Malbec Full, lush, plummy red, especially from Argentina

Merlot Juicy and plummy; part of the classic red Bordeaux blend

Nebbiolo The stern and tannic dark grape from north-west Italy

Pinot Noir A capricious grape, at best making elegant, silky reds with a haunting fragrance

Pinotage A love-it-or-hate-it sturdy, smoky red from South Africa

Sangiovese The main grape of Chianti; mouthwatering, sweet-sour red fruit flavours from Italy

Syrah/Shiraz Spicy and warm-hearted; at home in France's Rhône Valley, Australia, California, Chile...

Tempranillo Spanish strawberries and plums

Zinfandel California's all-purpose grape variety, often seen as a sweetish pink, but best as a spicy red

INSTANT RECALL: WHITE GRAPES

Chardonnay From ripe peaches and toast to steely, stony and austere: the classic international white grape in numerous styles

Chenin Blanc The quirky, fruity-minerally white grape from the Loire Valley

Gewürztraminer The uniquely spicy and exotic white, at its best in Alsace

Muscat Dry and sweet wines that actually taste of grapes

Pinot Gris Neutral in Italy (as Pinot Grigio), rich in Alsace, always with a hint of honey

Riesling The steely, citrussy aristocrat of white grapes, best in Germany, Austria, France's Alsace and Australia

Sauvignon Blanc Gooseberry and nettle tang, originally from France's Loire Valley but now better known in New Zealand, Chile and South Africa

Semillon Lemony, waxy dry whites and golden sweeties from Bordeaux and Australia

Viognier The sumptuous, apricotty white of the northern Rhône Valley

what makes each wine unique

It doesn't take much to make wine. In fact, a grape is quite capable of doing it by itself. The moment the skin of a ripe grape splits, the sugary juice on the inside comes into contact with yeasts that live naturally in the air and on the surface of the grape skin. Yeasts have a voracious appetite for sugar and as they eat their way through it they convert it into alcohol. The process is called fermentation.

But leaving nature to make wine for you like this is a bit like leaving your car out in the rain to get washed: the results will not be entirely what you were hoping for. Some 500 chemical compounds have been identified in wine, and most are produced naturally during fermentation. The winemaker's job is to ensure that the right compounds – the ones that taste good – are formed, and that the wrong ones – the ones that taste of rancid butter, or vinegar – are not.

Given 500 different components, it's not surprising that no two wines taste quite alike. But the winemaking process is only part of the story. The grape variety, the yield from the vine, the climate and the location of the vineyard all contribute to the flavour of the wine.

Climate and location

First off, grapes need sun, otherwise they can't ripen. And without sugar in the grapes there will be nothing to ferment into alcohol. The riper the grapes, the higher the sugar content and the more alcoholic the wine will be. If you're after a great big beast with a hefty wallop of ultra-ripe fruit, well – get that sunshine switched on to full.

But traditional wisdom asserts that great wines are produced only at the 'margin'. What does it mean? Well, we're talking about climate. It means that the most complex wines, the ones with perfume, appetizing balance, depth, and the ability to evolve with age, are produced In places where it is a marginal bet whether there will be enough sun to ripen the grapes at all. The grapes creep and stagger to ripeness through a long, unpredictable, not-too-hot summer and autumn. When it comes to traditional wines, like France's Champagne, Chablis, Bordeaux and Burgundy, I have to agree with the traditional view. But there are also many modern classics from California, Australia, Chile, Argentina and South Africa, where grapes ripen fully every year without much effort at all.

Perhaps the best of both worlds is to have cool-climate vineyards in areas with warm, reliable sunshine. How is that possible? Well, how about a coastal vineyard in northern California? Grapes soak up that famous Californian sun while simultaneously being cooled by the breeze and chilly mists that roll in from the Pacific. Or how about a high-altitude vineyard in the Andes? Plenty of clear skies and sun, but the higher you go, the cooler it gets, which slows down the ripening period and creates the balance we're talking about.

Every grape variety requires different conditions to ripen. Riesling can ripen perfectly in the cool valleys of Germany; Syrah can't. But Riesling would bake in the Rhône Valley, where Syrah gaily broils to perfect ripeness under the sun's bright glare.

And don't forget the soil, and the site. Waterlogged soil is cold and hinders ripening; well-drained soils promote it. Hillsides drain well and, if they're facing in the right direction, catch more sun; valley floors drain less well and often cop a snap of frost too. And these conditions can lie right next to each other, in the same village. They'll produce totally different wines.

Grapes and yields

The majority of the world's wines are produced from one or more of the 15 or 20 most popular grape varieties. The grapes have certain characteristics that are inevitably inherited by their offspring, the wines. Pinot Noir grapes give wines with red-fruit flavour. No black fruit, no citrus. You're a red-head, son, just like your old man. But the thrusting young Californian Pinot is a different chap from the cynical old Burgundian. Sauvignon Blanc gives green and tangy wines. Green is the colour of Sauvignon's eyes. But Sauvignon arrives at the party in different styles: bold and boisterous from New Zealand or South Africa, charming and subtle from France, mellow from northern California – it all depends on where she grew up and who shaped her growth.

Facing page: The Marlborough region in New Zealand's South Island enjoys long dry autumns (most years, that is).

This French term doesn't really have an English translation but it is at the root of the French attitude to wine. The **terroir** of each vineyard is what makes it unique: it can be defined as a combination of soil, climate and exposure to the sun. It thus sums up every possible factor: the type of topsoil and subsoil, the direction of the wind, the degree of shelter from frost, whether the ground slopes and how much, and whether it faces north, south, east or west. New World winemakers are more inclined to focus on **climate** as being the main determinant of wine style, with the soil sometimes being dismissed as merely the stuff that holds the irrigation water to keep the grapes growing. But the more good, different wines these guys taste, the more they realize flavour and personality need more than simply sunshine and a reliable water supply. That's when they thoughtfully kick the earth in their vineyards and think – perhaps there's something in this 'terroir' business after all.

After about 25 years vines become less vigorous and produce smaller, more concentrated crops. Australia has plenty of vines much older than that. These old-timers are in South Australia's Clare Valley.

The number of grapes each vine produces affects both the flavour of the wine and the price. Higher yields should mean lower prices. But do low yields mean higher quality? To a large extent, yes. A Pinot Noir vineyard in Burgundy where the vines are pruned hard every winter to prevent the vine producing too many bunches will make better wine, other things being equal, than one where the vines are allowed to crop too heavily. More grapes, in this instance, mean more dilute juice and less flavour.

But the equation is not always a straightforward one. Each vineyard, and each grape variety, has its own optimum yield. To allow the vines to produce more than that level means a drop in quality. It's a question of knowing your vines.

I'll give you an example. The warmer parts of Australia have heavily irrigated vineyards churning out wine like milch cows, and it's amazingly cheap. Clever winemaking and vine-growing techniques mean that it tastes pretty good, too. On the other side of the coin are the lovingly tended, 100-year-old vines boasted by the early-settled parts of Australia: these gnarled centenarians give tiny quantities of intense, concentrated, high-quality wines that cost a bomb. Their yield is perhaps one-twentieth of that of the irrigated vineyards. But if you treated those factory-farmed vineyards the same way as the centenarian ones, you still wouldn't get the quality of the latter. Yet the wine would cost nearly as much to produce.

And all this means...

Ideally, it all means perfect grapes. Or as good as the grower can get them: picked at optimum ripeness, with an optimum balance of sugar and acidity. Grapes like this, delivered in perfect health (no rot, no mildew) are at the absolute peak of their potential. Whether the wine lives up to that potential depends entirely on the skill and attentiveness of the winemaker.

Making wine

So much for the background; what about the sticky business of transforming fresh-picked grapes into the world's most delicious and intriguing drink? You won't see many jolly peasants treading the grapes these days; think, rather, of stainless steel, computers and laboratory-style hygiene. Constant experimentation with equipment and techniques is part and parcel of the modern wine industry, but for all that, winemaking remains a magical, messy process.

Grape juice

The first thing you need to do is get at the juice. A little controlled violence has to be applied in the form of a machine called a crusher, which breaks the skins of the grapes. If you are making white wine, the next job after crushing is to get the fermenting juice (known as the must) well away from all the skins and stems. They add tannin and colour to the wine – exactly what you don't want for a white wine. So you transfer the crushed mass to a press without delay and squeeze out all the liquid, then pump it into a container called a vat to ferment. Some winemakers put uncrushed bunches of grapes straight into the press to get even fresher juice.

Fermentation

Fermentation is the process in which yeasts – either natural ('wild') or specifically chosen – convert the sugar in the grape juice to alcohol, carbon dioxide and heat. The latter two bubble out and the alcohol remains in the juice.

The single greatest advance in winemaking in the 20th century was the advent of temperature-controlled fermentation – for which

Winemaking is hard work. Well, most of it is.

WINE TERMS **Winemakers**

The winemaking process, or **vinification**, is the point at which the natural events of fermentation are shaped and controlled with a view to creating a particular end product. The person who makes the decisions is the **winemaker**. The concept of the winemaker as an interventionist who determines the character of the wine is a modern one, developed in California and Australia in the 1970s. Previously it was an unsung role. An attentive winemaker can make decent wine even from unexceptional grapes, and a talented one can produce stunning wine from top-quality raw materials. A poor winemaker, on the other hand, can turn out dreadful wine even as neighbouring producers are creating classics. For this reason the name of the **producer**, the company or person that produces the wine, is a better guide to a wine's quality than the grape or the region.

read cool fermentation. Cool fermentation preserves fresh fruit flavours and is one of the reasons why inexpensive Australian or Chilean wine, grown in conditions that are too hot for comfort, still tastes fresh and fruity. Most modern easy-drinking whites are made in big refrigerated steel vats, but some top dry whites will be fermented in small oak barrels, which add buttery, vanilla richness.

You make red wine by fermenting the juice and the skins together, since the skins contain the colour as well as flavours, perfumes and the preservative tannin. This is generally done in a vat made of stainless steel, concrete or sometimes wood. Let the temperature go much higher than for whites to extract as much colour and flavour from the skins as possible. You'll have to stir the vat or pump the juice from the bottom over the skins floating on top, but otherwise just sit back and watch the deep purple colour ooze out of the skins. When the fermentation is over and you have all the colour and tannin you want, drain the free-running juice into a fresh container and put the remaining pulp into a press to squeeze out the rest.

For rosé wine, start as if you were about to make red wine, but separate the juice from the skins much earlier, so that the wine has just a tinge of colour. Then proceed as if you were making white wine. You can cheat by mixing a bit of red wine into a white wine, but that's not real rosé and it won't taste as good.

Fining and filtration

Fermentation is complete when all the sugar in the wine has turned to alcohol, or the alcohol level becomes high enough to kill the yeasts. Before bottling, most wine will go through fining and filtration so that it is nice and clear when it reaches the consumer. This could be done straight off with an ultra-fine filter but that would strip out a lot of quality and flavour from the wine too. Instead, winemakers get all the tiny particles that are making the wine cloudy to stick together and drop to the bottom (this process is called fining), and then use a gentler filter that will leave the wine clear but with quality intact. Traditional fining agents include egg whites, isinglass (a product of the sturgeon fish) and gelatine; they are not present in the finished wine, but if a wine is labelled 'suitable for vegetarians or vegans' it implies these haven't been used in the fining process.

WINE TERMS **Oak**

If wine is fermented or matured in oak barrels, it will acquire characteristic oak flavours from the wooden staves, particularly if the winemaker chooses brand new, fairly small barrels called **barriques**. Wine tasters describe these **new oak** flavours as toastiness, spiciness, butteriness, butterscotch and vanilla. Many of the world's best reds and whites are fermented or matured in oak; but large oak barrels that are reused from year to year add little to the flavour.

Barrels are expensive: an economical alternative is to submerge oak planks in a vat of wine, or to add oak chips in a kind of oversize tea bag while the wine is fermenting.

Stainless steel or concrete tanks, which don't affect the flavour, are preferable for fresh-tasting and ultra-fruity styles.

Blending

The winemaker has the opportunity to transform the wine by blending the contents of two or more vats together. That could mean putting together different grape varieties to add a whole new dimension of flavour.

Maturing the wine

The wine is still not ready to bottle: you need to mature it for anything from a few days to several years, depending on the flavour you are aiming at. Storing the wine in small oak barrels called barriques adds rich, toasty flavours. The newer the barrels, the greater their influence on the flavour. Oak-aging doesn't automatically make a wine better – it suits gutsy wines like Cabernet Sauvignon, but would overpower a delicate Riesling.

Stainless steel and concrete tanks are inert, so they add no flavour and preserve the wine's fruit; they are ideal for fresh-tasting wines such as tangy Sauvignon Blanc.

While they are maturing, wines, especially reds, benefit from a naturally occurring process called malolactic fermentation. A strain of bacteria converts the acid in the wine from harsh malic acid (the acid of unripe apples) to softer lactic acid, which is the main acid of milk. This isn't appropriate for some white wines, in which case the bacteria are filtered out or killed off with sulphur.

WINE TERMS Sulphites

One term you will always see on a wine label is 'contains sulphites', as sulphur dioxide is (almost) universally used as an anti-oxidant and preservative. It stops the juice oxidising (going off) when it comes into contact with the air. It is an essential tool for good winemaking.

The final amount of sulphur dioxide in the wine is always minuscule, but the label tells you it is there. Some people are more sensitive to it than others, and some winemakers are more heavy-handed than others.

Producing grape juice and then fermenting it into wine is a messy old business.

Making sparkling wine

All the very best sparkling wine is made by the method developed in Champagne in France. Any sparkling wine that is labelled 'traditional method', 'classical method' or something similar is made in this way.

The traditional or Champagne method

First you need to make some still wine, called the base wine, which is often unbearably acidic but has the potential to make good fizz, because carbon dioxide has the effect of softening wine and fully ripe base wine would produce flabby fizz. The next step is to create the bubbles. Put the still wine into strong bottles with a little yeast and sugar to start a second fermentation. Seal them with strong stoppers, because fermentation produces vast amounts of carbon dioxide gas, which builds up a lot of pressure in a sealed container. Since it cannot escape, the carbon dioxide dissolves into the wine, impatiently waiting for the day it will be released as jubilant foam and elegant trails of tiny bubbles.

Unfortunately the dead yeast leaves a decidedly un-celebratory deposit of gunge in the bottle. To get this out you first have to tip this muck towards the bottle's opening. Traditionally the bottles are stored in angled racks where they are turned and gently tapped by hand every day for a couple of months to achieve this. Mechanized racks now do the job in a few days.

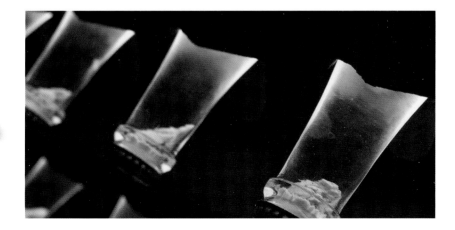

Right: This is the dead yeast gunge that has to be removed from the bottle before you can enjoy a glass of fizz.

Once all this sediment is in the neck of the bottle, you freeze the neck and whip out the stopper: the sediment will shoot out like a pellet but the bubbles stay dissolved in the wine. Add a little sweetening if you want to take the harsh edge off the acidity and push in the famous super-strong Champagne cork – and you've got Champagne-method bubbly.

Making sweet wine

For wine to be sweet, there must be a noticeable amount of sugar left in it after fermentation. This is known as residual sugar. The simplest method, for the simplest wines, is to stop the fermentation before all the sugar has been turned into alcohol – you just kill the yeasts with sulphur or remove them with a filter or a centrifuge.

Good sweet wines need grapes that are so ripe that the yeasts cannot ferment all the sugar before the alcohol level kills them off and the remaining sugar constitutes the sweetness in the wine. Intense sweet wines – notably Sauternes from Bordeaux – come from grapes affected by a fungus called botrytis or noble rot. It's 'noble' because rather than ruining the grapes like any other disease would, it reduces their water content and concentrates the sugar and acidity. If you have a warm autumn, you can also make sweet wines by letting the grapes shrivel on the vine. An Italian technique is to leave the grapes to shrivel on mats or racks for several months after picking before making the wine. The wines are called *passito* or *recioto*.

I love a glass of good fino sherry with its sharp, pungent tang.

Facing page: Opportunities to taste 19th-century Burgundies are as rare as hens' teeth nowadays. I once tasted an 1865 Romanée – a magnificent vintage. Mmmm...

Making fortified wine

Sweet or dry wines with 15 per cent alcohol or more are usually made by adding brandy or pure spirit to the wine. The practice of fortifying certain wines with extra alcohol was first developed in order to help them travel well.

Port

Red wines from the Douro were notoriously rough. By mistake someone added the fortifying brandy to the wine before the fermentation had finished. As I've already explained, yeasts die if the alcohol level rises too high (anything much above 16 per cent or so), so they were left with a sweet red wine which wouldn't go on fermenting. Genius. Port was born.

Sherry

Sherry is different from port: the brandy is added after the fermentation has finished, so the wine is dry. In barrel, fino sherry grows a layer of yeast called flor, which gives it its typical pungent, almost sour flavour. Sweet sherry is sweetened before bottling.

ORGANIC WINES

There is a strong move in grape growing, as in many other crops, towards organic methods of cultivation. All over the world there are growers who are avoiding using chemical pesticides, herbicides and fertilizers, and returning to natural methods. There are no international standards for what constitutes organic viticulture, but there are local organizations in many regions.

However, vines face tough problems in most parts of the world. Fungal diseases like downy mildew and powdery mildew can wipe out a crop, and insect pests can spread deadly viruses or themselves weaken vines. The risk of abandoning chemicals altogether can be just too great. So a popular alternative to full organic viticulture is to reduce the use of chemicals to the bare essentials. This is often called 'sustainable agriculture'.

Biodynamics takes the concept of working with rather than against nature a stage further than full organic viticulture. Vineyard practices are timed to gain maximum benefit from natural biorhythms, even taking account of the phases of the moon and the movement of the planets. No one is sure why it works, but it frequently does.

VINTAGE WINE

It's a phrase you often hear bandied about to suggest high living: drinking vintage wine, it is implied, is far, far smarter than drinking mere wine. Well, I've got news for you. Most wine is vintage wine.

Vintage wine is simply wine from a single year: the vintage is the name for the annual grape harvest. It does not carry any connotations of greater age or distinction, like vintage cars. If a bottle has a year on it that tells you when it was made, then it's vintage wine.

Not all wine is vintage wine, and not all is the worse for it. For example, most Champagne and other good sparkling wines are non-vintage, meaning that they're a blend of wines from two or more years. Blending different years here ensures consistency of flavour and style.

MEASURING CARBON FOOTPRINT

Gauging the carbon footprint of a wine means considering not just transport, but also the energy expended during production. A gleaming, well-staffed, modern winery is likely to have used far more energy per bottle than an artisan winemaker. Other factors include:

Transporting the wine

Let's have a quick look at logistics. The cost of transporting wine from New Zealand to Europe or the US is a relatively reasonable 13p (21 cents) per bottle. It is good value to ship wine in containers and shipping itself represents an efficient mode of transport. Transporting wine from, say, southern Italy to the UK is considerably more expensive, as the bottles will be trucked overland. Trucking wine is an expensive business.

Bottling at destination

Sometimes wine is shipped in sealed tanks from the source country and bottled at the destination. It makes sense. More wine can be shipped for less money and it's an efficient use of fuel. The carbon footprint per bottle is greatly reduced, and the price saving can be passed on to customers. As standards of bottling and techniques of transporting the wine improve, quality is rising and this is likely to become more common. New Zealand now ships a considerable amount of good bulk wine – something unheard-of a few years ago.

Heavy bottles and alternative packaging

Some producers like to put their wine in thick, chunky, distinctive bottles. Unfortunately, they couldn't be more environmentally unfriendly if they tried, and anyone with an interest in being green should steer well clear of them. Anyway, the wine inside is more than likely to be thick and chunky as well. Heavy bottle producers like that kind of wine. I don't.

Glass is wonderfully inert and innately beautiful but also heavy and fragile. Could plastic be an alternative? Or even juice-style cardboard containers? So far I'm not convinced. But with the climate change crisis we will have to see greater acceptance.

From grape to glass — a tale of two wines

What I want to do here is tie everything together, to trace two different wines from grape to glass and bring the whole process to life. The point is not to compare the wines but to contrast the stories. It is a real and personal business.

On the one hand, I'll look at a **big-selling Sauvignon Blanc from New Zealand**: high-volume, popular wine to retail in the UK at £5–£10 and in the US at between $10 and $20. And on the other, I'll look at a **small producer in Burgundy**, making a fraction of the quantity at over four times the price. In other words a decent producer of what is only mid-priced wine in Burgundy.

Below left: Marlborough, a modern wine region created as recently as the 1970s. Below right: Vineyards have been cultivated in the heart of Burgundy, here in the village of Pommard, since the early Middle Ages.

Background

Our Kiwi Sauvignon, let's call it **OZZIE'S HILLS**, is based at a large, purpose-built, state-of-the-art winery in Marlborough, which houses industrial-scale crushers and pressers, long rows of enormous fermentation vats and layered cellaring facilities. It is the workplace of wine professionals, from winemakers to accountants, scientists to cellar door managers. It is a slickly run operation.

The company owns a substantial portion of land in Marlborough but not enough to satisfy demand, so they also buy grapes from specialist contract growers. **Ozzie's Hills** themselves started out as contract growers in the 1980s, and have managed to successfully turn their hand to winemaking.

Over in Burgundy, **MONSIEUR LE CLARKE** runs the family business from home. He employs three people: his wife, his son and a reliable chap called Jacques from the village. The effortlessly charming Madame le Clarke

Above: Traditional Burgundian basket press. Facing page: Stainless steel vats are used at most New World wineries.

runs the 'office' in a constant battle with their temperamental home computer, while his son is learning the ropes of the business. He makes the odd balls-up but has a useful degree in enology – which is winemaking to you and me. **Monsieur le Clarke** himself is only happy in the vineyards or the cellar, and that's where you'll always find him. His wife tried to make him use a mobile phone, but he said he can't have any interruptions when he's looking after his vines.

All the winemaking equipment is kept in the garage, next to the tractor. The beautiful house has been in the le Clarke family for 250 years, which is about as long as the family has been making wine.

Vineyards, climate and grapes

The Marlborough vineyards sweep across rolling hills and valleys for as far as the eye can see. The growing season starts in September/October and summer consists of long warm days of bright sunshine that ripen the grapes fully, while cool breezy nights maintain the essential balance. This combination creates a wine bursting with flavour but also crisp and dry. Much top-spec technology is utilized to help grow the best-quality grapes in large quantities. Great gleaming tractors make short work of zipping up and down the rows. Helicopters may be used for spraying.

M. le Clarke, meanwhile, has no outright vineyards to manage but owns many parcels of vines spread across 18 different vineyards in three adjacent villages. This is the norm. Napoleonic laws of inheritance have resulted in fractured ownership of land. While M. le Clarke tends his rows of grapes very carefully, the rows on either side of his are not so well loved. Quality varies enormously within every vineyard. Each parcel of vines is made into separate wine.

The climate in Burgundy is much more marginal than in New Zealand, which makes growing grapes more precarious. The growing season begins in April/May and all fingers are crossed for a warm, long summer. Delicate Pinot Noir, **M. le Clarke**'s main interest, seems to give its best in exactly this kind of climate. He has one small tractor to help with spraying but it's old and cumbersome. Some of his neighbours are talking of returning to using horses. He thinks they may have a point. Free manure, for a start.

Making the wine

In New Zealand the grapes are picked in late February and March by machine harvesters that gently shake the grapes from the vine. The **Ozzie's Hills** winemakers wait to direct the process in the winery, having spent the last six months abroad, honing their skills in the northern hemisphere.

Fermentation at cool, controlled temperatures in stainless-steel vats is the next step. Their adoption in New Zealand from the dairy industry revolutionized winemaking in the 1980s. The stainless steel vats are inert and allow the winemaker to maximize the flavour of fruit and freshness in the grape. Filter and bottle it

really young – maybe just a month or two – and the result is an explosion of crisp green Sauvignon flavours from the glass.

Back in Burgundy, harvest is in September and **M. le Clarke** organizes a team of experienced pickers to help him hand-pick the grapes. Some of the pickers come from families who've been helping with the harvest for a hundred years. They know the vines almost as well as M. le Clarke does. If anything's not right, they'll tell him. He's overseen 28 vintages in his time and saw many more as a boy. There is little he hasn't seen.

Once the harvest is in, he sets about making the wine in his garage on his annually primed and cleaned equipment. He has one new piece of equipment: a basket press for gentler separation of the juice from the skins – very important for Pinot Noir. Funnily enough, the design of the basket press, with its slatted wooden sides, is almost exactly the same as that of the one his grandfather used. In Burgundy, progress is often a case of going back to see what worked best in the old days.

Some new French oak barrels have been purchased from a local cooper for maturing the wine, and are stored in cool, underground cellars. The main cellar is beneath the house, but as he's gradually bought more parcels of vineyard he's needed to expand and so also rents a cellar underneath the priest's house. Any difficult wines are stored there, and they do seem to calm down and develop a delightfully tranquil nature under the divine influence of the prelate. Actually, M. le Clarke stores only his top wine in 'new' oak, because he doesn't want too much vanilla and toasty spice in his Burgundy; it will swamp the subtleties of all his different vineyard sites. He uses barrels for several vintages before selling them off to a merchant in the nearby town. He knows the exact state of each barrel, in each cellar. Maturation may go on for many months and he will often be making winemaking decisions well into the following growing season, further complicating the balancing act of what to do and when. He waits and waits until the wine feels right, and then it is ready.

Bottling

Ozzie's Hills will be bottled under screwcap, thus essentially eliminating any chance of cork taint. The embracing of screwcap technology is fully indicative of New Zealand's forward-looking mentality, and has helped push reluctant consumers toward modernity.

M. le Clarke has not yet learnt the French word for screwcap, and has never tasted a screwcapped bottle of wine. For him, it is cork or nothing.

PART TWO
ENJOYING WINE

Wine is part of everyday life and treating it with reverential awe won't make it taste any better. The rituals of opening, serving, tasting, buying and storing wine are mostly built on sound reasoning, but they are meaningless if they don't help you to enjoy yourself and get the best out of your wine. If you don't get pleasure out of a glass of wine, there's no point to it. But for some of you, these rituals of serving and the responsibility of owning and storing wines will add to the pleasure. And you may take pleasure in arguing the toss in wine shops and restaurants with sales assistants and wine waiters. Fantastic. But if you don't get a buzz out of such things – don't worry. Just have confidence in the fact that the most important thing is that you are happy and having fun yourself. In this book I try to make life easier for everyone who enjoys wine, at whatever level.

buying and storing wine

I have a chaotic jumble of bottles under the stairs in my house, and stray bottles tucked into odd corners in the kitchen, the box room and behind the TV. But however much wine I accumulate, it's never going to stop me dropping into my local wine shop to browse, have a chat and pick up a bottle for the evening. This is the way we buy most of our wine these days, not by the case, not for laying down, just as part of our daily shopping.

OZ'S TIPS FOR FINDING OUT MORE ABOUT WINE

A selection of useful internet sites
- www.wine-searcher.com
- www.decanter.com
- www.winespectator.com
- www.winemag.com

A few good wine blogs
- www.wineanorak.com
- www.jancisrobinson.com
- www.wineloverspage.com
- www.wine-pages.com
- www.natdecants.com
- www.quaff.com.au
- www.matchingfood andwine.com

Where to buy wine

Shopping for wine can be so much more, though, than a dash to your local store: it can be a pleasure and a leisure pursuit in itself. Here are some of the options, starting with the easiest, buying from your home.

Using the internet and mail-order shopping

For sheer range of choice, the best thing to do is stay at home. Seriously. The internet has revolutionized wine buying. Plenty of established merchants and internet-only wine 'e-tailers' have websites which you can browse at leisure, comparing prices and digging out far more information on individual wines than you'll be likely to find on a shop shelf.

Of course, it's just an advanced version of traditional mail-order shopping, which has been a mainstay of wine retailing for years. Both methods have the advantage that you don't need to worry about carting the wine home and, more importantly, give you access to a vast number of wines not available in your local area.

And if you want to experience the warm sense of being part of a like-minded fellowship, well, there are a significant number of wine clubs out there that will not only sell you wine but will also keep you involved, with newsletters, tastings and events.

A good wine shop

What the internet lacks is the quiet meditative atmosphere of a really good wine shop – the cool, even slightly musty air, the calming lighting, the stillness. It slows the pulse rate and gives you the space and time to browse, choose with care and touch and dream about bottles you may never be able to afford. These are all signs of a shop that stores the wine in appropriate conditions and has knowledgeable staff. You may pay a bit more for your wine here, but this is where to come when you need inspiration.

Most shops offer a discount on a 12-bottle case, and this is the minimum quantity you can buy from many internet and mail order merchants. You don't have to buy a whole case of the same wine: you can usually order a selection of bottles (called a mixed case).

OZ'S TIPS

Good shops, bad shops

A good wine shop

- has clued-up staff and plenty of information about the wines
- is cool and not too brightly lit
- is prepared to advise you to buy a cheaper wine
- holds regular wine tastings
- offers a mixture of young and mature wines

A bad wine shop

- has uninformed staff
- has wine standing upright on the shelves that has been gathering dust and gently cooking for months on end
- has pushy staff who try to make you buy a more expensive wine than you intended
- only sells brand-name wines
- gives more space to beers, cigarettes, groceries and snacks

This is the kind of wine shop I enjoy – it's well stocked and laid out and the lighting is not too strong.

A good supermarket display with clear signs and a wide range of wines on offer.

A good wine shop doesn't have to have been established for hundreds of years. Many corner shops have some good wines, and the best of the franchise operations try to encourage the operators to stock decent stuff. Many of the best independent merchants have actually been established for less than a generation and many operate out of an industrial estate. Wine warehouses may not look very sophisticated – they're not trying to – but they usually offer very good ranges of wines, as do the larger branches of the supermarkets. And if you're getting the wine bug, wine brokers offer keen, up-to-the-minute prices, but usually only on top-end stuff and for orders of at least a case or to a minimum value. They advertise in wine magazines and online wine sites.

Getting good service

If you want to know about any of the wines in a shop, ask. Enthusiastic and knowledgeable staff are usually bursting to tell you about their wines. If none of the staff knows anything about the wines, or you get the impression that they are blustering, it's probable that they don't handle the wines too carefully either. Shop elsewhere.

However well a merchant does handle the wines, it's impossible to guarantee that every bottle is faultfree. Most shops will happily exchange the wine for a replacement bottle if you suspect a fault after opening the wine.

It's worth buying regularly from one merchant. Let them know which wines you liked and which you weren't so keen on. The more a merchant knows about your preferences, the better he or she will be able to guide you.

Getting information

Wines are reviewed on TV, on the radio, in newspapers and magazines and on dedicated wine websites, but sharing your experiences with friends is one of the best ways of gathering recommendations. Some shops have informative cards on the shelves and many wines have detailed descriptions on the back label.

All wine merchants publish lists of the wines they stock. The simplest name the wines and their prices, and give details of the merchant's terms of business. More ambitious lists review all the wines (sometimes with the whiff of marketing hype) and may include details about the merchant's pet wine regions and winemakers.

Most merchants hold regular wine-tastings. Some are formal occasions, others simply a matter of opening a few bottles for customers to sample during shop hours. Surprisingly few merchants will pressure you to buy any of the wines being tasted.

Auction houses

A wine sale catalogue from a top auction house will have wine enthusiasts drooling over wine names they certainly don't see in their local wine shop every day. Better still, the lots are often of mature vintages that are difficult to buy elsewhere. Top auction houses today make a considerable effort to check the provenance of their wines. If you've never bought wine at an auction before, a good place to start is at a local auctioneer rather than at the famous international houses of Sotheby's, Christie's or Acker Merrall & Condit who hold regular auctions in London, New York and Hong Kong. Online wine auctions are also popular, too, and have similar pros and cons to live auctions.

WINE TERMS **Bin ends**

Bin ends are simply leftovers: they're the last bottles of the old vintage, and the wine merchant wants to clear them out to make room for the new vintage. Or the merchant bought too much of a particular wine, and wants to shift it. Or they're just odds and ends that are taking up space. Either way, they may be offered at reduced prices. Often they're a bargain – but there's always a risk they may be past their best.

OZ'S TIPS

Buying direct from the producer

Some châteaux and wineries are only too happy to sell wine from the cellar door or by mail order. For some, it's the only way they sell it. If you're visiting, call first to check opening times and if necessary to make an appointment. But beware: even in this age of online shopping you can still run up against archaic trade barriers. Wherever you live you'll generally have to pay a customs duty on wine shipped to you from abroad. And in some US states it is actually illegal for consumers to buy wine direct from outside the state.

IDEAS FOR WINE TOURING

Two general websites to get you started

- www.winetravelguides.com
- www.travelenvoy.com/wine.htm

Country by country websites

Most of the sites below have links to regional organizations with more ideas for wine routes, wineries to visit, seasonal events and so on.

Europe
- www.englishwineproducers.com
- www.vins-bordeaux.fr
- www.bourgogne-wines.com
- www.champagne.fr
- www.italianwinetours.com
- www.winesfromspain.com
- www.viniportugal.pt
- www.germanwine.de/english.html

North and South America
- www.appellationamerica.com
- www.wineinstitute.org
- www.newyorkwines.org
- www.washingtonwine.org
- www.oregonwine.org
- www.winesofchile.org
- www.winesofargentina.org
- www.winesofbrasil.com

Rest of the world
- www.wineaustralia.com
- www.visitvineyards.com
- www.newzealand.com/travel and www.nzwine.com
- www.wosa.co.za

Wine touring

Many of the world's most stunning vineyard areas make great holiday destinations, too, and I can think of few greater pleasures for wine lovers than tasting wine in the place it's made. Specialist wine tours are a fantastic way to learn about wine in a way you'll never forget, and it's all done for you – visits planned, experts to show you around, translators on hand – but independent travellers can have just as much fun, too.

In France, Alsace, Burgundy and the Loire Valley are perhaps the most delightful regions for the wine lover, but wherever vines are grown in France you're likely to see signs by the road saying *dégustation et vente* (tasting and sales) or *vente directe* (direct sales). In Bordeaux, by all means visit the famous châteaux – you'll need to make an appointment and the top ones won't let you in, anyway. They don't usually let *me* in – who could blame them? But the less famous ones will welcome you. In Champagne most of the big houses in Epernay and Reims offer guided tours.

Cantinas (wine cellars) can be found all over Italy, but Piedmont, Tuscany and the Veneto are the regions that have been at it the longest, and are most geared up for tourists. In Spain you'll find *bodegas* set up to welcome tourists, particularly in three main regions: Rioja, Penedès, inland from Barcelona and famous for Cava fizz, and the town of Jerez in Andalucía with its sherry bodegas.

Wine tourists in South Africa, Australia, New Zealand and many US states, in particular California, are well catered for by friendly people, and many wineries offer fine dining experiences, too.

Storing wine

Very few of us have a big, dark, cool cellar under our house where we can lay down wines to mature for years on end. Just as well then, that plenty of modern wines aren't designed to benefit from extended aging anyway. It's still worth keeping a few bottles in a rack to save running down to the shop all the time. Store the wine you buy out of direct sunlight and away from major heat sources and it will be happy for a few months.

However, a fiercely tannic red will only reveal its sweeter nature after several years, and many high-quality white wines develop with time. If you just keep them standing about the house for years on end, the light, warmth and dry air will conspire to ruin the wine.

You need somewhere fairly cool and humid that isn't subject to fluctuations in temperature or to vibration, and you need darkness (draping a blanket over the bottles will also help keep their temperature fairly even). Lay the wine on its side to keep the cork damp and swollen, which preserves the airtight seal. An understairs cupboard is a good storage place. For perfect conditions you could buy a temperature- and humidity-controlled cabinet or even have a cellar installed under your house, but both options are expensive.

For more expensive purchases, you can pay your wine merchant to store the wines. Make sure that you receive a stock certificate and that your cases are clearly identified and stored separately from the merchant's own stock.

Simple racking systems like this one are not expensive and are easy to install. I spend far too much time drooling over the bottles on my racks.

OZ'S TIPS

Finding out about vintages

Some of the world's most sought-after wines come from places where the grapes are poised on a knife-edge of ripening or failing every year. These are the regions where vintages really matter, because the wines can be so different from one year to the next. In regions with a more reliable climate, the vintage year on the bottle is really no more than an indication of the wine's age.

You'll find vintage charts, giving a mark out of ten to each vintage in the world's main wine regions, in many places – you may even have one in your diary. How closely should you follow them?

The answer is that such general information can only ever be a rough guide. Weather conditions are not necessarily the same for a whole region, and in any case a good producer will make better wine in a poor year than a lazy one will make in a good year. So consult vintage charts for general advice – but don't treat them as gospel.

Age and maturity

As wine lies in its bottle, it evolves. Tannins soften, acid mellows, red wines grow paler and develop sediment, whites darken to a rich, nutty amber. Wines with plenty of acid and tannin will become more approachable and less fierce-tasting with time, and if they have the vital extra ingredient – loads of intense fruit flavour – the true quality of the wine will be revealed only after a few years' aging in the bottle.

But older wine is not always better wine. For most wine the best vintage is the most recent one. Everyday wines simply taste more and more stale, faded and dull as the

understanding wine labels

A wine label is not just the attractive final touch to the bottle or an advertisement for the producer's sense of style, it is a guide to the contents of the bottle and should give you a pretty good idea of the style and flavour of the wine inside. However, there are certain legal requirements that vary from country to country, which I will cover briefly in the following pages.

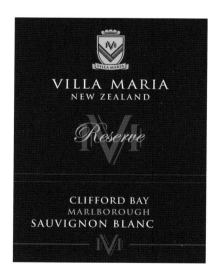

This is a typical New World label where the name of the producer, here Villa Maria, and the grape variety, here Sauvignon Blanc, are more important than that of the region (Marlborough) and wine name (Clifford Bay).

You can see for yourself whether the wine is white, red or rosé. Next I would want to know which grapes the wine is made from, where they were grown, who made the wine and when. With this information, you'll be in a position to know what you're getting.

It seems simple enough to offer this passport-style information, and many wine labels lay it all out with commendable clarity. Others can seem seriously obscure, though really it's only a question of understanding a little more about how the world of wine works.

What will it taste like?

The simplest labels to understand are those that state the grape variety. Most labels of New World wines do this, although there's also a fashion for naming top-class wines after a bin number or a vat number or the vineyard or the proprietor's daughter. But in such cases the back label often gives the game away and tells you the grapes used. The grape variety is the biggest clue the label gives to the taste of the wine. The next biggest is the place. If you've read as far as this you'll know that Sauvignon Blanc from New Zealand has a particular style and flavour; when you see a bottle you know more or less what to expect.

In the case of European wines, the grape varieties are often not stated. However, they tend to be defined by the rules that apply in the region that the wine is named after. That's why I've put together the Appellation Decoder on pages 186–188 to link classic wines with their grape varieties. Because what you need to be able to do, when looking at a wine label, is put it in context.

I mentioned the term terroir on page 52. Terroir is the basis of the French appellation or 'control of origin' system. In the French view, terroir is what makes each vineyard different from its neighbour. So it makes sense to take an area that shares more or less the same terroir and give it one name (or appellation), then take another area with basically a slightly different terroir, and give it another name. Even if the grapes are the same, the style of the wine should be different. For example, five neighbouring appellations in the northern Rhône Valley produce red wines based on the Syrah grape but each (in theory) has its own unique character.

Which producer?

The producer is the company or person that makes the wine. They have control over the choice of grapes and who makes the wine and how, and so are responsible for the quality of the wine. High quality doesn't necessarily mean a high price: one thing that marks out a good producer is how much better the wines are than poorly made or unexciting ones of a similar price. A poor producer can follow all the rules and come up with poor wine; a good producer will make creditable wine in almost any circumstances.

There are thousands and thousands of wine producers in the world and you can't hope to know all of them, or even all the good ones, even in one country. If you know nothing about the producer of the wine then buying it is a risk. It's a matter of taking advice and experimenting to find producers whose wines you like. You'll find some of my recommendations in the The World of Wine section on pages 106–185.

Easily recognized brand-name wines offer a safe route out of the producer maze. The quality of these wines is generally good these days, although they can be overpriced. But if I buy a brand name, I'm buying a non-specific wine, blended to a happy-medium sort of a taste. It will probably be perfectly nice, and reliably so, but it's unlikely to be exciting.

European appellation systems make it difficult for the less knowledgeable wine lover to tell from the label what grape varieties have been used in the wine. Red Rioja is made principally from a blend of Tempranillo and Garnacha (Grenache) grapes, but this classy example, Castillo Ygay, is mainly Tempranillo with a little Mazuelo to bring a hint of acidity to the blend. Yet the label doesn't tell you.

WINE TERMS **Dry, medium or sweet?**

For wines from all countries except Germany, you can generally assume that the wine is dry unless otherwise stated. However, the wines from Alsace in France are currently involved in a bit of a rumpus because a lot of them are quite sweet yet don't say so on the label. With global warming, and a general trend towards very ripe flavours – especially in the US – you might think that quite a lot of the wines you taste, for instance, Sauvignon Blanc and Chardonnay, are not quite dry. And you'd be right.

FRANCE
Brut is very dry; **Sec** is dry; **demi-sec** off-dry; **doux** or **moelleux** sweet; **liquoreux** very sweet. Be aware that wines from appellations that apply specifically to sweet wines, such as Sauternes, make no mention on the label of the fact that the wine is sweet.

ITALY
Secco is dry, **semisecco** is medium-dry. Medium-sweet is **abboccato** or **amabile**. Sweet wines are **dolce**.

SPAIN
Seco is dry, **semi-seco** medium and **dulce** sweet.

GERMANY
Wines here tend to be at least slightly sweet unless otherwise stated. The terms **Kabinett**, **Spätlese**, **Auslese**, **Beerenauslese**, **Trockenbeerenauslese** and **Eiswein** refer to ascending levels of sweetness. **Trocken** is dry while **Halbtrocken** off-dry.

AUSTRIA
Dry wines are more common here than in Germany, but with a warmer climate, they are also a little fuller and riper. Austrian sweet styles are, in ascending order of sweetness: **Spätlese**, **Auslese**, **Beerenauslese**, **Ausbruch**, **Trockenbeerenauslese** and **Eiswein**.

Classifications on the label

The most pressing question, the one that none of the information on the label will answer directly, is whether the wine is good, bad or indifferent. And, try as they might, official classification systems don't help much with indicating the quality of the wine.

The most basic way of classifying wine is by the place of origin. Outside Europe most countries are settling for something like the US AVA (American Viticultural Area) system. Each area is supposed to be homogeneous in some way – climate, for example – but in practice many AVAs have boundaries that simply follow county lines. This sort of system guarantees the geographical origin of the wine, but carries no quality connotations.

All the European systems are based to some extent on the concept of terroir (see page 52). To ensure that the intrinsic character of each region's wine is maintained, it is deemed necessary to regulate most aspects of wine production.

The most strictly regulated wines in France (and each European country has an equivalent classification – see the box on page 76) are Appellation Contrôlée wines. The words Appellation Contrôlée on a label are not, however, a guarantee of quality – they simply guarantee that the wine is from the region, uses the correct grape varieties and vineyard and winemaking practices, and has been made in accordance with the rules of that region. This is why you can't grow any old grape varieties in Bordeaux and then claim the Bordeaux appellation. Rules for IGP wines (these used to be called vins de pays) are far more relaxed; and Vin de France (formerly vin de table) can be pretty much anything that won't kill you.

Interestingly, it is at the top end that fraud is of the most concern. As the price of top wines has spiralled upwards, and as they are sold more and more to new markets like China and Russia that don't have a long experience of how the labels, corks and capsules should look and how the wines should taste, fraudulent bottles have become surprisingly common. Top producers are now employing various techniques in labelling, capsuling and corking their top bottles that guarantee authenticity and help to trace any fraudsters.

OZ'S TIPS

Imposters!

Rules about how wines may be described on labels are tighter than ever. It's true that sparkling wines from America, North and South, can call themselves 'Champagne' as long as they're not shipped to Europe, but there has been progress. Australia has virtually phased out the misleading use of classic European wine names – Chablis, Sauternes and so on – for its own wines.

What we have to look out for now is wines from unfashionable areas being repackaged to look like wines from fashionable ones. It's quite simple and quite legal: you take your Eastern European white and red, give them a brand name like Kangaroo Creek and leave the details of where they were made for the small print.

No, it's not a capital offence. And as long as the wine tastes as modern as the packaging, I can't entirely condemn it. But it's a shame that they think we'll only buy their wine if it looks like something else. Especially when experience shows we'll buy anything, if it's good enough.

WINE CLASSIFICATIONS: EUROPE

The French appellation system is the most widely known system of quality control. Other European countries have roughly equivalent gradings, though some have more categories. Quality within any of the bands is not consistent and a good example of a simple wine will be better than a poorly made wine that has complied with the rules to achieve a higher status.

	FRANCE	ITALY	PORTUGAL	SPAIN	GERMANY	AUSTRIA
Special-quality wine	No category	Denominazione di Origine Controllata e Garantita (**DOCG**)	No category	Denominación de Origen Calificada (**DOCa**)	Qualitätswein mit Prädikat (**QmP**), but since 2007 called Prädikatswein – divided into 6 styles	Prädikatswein – a superior category of Qualitatswein – is divided into 7 styles
Quality wine	Appellation d'Origine Contrôlée (**AC/AOC**) or Appellation d'Origine Protégée (**AOP**)	Denominazione di Origine Controllata (**DOC**) or Denominazione di Origine Protetta (**DOP**)	Denominação de Origem Controlada (**DOC**) or Denominação de Origem Protegida (**DOP**)	Denominación de Origen (**DO**) or Denominación de Origen Protegida (**DOP**). Vino de Pago is a new category for single-estate wines	Qualitätswein bestimmter Anbaugebiete (**QbA**) comes from one of 13 designated regions	Qualitätswein covers wines from a named region. In addition, DAC is a regional appellation for wines of a particular style from a particular region
Regional wine	Indication Géographique Protégée (**IGP**), previously known as Vin de pays	Indicazione Geografica Tipica/Protetta (**IGT/IGP**)	Vinho regional or Indicação Geográfica Protegida (**IGP**)	Vino de la tierra (**VT**) or Indicación Geográfica Protegida (**IGP**)	Landwein	Landwein
Basic wine	Vin de France; this replaced the vin de table category in 2009	Vino da tavola	Vinho	Vino (previously vino de mesa)	Deutscher Wein (previously Tafelwein)	Wein (previously Tafelwein)

What the label tells you

The majority of modern wines will tell you what grape was used to make the wine, and what country the grapes were grown in. These are the two most important indicators as to the style of the wine. The producer's name is also crucially important: as in any walk of life, some are better than others. You should also find the year the grapes were harvested – the vintage. After that, here is a list of things you may find: the region and the country the wine comes from; the wine's classification, if it has one; the alcohol level, increasingly important in our health-conscious age; and where the wine was bottled – ideally by the producer, next best is in the region of production, and least good is in a country thousands of miles away from where the grapes were grown. However, with worries about carbon footprint, the quality of wines shipped in bulk is already improving.

A good label should give you lots of clues about the wine, but beware of florid marketing hype on the back label.

Five things to be wary of on a label

1 Reserve In some countries (notably Spain and Italy) reserve wines are matured in oak for longer than the standard wines and a full set of rules is in force. Elsewhere the term might be used to indicate this style of wine, but then again it might just mean nothing at all.

2 Supérieur Surely a superior wine is better? Sorry, wrong. This French term and its Italian equivalent **superiore** indicate only that the wine has a slightly higher alcohol content than the ordinary wine of the same name.

3 Grand Vin In Bordeaux, Grand Vin indicates that it is the main wine of the property, as opposed to a second wine. It does not mean 'great wine'.

4 South-Eastern Australia No, there's nothing wrong with this – just bear in mind that South-Eastern Australia includes the vast majority of Australia's wine-producing areas – just about everything except Western Australia. So while the name of the wine might imply a particular place and the label might imply a specific appellation, it's not as specific as all that. Far from it. It's like saying 'this wine could come from anywhere in France except Champagne and Alsace'.

5 Anything that claims to be special – exceptional, classic, a limited release, from the founder's bin... Just ignore these terms and stick to the basics of who, what, when and where in deducing the likely quality of the wine.

European wine labels

The front label varies with the type of wine and from country to country but it should tell you all the necessary information about the wine. The two European wine labels here show two very different approaches.

PLANETA a modern, dynamic producer from Sicily

1 Name of the producer this modern label from a go-getting company is more reminiscent of labels from outside Europe, especially from California and Australia. The producer name is the most important element on the label.

2 Name of the wine 'Burdese' gives the consumer no clue as to the style of wine inside. I would hope the back label explains more!

CHÂTEAU LAFON-ROCHET a traditional Bordeaux producer

1 Classification This tells you that the wine was included in the famous 1855 Classification of the red wines of Bordeaux.

2 Traditional imagery The vast majority of Bordeaux labels still feature a straightforward illustration of the château building. Any that do not are probably making a statement about their modern approach.

3 Château name Any wine estate in France, especially in Bordeaux, can take a château name, regardless of whether it has a grand building. Castello is the equivalent word in Italy, Castillo in Spain and Schloss in Germany.

4 Appellation European wine regulations expect the appellation name to tell you all you need to know about the taste of the wine, its quality classification and place of origin. St-Estèphe in Bordeaux is best known for its slow-maturing, tannic red wines based on Cabernet Sauvignon.

5 Vintage The year the grapes were harvested. In most parts of the world the year's weather influences the style of wine, its ripeness, alcohol level and longevity. It's also important to check the vintage to see whether the wine is ready to drink.

6 Château bottling Once rare, this is now the norm in Bordeaux, and means that the wine was bottled on the estate. Anything not bottled at the château or '*à la propriété*' is most likely an undistinguished offering from a large merchant or co-operative.

7 Meaningless statements 'Grand vin de Bordeaux' sounds good but in fact says nothing about the quality of the wine. 'Grand Vin' on its own on a Bordeaux label indicates that the wine is the château's main wine, rather than one of its lesser ones, but again says nothing about its quality.

8 Alcohol level the regulations for each appellation specify the required minimum alcohol level.

9 The quantity of wine in the bottle 75cl is the standard bottle size for wine.

German wine labels

For some time now German producers have been moving away from traditional Gothic script on their wine labels to a design that is more user friendly, especially to consumers outside Germany. Optional information is moved to the back label.

LOOSEN

1 Name of the producer Dr Loosen is a top German producer making exciting wines.

2 Vintage This style of wine is best drunk young so the year of vintage is clear to read.

3 Grape variety The grape variety is the most prominent name on the label. Riesling is Germany's best white grape.

LANGWERTH VON SIMMERN

This beautiful label is an example of the more traditional style of German label. But all this information still gives the less knowledgeable consumer little indication of the flavour of the wine inside the bottle – except that it's probably sweetish.

1 Name of the producer Freiherr Langwerth von Simmern based in the village of Eltville.

2 Gutsabfüllung means 'bottled by'.

3 Village and vineyard site The vineyard name usually follows the name of the village. Marcobrunn is a famous Riesling vineyard in the village of Erbach in the Rheingau.

4 Auslese indicates the level of sweetness. Auslese wines are usually fairly sweet.

5 Grape variety The name Riesling is in small letters and is not seen to be a selling point.

GERMAN WINE STYLES

Prädikat (the top overall classification) comes in six styles or grades, defined by the ripeness of the grapes used.

Kabinett The lightest Prädikat wine. It will be slightly sweet unless labelled as **Halbtrocken** (off-dry) or **Trocken** (dry).

Spätlese ('late-picked') Many are sweetish, though Halbtrocken and Trocken versions are also common.

Auslese ('selected') Wine made from selected bunches of very ripe grapes. Most are fairly sweet but some are dry.

Beerenauslese ('selected berries') Luscious sweet wine made from selected single grapes, almost always affected by the noble rot fungus.

Trockenbeerenauslese ('shrivelled selected berries') Intensely sweet wines made from individually picked grapes shrivelled by noble rot.

Eiswein ('ice wine') Made from frozen grapes picked in winter. (Honest! Sometimes they're picked on Christmas Day!)

Other wine labels

Labels from wine regions outside Europe are usually clearly laid out and easy to understand.

HOWARD PARK

1 Name of the producer Wines produced outside the traditional appellation areas of Europe often promote the producer name over that of any region.

2 A simple graphic image is commonly used for wine labels in the same way as a European coat of arms.

3 Wine name The name doesn't give the consumer a clue as to the style of wine inside the bottle, but I know that Abercrombie is Howard Park's flagship wine.

4 Grape variety Cabernet Sauvignon is a key selling point on this label, and is one of Western Australia's success stories.

5 Region Western Australia is a key wine state in Australia.

Back labels

Buying wine would be far easier if the label told you how the wine tasted; some back labels do. Many retailers also have helpful systems for grading each of the wines they sell on a scale from bone dry to very sweet for whites, and from light to full-bodied for reds. Back labels can tell you how oaky the wine is and which grape varieties were used to make it. Or they can tell you whether the wine is suitable for aging and what foods will go well with it. But they can also be complete waffle and marketing gobbledegook.

It's up to you to make the distinction between useful information and the interventions of an enthusiastic marketing department. Treat back-label information as a general guide to the wine and don't let yourself be drawn in by florid accounts of the winemaking.

REGULATIONS OUTSIDE EUROPE

In the US, South America, Australia, New Zealand and South Africa, regulations govern statements about the place of origin of the wine and the grape varieties used. They help to ensure that the labelling is honest, but don't generally tell you anything about quality.

The US uses the AVA (American Viticultural Area) system which merely requires that at least 85% of grapes in a wine come from the specified AVA. Canada has a quality-based system; look for the letters VQA on the label. In Australia the Label Integrity Program (LIP) guarantees all claims made on the label and the GI (Geographical Indication) system is being rolled out across the country. In New Zealand labels guarantee geographic origin and in South Africa the Wine of Origin (WO) system specifies regions, districts and further subdivisions.

opening the bottle

The gentle creak, squeak and pop of a cork being pulled – that's a sound I like a lot. It's the overture to a celebration, the moment when work stops and the evening begins. Even the most hopeless corkscrew will work most of the time, but a well-made one is less likely to wreck the cork or leave cork crumbs floating in your wine.

BOXES, CARTONS AND CANS

Wine boxes with a tap on the side are a perfectly sound idea, especially if you just want a glass or two per day. The technology is fine; the problem is that the choice is limited and the wine in the box is rarely exciting.

Cartons like the ones used to store milk are effective, but they're awkward to open and, again, the wine put into them is nothing to write home about. As for **ring-pull cans**, don't even think about it – yet. But for a party or a picnic drink, the idea is fine: it just needs more serious technology applied – and better wine in the can.

Don't be a cork snob – bottles come with all sorts of seals nowadays. But I do still love a good, old-fashioned real cork.

Choosing a corkscrew

Look for a corkscrew with a comfortable handle, an open spiral and a lever system that you like using. Corkscrews with a solid core that looks like a giant screw tend to mash up delicate corks or get stuck in tough ones. With a simple T-shaped corkscrew the effort of pulling the cork can turn into a circus-strongman act, but it does bring a certain sigh of satisfaction when – if – you remove the cork without giving yourself a hernia.

Using a corkscrew

First tear off or cut away the metal foil or plastic seal around the top of the bottle, known as the capsule. You can buy a device called a foil cutter for this job; some corkscrews include one in the handle. Wipe the lip of the bottle if there is dirt or mould around the top of the cork.

Press the point of the corkscrew gently into the centre of the cork. Turn the corkscrew slowly and steadily and try to drive it in dead straight. If it veers wildly off-course at the first attempt, it is better to unwind it and start again than to press on and risk breaking the cork. With some, like Screwpull, you just keep turning and the cork is pulled out. With others, stop turning as the point emerges at the bottom of the cork and then ease the cork out gently.

The standard restaurant corkscrew is called a **waiter's friend**. It has a lever at the top to help ease out the cork and folds away neatly. I find it the simplest, most compact opener – I never go anywhere without one.

The **Screwpull** brand is a very simple design, which has never been bettered. It relies on the high quality open spiral for its effectiveness. This long-handled version gives you extra leverage and makes light work of even the stiffest corks, although the foil-cutting knife is a bit tricky to use.

The most irritating design is the ubiquitous '**butterfly**' – not only does it feature the sort of thick, solid-cored screw that mashes up corks, but I always find it impossible to remove the cork in one sweep of the lever arms.

OZ'S TIPS

Don't be a cork snob

The only requirements for the seal on a bottle of wine are that it should be hygienic, airtight, long-lasting and removable. Cork has been successsfully employed since Roman times at least, and I do love the ritual of extracting a cork from a good bottle, but cork is simply the bark from the cork oak tree and as such is prone to inconsistency, infection and shrinkage. Modern alternatives lack cork's cachet and mystique, but they will give you fresher wine on a regular basis.

Screwtops are seriously challenging cork for supremacy. They are consistent and inert, so the wine is reliable every time. They don't let oxygen in so the wine stays fresher longer and, in fact, wines age more slowly under screwcap. Their only major drawback is that the wine can develop a sulphide-y off-odour, but this is due to lack of oxygen and can easily be addressed by the winemaker.

Plastic corks are OK for early-drinking wines, but no one is convinced of their ability to age.

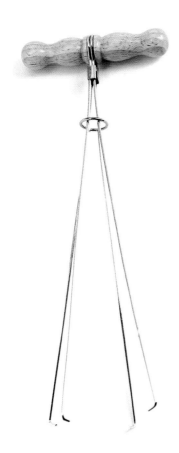

If you're very lucky, you might own this device called a butler's friend which is brilliant at fishing out pieces of broken cork.

Opening sparkling wine

The pressure in the bottle does the work, so all you have to do is control it. If you don't, you'll get a loud pop, a rush of foam and a half-empty bottle of rapidly flattening fizz. You might injure somebody, too.

Tear off the foil to reveal the wire cage that restrains the cork. Place one thumb over the top of the cork and undo the cage. From the moment the cage is released there is an ever-present danger of the cork shooting off, so point the bottle away from people, windows and other breakables.

Some people say you have to turn the bottle, not the cork. Well, I say grasp the cork with one hand and hold the bottle firmly with the other. Then either turn the cork, or the bottle, whichever grabs you, but the most important thing is, keep a thumb or a hand over that cork to stop it flying out and removing someone's eye. If you keep a lot of downward pressure on the cork you should be able to ease it out gently – and you may even experience that ol' timers' delight, the cork slipping out with a sigh like a contented woman. Hold the bottle at an angle of 45° for a few moments to calm the initial rush of foam, then pour the first glass.

Always make sure the bottle is thoroughly chilled before you attempt to open it. A warm bottle is quite likely to explode its cork in dramatic fashion, however hard you try to restrain it.

Broken corks

To remove a broken cork that is still wedged into the bottle neck, drive the corkscrew in at the sharpest available angle and press the cork fragment against the side of the neck as you work it gently upwards. If you're having no luck, push the cork down into the wine. You might get bits of cork in your glass, but the wine will taste none the worse for it – just fish them out.

If a sparkling wine cork breaks in the bottle, then your only option is to resort to a corkscrew. But take the cork out very cautiously – remember, there's still all that pressurized gas in the bottle.

serving wine

If you want to taste wine at its best, to enjoy all its flavours and aromas, to admire its colours and texture, choose glasses designed for the purpose and show the wine a bit of respect.

Glasses

The ideal wine glass is a fairly large tulip shape, made of fine, clear glass, with a slender stem. Anything that approximates to this description will do. When you pour the wine, fill the glass no more than halfway so that you can swirl the wine around and allow the aromas to develop. For sparkling wines choose a tall, slender glass, as it helps the bubbles to last longer.

Coloured glass obscures the colour of the wine, flared glasses dissipate the aromas rather than concentrating them, and heavy, thick glasses are, well, heavy and thick.

Detergent residues or grease in the glass can affect the flavour of any wine and reduce the bubbliness of sparkling wine. Always rinse glasses thoroughly after washing them and allow them to air-dry or keep a lint-free cloth for drying glasses only – Ulster and Chinese linen are traditional choices. Ideally wash the glasses in really hot water and use no detergent at all. Store your wine glasses upright to avoid trapping stale odours.

Decanting

There are three reasons for putting wine in a decanter: one, to separate it from sediment that has formed in the bottle; two, to let the wine breathe; three, to make it look nice. You don't need a special decanter, a jug is just as good. Equally, there's no reason why you shouldn't decant the wine to aerate it and then pour it back into the bottle again for serving.

A bottle of mature red wine that contains sediment needs careful handling. Stand it upright for a day or two before you want to serve it, to let the sediment settle to the bottom. You can serve the wine

Careful decanting is only necessary when the wine contains sediment. Stop pouring when the dark grains or sludge reach the neck of the bottle.

straight from the bottle if you pour it carefully, but it's safer to decant it. Place a torch or a candle beside the decanter and, as you pour the wine, position yourself so that you can see the light shining through the neck of the bottle. Keep pouring in one steady motion and stop when you see the sediment rushing into the neck.

Breathing

Most wines do not need to be opened early in order to let the wine breathe. A few fine red wines – top-class red Bordeaux, top Italian reds, top Syrah/Shiraz and a few others – can benefit from it, but almost all inexpensive ones, and all white wines, can simply be opened and drunk. There are no set rules, however, and only experience will tell you if a wine will improve with breathing.

The reason for letting a wine breathe is that contact with oxygen in the air makes the flavours more open. But if you leave the wine for too long before you drink it you may find the flavours going flat and dull from excessive oxidation. If you're the sort of person who plans ahead, open your reds an hour or so before you intend to drink them. That way they won't suffer from oxidation, and they may even improve. And always beware of opening even top wines too early. Very old examples can lose all their flavour if they are exposed to the air for too long.

SERVING TEMPERATURES

Wine should be warm enough to be flavoursome and cool enough to be refreshing. High-quality whites taste good at higher temperatures than lesser whites of the same style. It is better to serve a wine too cool and warm it in your hands than to serve it too hot, when the flavours fall apart.

WARM

No wine tastes good above a comfortable room temperature of about 20°C (68°F)

ROOM TEMPERATURE

Intense, blackcurranty reds, spicy, warm-hearted reds, heavier mouthwatering, sweet-sour reds and warming, fortified wines

over 20°C   **15° to 20°C**

Simply uncorking the bottle and leaving it to stand will have little or no effect, as only a small surface area is exposed. Pouring off a small amount will help, but decanting will expose the wine to far more air. For instant results with a wine that has been uncorked just this minute, a quick swirl of your glass will work wonders. Interestingly, many screwcap wines taste better on the second glass because they've been bottled with virtually no oxygen, and they need a few minutes to wake up. If a wine has a rather sweaty, meaty smell – the expert term is 'reduced' – put a copper coin in the glass and swirl it round. The wine will taste as fresh as a daisy in a minute or two.

Leftovers

You can keep leftover wine for several days without it losing much of its flavour. All you need to do is hold off the effects of oxidation. The simplest way is to push the cork back in and stick the bottle in the fridge. Alternatively, you can buy reasonably effective devices which suck out the air or which inject a dense inert gas.

Special stoppers are available for recorking sparkling wine, but a conventional cork does the job well enough. Either way, keep the wine well chilled.

If you have two leftover bottles of the same wine, pour the contents of both into one. The fuller the bottle the longer the wine will last. White wines last better than reds.

OZ'S TIPS

Quick tips for temperature

A fridge takes two to four hours to chill a bottle of wine, so it's not much use in an emergency. The quickest way to chill a wine is by immersing it in a bucket filled with a combination of ice and cold water. This is much faster than ice on its own. Add salt to the water for even quicker results. Wine chills down fairly swiftly in a freezer, too – but don't let it freeze solid.

If a wine is too cold, the best thing to do is to pour the wine and then cup the glass in your hands for a minute or two. Don't put the bottle next to a strong heat source like a radiator. Never put it in a microwave.

COOL ROOM TEMPERATURE	**COOL**	**COLD**	**CHILLED**	**WELL CHILLED**
Silky, strawberryish reds	Juicy, fruity reds, light mouthwatering, sweet-sour reds, tangy fortified wines and golden sweet wines	Intense, nutty whites, ripe, toasty whites and aromatic whites	Green, tangy whites, sparkling wines, delicate rosés and the lightest tangy fortifieds	Bone-dry neutral whites and cheap sparkling wines
13° to 15°C	**11° to 13°C**	**8° to 11°C**	**6° to 8°C**	**4° to 6°C**

how to taste wine

At last. You must have thought we were never going to reach the business end of things – opening your mouth and taking a deep draught of delicious wine. That's if it is delicious. You're the only one who can say – it's your palate. But as you try more and more wines, your awareness of flavour and your personal preferences will develop. And the good thing is that you'll be able to apply this knowledge when choosing wine in a wine shop or restaurant.

OZ'S TIPS

Tasting skills

Keep your nose alert Make a conscious effort to remember the smells you encounter in daily life and give them names. These smells form the basis of your tasting vocabulary and are the key to disentangling the elusive smells in wine.

Remember fruit flavours Fruit aromas and flavours are common in wine and it pays to be familiar with blackcurrants, blackberries, cherries, raspberries, strawberries and plums for red wines, and with lemons, limes, apples, apricots, peaches and tropical fruits for whites.

Make notes Keep a record of the wines you have tasted and your assessments. Two or three key words in your diary will do.

But what's so special about wine that you have to go through a whole ritual just to say what it tastes like? Well, wine doesn't just taste of wine. Any number of aromas and flavours mingle together in the glass – we're talking dozens, sometimes hundreds – and if you just knock it back the same way you do a cold beer or a soft drink, you could be missing most of whatever flavour the wine has to offer.

Giving wine a bit of thought while you're drinking it is by far the best method for finding your way around the grapes, regions and styles of the wine world. THINK WHILE YOU DRINK. It's more fun than studying and one delicious sip will stay in your memory far longer than any book. In fact, you'll enjoy this book much more if you've got a glass by your elbow – and my words will probably make more sense, too. If you get really interested in wine, you can join wine-tasting groups, but let's start with you, and ideally a friend or two, getting used to thinking while you drink and, above all, enjoying it. You'll soon work out what you like and knowing what you like should give you the confidence to try more and more styles.

Look at the wine

Pour the wine into a wine glass so that it is about a third full. A big tulip-shaped glass that is broad near the base and narrower at the top will help to concentrate the aromas of the wine. Tilt the glass against a white background so you can enjoy the range of colours in the wine from the centre to the rim. But don't spend too long on this: you're wasting good drinking time.

Smell the wine

Give the wine a vigorous swirl in the glass to release the locked-in aromas. Stick your nose right into the glass and inhale steadily and gently, as if you were smelling a flower.

These initial split seconds of inhalation will reveal all kinds of familiar and unfamiliar smells. Always interpret them in terms that mean something to you. If the smell reminds you of honey, or chocolate, or apples, or raspberries, then those descriptions are sure to be right for you. Remember, it's your nose that counts here. It doesn't matter if someone else interprets the smells differently – that's their nose – and anyway, it's all part of the pleasure of wine. It's only by reacting honestly to the taste and smell of a wine that you can build up a memory bank of flavours against which to judge future wines and to help you recognize wines you have already encountered.

At first you may find that you can't put a name to smells you do recognise or that there are too many smells to untangle in your mind, or even that the wine smells of nothing much at all. Your nose tires quickly, so give it a break after a few seconds, then go back to the wine. It's worth jotting down a note of your thoughts before you forget them – a glance at the notes can bring the aromas flooding back weeks later. And if you're with friends, say what you think and listen to what the others say. Everyone's view is valid and useful.

OZ'S TIPS

Make tasting a habit
Whenever a glass of wine comes your way, take a moment to look at it, smell it and taste it. If you're having a meal, consider how the wine and food interact. Do they draw an extra dimension of flavour out of each other or does one knock the other flat?

Hold your own tastings Get together with some friends to compare a range of wines. With everyone pitching in their ideas, you'll end up with a broader view of what a wine is like. And you'll have much more fun. Start by investigating the differences between two or three grape varieties. Then try comparing several wines from the same variety or from the same region.

Take a sip

At last! It's time to drink the wine. So take a decent-sized sip – enough to fill your mouth about a third full. Draw a little air through your lips and suck it through the wine to help separate the aromas from the liquid, then start to enjoy all the personality and flavour that the fumes impart.

The tongue can detect only very basic flavour elements: sweetness at the tip, acidity at the sides (saltiness too, but you won't find that in many wines) and bitterness at the back. The real business of tasting anything, not just wine, goes on in your nasal cavity. So hold the wine in your mouth, and consciously breathe out through your nose. The nasal cavity has millions of receptors searching for every scent and flavour known to man and ready to transmit the aroma straight to your brain. If you're not sure about this nasal business – hold your nose and take a mouthful of wine. Can you taste anything? No. Then release your nose, breathe out through it – and your mouth will fill with flavour. All the flavours that give us so much pleasure in our daily eating and drinking are carried from our mouth to our brain by aromas we breathe up into our nasal cavity.

Evaluate the wine

Ideally make a few notes: jot down first impressions, then record the taste that develops after the wine has been in your mouth for a few moments. First note any sweetness, acidity and tannic bitterness that your tongue detects. Some flavours are upfront and unmistakable, others shift subtly, just out of reach. A few words jotted down and the flavour can come flooding back. And if you really want to become a good wine taster, your memory is as important as your palate. And stay relaxed. This is supposed to be fun. The more tense you are, the less likely you are to enjoy the wine – or remember what it tastes like.

Swallow or spit it out

Why do wine tasters spit wine out after they have tasted it? Quite simply, it's the only way to taste a lot of wines and remain sober. I often have to taste and make notes on 100 wines at a time and the spittoon can easily hold the equivalent of two to three bottles of wine – all spat out by me. Winetasters like a drink as much as the next person – but not when we are 'tasting'. We're trying to stay sober and make accurate, useful judgements on all the wines that we can refer to later. If you're visiting a producer's cellar or attending a professional wine-tasting, believe me, spit.

At home, if you've organized a tasting session – well, if no one's driving – you could all just sit around the kitchen table and get happy. But if you want to do it the proper way, you don't need a special spittoon, just use a bucket, preferably placed on some newspaper; if you and your friends aren't practised spitters you could make a right old mess otherwise. And when you've spat – OK, or swallowed – make one final mental or actual note on any lingering aftertaste. And decide whether you liked the wine or not – and why.

All wines have some basic elements in common:

Acid and sugar are present in the juice of the grape. The sugar is turned into alcohol during fermentation, but some can remain. A lot of leftover sugar makes for a sweet wine. Acid sounds unpleasant and aggressive, but when present in the right proportion it makes the wine intense and refreshing. All wines contain acid, as do all fruits.

Tannin is the stuff in red wines that stains your teeth and dries your mouth, but in the right amounts can do marvellous things to the flavour and texture of the wine. White wines don't have noticeable levels of tannin. Tannin and acid both have the added benefit of acting as preservatives, and wines with high levels of either (or both) have the potential to last for many years in the bottle.

Alcohol isn't just there for the sake of getting you lit up. It balances other flavours, for example softening the attack of the acid, and makes the wine feel richer in your mouth. And without it, you'd just be downing a glass of grape juice.

TASTING BASICS

Nose is the name for the smell of the wine. Alternative terms are **aroma**, usually used of young wines, and **bouquet**, usually used for mature wines. But hey, **smell** will do.

Palate is the taste of the wine in your mouth. Call it **taste** if you prefer.

Sweetness or the lack of it is the first sensation as the wine hits the tip of your tongue. Sweetness always needs to be balanced by acidity or it will be cloying. All but the very driest of wines will have some sensation of sweetness.

Acidity makes wine taste crisp and refreshing. You notice its effect on the sides of your tongue. It must be balanced by sweetness, alcohol or body: if a wine has too little of these, too much acidity will taste unpleasantly tart. A wine with too much sweetness, alcohol or body and too little acidity will taste flabby and flat.

Tannin is the mouth-drying substance found in red wines. It mostly comes from the skin and pips of the grapes. When it is balanced by good fruit flavours it adds enormously to the mouthwatering, savoury character of good red wine. Too much and the wine will taste hard and bitter. Not enough and it can taste as soft and innocuous as fruit juice.

Alcohol is found in all wines, but levels vary from as little as 8% for a light German Riesling to maybe 15% for a rich, ripe Aussie Shiraz – and higher for fortified wines. High alcohol levels make wine feel rounder in your mouth. It is possible by scientific methods to reduce the level of alcohol in wines by a degree or two without ruining the flavour, but too much de-alcoholization leaves a drink that is devoid of alcohol's round, warming texture and usually tastes like a less interesting version of grape juice.

Fruit flavour in wine comes from the grapes, yet wine seldom tastes of grapes. Indeed, most wine grapes don't taste of much until fermentation transforms them. Then the resulting wine can develop hundreds of flavours, but we have to borrow language from elsewhere to describe them. Often we use fruit flavours – plums, strawberries, blackberries, limes and many others. But we also find flavours like nuts, coffee beans, chocolate and fudge, biscuits and bread, herbs and leaves, coal dust and smoke – honestly, the number of flavours in wine goes into hundreds – and they're borrowed from every walk of life.

Weight or **body** describes the different impressions of weight and size wines give in the mouth. This is what is referred to by the terms full-, medium- and light-bodied. Different wine styles will be at their best with different body and weight. And more is *not* always better.

Length is the flavour that persists in your mouth after you've swallowed the wine. A flavour that continues or even improves for some time after the wine is gone is a mark of quality.

Balance is the relationship between all these elements of the wine: sweetness, acidity, tannin, alcohol, fruit and body. An unbalanced wine will taste as though it is lacking something – and it is.

There's more to describing wine than saying it's good or bad. Tasting terms are a way of sharing our perceptions of a wine's qualities; they should never be a secret code for experts. Fruit flavours are direct comparisons, so if I know the fruit, I will recognize the flavour you are talking about. The same goes for honey or nuts. These less obvious terms are useful too.

Aggressive A wine with acid that makes your gums sting or that dries up the back of your throat due to an excess of tannin.

Aromatic All wines have an aroma, but an aromatic wine is particularly pungent, *floral* or *spicy*, and is usually from an aromatic grape variety like Gewürztraminer.

Astringent A wine in which the mouth-drying effect of tannin is very marked.

Big A full-bodied wine with lots of everything: fruit flavour, acidity, tannin and alcohol.

Bold A wine with distinct, easily understood flavours.

Buttery Oak barrels and malolactic fermentation (see page 55) can both give a buttery taste.

Chewy Wine with a lot of tannin and strong flavour, but which is not *aggressive*.

Clean Wine free of bacterial and chemical faults. Also describes simple, refreshing wines.

Complex A wine that has layer upon layer of flavours.

Crisp A refreshing white wine with good acidity.

Deep Subtle, *rich*; allied to *complex*.

Dry Not at all *sweet*.

Dull A wine with no well-defined, pleasing flavours. Often a sign of too much exposure to oxygen.

Dusty A dry, slightly *earthy* taste sometimes found in reds. Can be very attractive if combined with good fruit.

Earthy A smell and taste of damp earth – appealing in some French reds from the Loire Valley and Bordeaux.

Fat Full-bodied, unctuous.

Firm Well-balanced, well-defined wine; the opposite of *flabby*.

Flabby Lacking in acidity, feeble.

Floral Several whites have an aroma like fllowers or blossom.

Focused A wine in which all the flavours are well defined.

Fresh Young wine, with lively fruit flavours and good acidity.

Full A weighty feel in the mouth.

Grassy Commonly used though not strictly accurate term for the green leaf, lime zest or capsicum flavours typical of Sauvignon Blanc.

Green Can mean unripe, in which case it's pejorative. But green leaf flavours are common in cool-climate reds, and greenness in association with flavours such as gooseberries or apples implies the fresh, tangy flavours found in many white wines.

Hard A red with a lot of tannin or a white with too much acid. Uncompromising rather than *aggressive*, but rarely enjoyable.

Jammy Red wine in which the fruit has the boiled, cooked flavours of jam.

Light Low alcohol or little body. Not necessarily a bad thing.

Meaty A heavy red wine with solid, chunky flavours. A few wines actually do taste of grilled meat or bloody beef.

Minerally How you might imagine a lick of flint or chalk to taste. Common in wines from Germany and Austria, and from Chablis and the Loire Valley in France.

Neutral Little distinctive flavour.

Oaky The slightly sweet vanilla flavour in red and white wines that have been fermented and/or aged in new oak barrels. Oak also adds tannin.

Petrolly A surprisingly attractive petrol- or kerosene-like smell that develops in mature wines made from Riesling.

Piercing Usually refers to high acidity. But vibrant fruit flavours can also be piercing.

Powerful A wine with plenty of everything, particularly alcohol.

Prickly Slight fizziness caused by residual carbon dioxide gas, meaning that fermentation is not quite finished. Very refreshing in simple whites but a fault in red wines.

Rich Full, well-flavoured, with plenty of alcohol.

Ripe Wine made from well-ripened grapes has good fruit flavour. Unripe wines can taste *green* and stalky.

Rounded Any wine in which the flavour seems satisfyingly complete, with no unpleasant sharpness.

Soft A wine without harsh tannins or too much acidity, making it an easy-going drink. Often a good thing, but a wine can be too soft.

Spicy Exotic fragrances and flavours common in Gewürztraminer; also the tastes of pepper, cinnamon or clove in reds such as Australian Shiraz. Spiciness can be an effect of oak aging.

Steely Good acidity and a wine that is firm and lean, may be *minerally* but not *thin*.

Stony A dry, chalky-white taste, like *minerally* but without quite the excitement.

Structured 'Plenty of structure' refers to a wine with a well-developed backbone of acidity and tannin, but enough fruit to stand up to it.

Supple Both vigorous and smooth. A description of texture rather than flavour.

Sweet Not only a wine with high levels of sugar, but also the *rich* and *ripe* quality of some of the fruit flavours in many modern dry wines.

Tart A very sharp, acid taste like an unripe apple.

Thin, **lean**, **stringy** Terms for high-acid wine lacking in flavour.

Toasty A flavour like buttered toast that results from maturing a wine in oak barrels.

Upfront A wine that wears its heart on its sleeve: expect obvious flavours, not subtle ones, but sometimes that's just what you want.

how to spot a faulty wine

There are fewer poor wines nowadays because winemaking is better understood today than ever before. This is a result of a new generation of winemakers, in particular from Australia and California, who have studied the science of winemaking and then set off to work in vineyards around the globe sharing their knowledge. Even so faulty bottles do crop up. You can spot faults in the same way as you can any wine flavour, by using your senses of sight, smell and taste.

Use your eyes

Whatever its colour, wine should be clear and bright. Cloudy wine usually indicates bacterial spoilage, but it's extremely uncommon these days. Don't confuse cloudiness with shaken-up deposit: an aged red wine that has developed a dark, powdery or gritty deposit just needs to stand upright until the deposit settles again.

The colours of wines vary according to their grape variety and the climate in which they were made. But if a white wine you expect to be pale has a brownish-yellow tinge, or if a young red has a brownish tinge, then beware: it's probably oxidized. Oxidized wine tastes dull and flat.

If wine has seeped past the cork, making the neck of the bottle sticky, then it probably hasn't been very well kept and air might have got in. This, too, can mean oxidized wine.

Use your nose

These smells are all tell-tale signs of trouble:

Sherry-like smells Only sherry should smell of sherry. Such smells on unfortified wines can indicate oxidation.

Vinegary smells If it smells like vinegar, then that is what it is turning into.

Rotten eggs This horrible, horrible smell of hydrogen sulphide can form during fermentation and is a sign of poor winemaking.

Mouldy, musty smells This is 'corked' wine, caused by a contaminated cork. A slight cork taint may just dull the wine but not make it undrinkable.

Reduced smells You get this slightly meaty, cheesy smell sometimes, especially on screwcap wines. It's a sort of sulphide usually created by the wine not having enough oxygen, rather than too much. I always carry an old copper coin with me. If the wine is 'reduced', pour yourself a glass, slip in the coin, swirl the wine about and in a minute or two all the sulphidy smells will have disappeared. It's something to do with smelly sulphide reacting with copper to create odourless copper sulphite. I think. And do remember to remove the coin from the glass before drinking the contents.

Use your taste buds

Your palate should normally confirm what your nose has already told you – but sometimes a fault will show more on the nose than on the palate, or vice versa. Use nose and palate in conjunction when judging a wine.

UNSIGHTLY BUT NOT FAULTY

Pieces of cork floating in your wine glass are nothing to do with cork-tainted wine. They are unsightly but have no effect on the flavour.

White crystals often form on the cork and at the bottom of bottles of white wine. These natural deposits, called tartrates, are harmless and do not alter the taste of the wine.

Sediment often develops in red wines after a few years in the bottle and is a 'good thing'. Sediment is best dealt with by decanting.

drinking wine in a restaurant

The key here is: if in doubt, ask. This applies regardless of the sort of restaurant you're in. If there's a well-informed wine waiter or sommelier (that's the person who is in charge of the wine) and the wine list seems to have been put together with care, then he or she will be only too pleased to tell you anything you want to know – and will probably have some suggestions about which wines will go particularly well with the food you have chosen.

OZ'S TIP

Restaurant dilemmas

If you're in a restaurant and everyone is ordering different food, even the most resourceful expert is going to have difficulty choosing one ideal wine. In this situation, the traditional combination of a bottle of white and a bottle of red should see you through.

A lot of restaurants, of course, have neither a particularly good wine list nor a decent wine waiter. If the list doesn't tell you the producer, or the vintage, or some other vital piece of information about a wine, ask to see the bottle. At least you can then make your own mind up. The quality of a wine list is not measured by its length. A short, well-chosen list is often better, as is one that specializes in the wines of one region.

Ordering your wine

So, you've decided what you're going to eat, and you've had a look at the wine list and decided what price you want to pay. This is very important. Being pressured into paying more than you can afford can ruin your evening. And a good wine waiter wants to know your price limits so that he can work within them. What you don't know is what any of it tastes like. The wine waiter approaches. How do you begin? Try something like this: 'Oh, hi. Look, we're both having fish, but we want to drink red. We were thinking about this Chilean Merlot, but perhaps it would be too heavy. What would you recommend?'

That's a very broad outline, and you don't have to blurt it all out at once, but the point is that you've given the waiter all the clues he or she needs – food, style and price range – to make an appropriate suggestion. And now you've broken the ice you can come to a final decision calmly rather than in a state of blind panic. The worst thing, if you don't know what to choose, is to sit staring in terror at the wine list, and refuse to ask because you think you'll lose face. You won't.

However, it is a good idea to make a preliminary choice before you seek advice: if you don't like the advice you get, it will leave you with something to fall back on.

When the bottle comes and is shown to you, check it. Sometimes the wrong wine arrives because somebody misheard. Sometimes the vintage has changed, and nobody's told you. If it's not the vintage you ordered, query it. If you don't want the replacement, choose something else.

When the waiter pours the wine, sniff it and taste it. You're checking to see if it's faulty, not if you like it. Take your time. If you suspect it might be faulty, express your doubts, take another taste

OZ'S TIPS

Good restaurants, bad restaurants

A good restaurant for wine

- gives full details of the wines on the wine list
- offers wines that have been carefully chosen to go with the food
- will replace a faulty bottle with good grace
- serves good house wine and a selection of interesting wines by the glass
- will provide decent glasses to help you enjoy the wine it serves

A bad restaurant for wine

- gives no specific information about the wines
- challenges your judgement if you complain
- has uninformed or overbearing staff
- tries to make you spend more than you want to

and perhaps ask the waiter to try it. If it is faulty they should immediately replace it.

This is where most of the problems with wine waiters arise. Bad wine waiters refuse to accept that a faulty wine is faulty. Bad customers insist that a wine is faulty when there's nothing wrong with it – it may just be unfamiliar.

If you have a disastrous experience (and everyone who eats in restaurants has a bad wine waiter story) don't pick a row: it will spoil the evening. A quiet, reasoned complaint to the manager at the end of the meal will do more good. And if you've had bad service, don't leave a tip.

OZ'S TIPS

Top 10 restaurant tactics

1   Try a glass of house w ne first – it allows you to take your time when choosing the wine and if it's good you could stick with it.

2   Order water to quench your thirst so you can savour the wine.

3   Discuss your choice of wine with the wine waiter if there is one. Don't treat him or her as an enemy – or a hired slave.

4   If you're going to have two bottles, don't blow your budget on the first.

5   Don't worry too much about matching the wine to your food: New World Cabernet Sauvignons, Shirazes and Merlots are good all-round reds; New World Chardonnays, Sauvignons and Semillons are useful whites; and Alsace whites go well with a great variety of dishes. This is particularly important in Asian restaurants where the flavours of the national cuisines have evolved without any wine culture. You could say the same for Cajun, Mexican and Caribbean food. With these foods you don't want hard edges on your reds, or vanilla oakiness on your whites. Fruit and balancing acidity are the most important factors here, and if I had to choose two, I'd say New Zealand whites and Chilean reds do this best.

6   On an uninspiring list, opt for wines from Australia, New Zealand or South America – they are the most likely to be reliable and good value.

7   Take a chance on up-and-coming regions of Italy, Spain or Portugal – Sicily or Puglia in Italy, wines from the Garnacha grape in Spain and wines from Alentejo, Beiras or Dão in Portugal – they could well be the best value on the list.

8   Feel the temperature of the bottle when it arrives. If the wine is too warm, whether it's red or white, ask for an ice bucket; and if it gets too cold, don't feel you have to keep it in the bucket just because the waiter has put it there.

9   Don't be bullied by over-assiduous waiters – make sure the bottle is within your reach and top up your glasses when *you* want to.

10   Enjoy yourself: you're the one who's paying.

matching food and wine

Good wine is tasty on its own, but to get the best out of wine you need a group of friends around, and a bite to eat. So, how do you go about choosing the wine for the meal? The pleasures of eating and drinking operate on so many levels that there's far more to perfect wine and food partnerships than clinical flavour matching. If you're in the mood for Champagne then don't let anyone stop you drinking it, whatever you're eating; and if the spirit of place, or the weather, or the company you're in begs for a particular wine, go for it.

Wine affects the flavour of food; food affects the flavour of wine – pretty obvious, I suppose. When the fundamental characteristics of the wine and the food are in harmony, the flavours of both should sing out. Sometimes a well-judged contrast does the trick just as well as a perfect match. Frankly, most combinations are perfectly enjoyable and a few are sensationally good, but a real mismatch can take the fun out of both the food and the wine.

Fortunately, it's easy to avoid disastrous pairings. Don't drink dry wine with sweet food – the wine will taste unpleasantly thin and acidic – and stick to red meat if the wine is a high-tannin red, such as Barolo from Italy, Dão or Bairrada from Portugal, or red Bordeaux. Fish is fine with low-tannin reds such as young Pinot Noir, but too much tannin with your fish will give a metallic taste. And that's about it. Now you can get on with looking for combinations that bring out the best in both the wine and the food.

Sense of place

My best memories of sublime wine and food partnerships come from picnics while travelling in France and Italy. I'll stop in the villages of Tuscany or southern France to pick up bread, sausage, cheese and tomatoes, buy wine straight from the local winemaker's barrel and gulp it all down ten minutes later at the side of a country lane. Wine and food will never taste better than this.

Weight As well as matching the taste of the wine to the flavour of the food, it's a good idea to match the weight (or body) of the wine to the intensity of that flavour. A heavy, alcoholic wine suits hefty food; choose a light wine for delicate dishes.

Acidity The acidity of the food should balance that of the wine. High-acid flavours, such as tomato or lemon, need matching acidity in the wine. You can also use an acidic wine to cut through a creamy or oily dish, but make sure the wine has plenty of flavour, like New Zealand Sauvignon.

Sweetness With desserts and puddings, find a wine that is as sweet as or sweeter than the food. Some savoury foods, such as carrots, onions and parsnips, taste slightly sweet, and if they are prominent in the dish a really ripe-fruited wine like Viognier will work well.

Age/maturity A mature wine will have developed a complex taste and aroma over the years. To get the most enjoyment out of it, keep the food simple – plain grilled or roast meat is ideal.

Sauces and seasonings Always bear these in mind. It may be more important to match the wine to a rich sauce or spicy seasonings than to the main ingredient. As a general rule tannic reds and oaky whites don't like spicy sauces of any kind.

Oak A heavily oaked wine can ride roughshod over food that isn't richly flavoured, and really isn't the thing with spicy Asian food.

The magic resides in the simplicity of the meal and the joy of basking in the same sunlight that is ripening the vines. There's a lesson to be learnt from this for wine and food matching at home. Regional wines and foods aren't necessarily ideal matches from a scientific point of view, but a technical approach takes the fun out of the wine and the food. It's much better to make a bit of a holiday of your meal and think along the lines of southern French wine with Provençal food or a light Italian red with pizza.

International cuisines

Wine and food are both international travellers these days and they pick up new friends wherever they go. Many of the food styles popular around the world today grew up in cultures that don't have wine in their repertoire. Rich and spicy Asian, Indian, African and Mexican dishes and the mixed cuisines of fusion food and Pacific Rim cooking demand wines with a character that the traditional wine cultures of Europe never had to provide. But fruit-driven modern styles can deliver the perfect match.

Nevertheless, some European classics *do* deliver the fruit: Alsace wines, particularly Gewurztraminer and Pinot Gris, and German Riesling. Riesling from any country is a good choice, as are the intense Sauvignon Blancs from New Zealand and South Africa. Juicy fruity reds like Garnacha from Spain, Merlots from Chile and the lighter Malbecs from Argentina can do the trick, and the less powerful California Zinfandels are a good choice.

Wine and cheese

I'm really not sure why cheese is always seen as a natural partner for wine. Only occasionally do I come across an exciting combination. The enduring cliché, perpetuated by a host of back labels, that red is the wine for cheese, is even more perplexing, as white is frequently a better partner. Red wines are OK for hard cheeses like mild Cheddar or Gouda and bland ones such as mozzarella. For mature Cheddar and other strong hard cheeses you need a powerful red like Rhône Syrah or Australian Shiraz, or even port. Goat's cheese is better off with white Sancerre or other wines made from Sauvignon Blanc. Ripe cheeses like Brie or Camembert are hostile to most wine flavours, but sparkling wines can tame them. Otherwise, I'd drink Normandy cider. Strong blue cheeses call for sweet wines: the classic combinations are port with Stilton and Bordeaux's sweet white Sauternes with Roquefort.

Vegetarian dishes

The clean, bright, appley flavours of Pinot Blanc from Alsace and the simple fruitiness and low tannins of reds like Grenache and Tempranillo make them good all-rounders for modern vegetarian cooking. Dry rosé is a good idea, too. Anything spicy calls for fruity and acidic reds and whites. So do tomato-based sauces. Cream and cheese sauces need softer wines: Semillon or ripe, toasty Chardonnay would be good. Salads with vinegary dressings can be murder on wine. Go for tangy whites, such as dry Riesling or Sauvignon Blanc.

WINE'S WORST ENEMIES

Artichokes, **chillies**, **oysters**, **kippers** and **mackerel**, **salsas** and **vinegars**, **salted peanuts** and **chocolate** can all flatten the flavours of wines. If you want to drink wine with these foods, the general rule for reds is to avoid very tannic wines and go for juicy young ones instead; or choose whites with plenty of fruit and fresh acidity.

With mackerel and kippers try a dry fino sherry, and with chocolate go for fortified Muscats, the Italian sparkling wine Asti or perhaps some port. Vinegary dressings, chillies and salsas need a match for their acidity, so team them with Sauvignon Blanc or dry Riesling. Oysters need bone-dry whites.

Eggs can be tricky to match with wine. Choose light, unoaked Chardonnays or neutral whites – oaky and very fruity ones don't work so well. Only the very lightest reds, such as Beaujolais or Bardolino, go well with eggs.

Red wine and food: some suggestions for the wine styles described on pages 12–16.

	Juicy, fruity reds	Silky, strawberryish reds	Intense, blackcurranty reds	Spicy, warm-hearted reds	Low-tannin, mouthwatering, herby reds	Earthy, savoury reds
EXCELLENT MATCH ✓✓✓	Roast or grilled red meats Barbecues Roast or fried chicken Ham Roast pork Spicy food Indian and Tex-Mex food Cold meats and pâtés Pizza Grilled fish Creamy or cheesy sauces Spaghetti Bolognese and lasagne Soft cheeses Tomato-based dishes	Red meat in rich sauce, e.g. boeuf bourguignon Roast game birds Roast or grilled red meats Chicken in red wine sauce or cooked with garlic Substantial fish, such as grilled salmon or tuna Roast pork Rich, lightly spiced Oriental dishes	Roast or grilled red meats – especially lamb Venison Duck and goose Roast chicken and turkey Cold roast beef Red meat in rich sauce	Peppered steak Sausages Warming, herby stews Duck and goose Roast or grilled red meats Venison stew Barbecues Hard cheeses Indian food Tex-Mex food Chilli con carne Spaghetti Bolognese Salami Roast chicken or turkey with stuffing	Pizza Lasagne Tomato-based dishes Spaghetti Bolognese Cold meats and salamis Roast pork Garlicky and herby dishes Roast or grilled red meats Grilled fish	Rich game dishes Warming, herby stews Roast or grilled red meats Mushroom or meat risottos Roast chicken or turkey with stuffing
OK MATCH ✓						
DISASTER WARNING ✗	Only the standard warning that goes for all dry reds – avoid sweet foods.	These wines lose their charm with fiery spicy food.	They overwhelm fish, taste bitter with tomatoes and spicy foods, and don't suit cold pork or chicken.	These are food-loving wines, but they will swamp delicate food.	No problems – these wines are real all-rounders.	These wines only come into their own with robust, meaty meals. They clash with cold pork or chicken.

White wine and food: some suggestions for the wine styles described on pages 19–22.

	Bone-dry, neutral whites	Green, tangy whites	Intense, nutty whites	Ripe, toasty whites	Aromatic whites	OTHER WINE STYLES
EXCELLENT MATCH ✓✓✓	Plainly cooked fish and shellfish Grilled chicken Spaghetti carbonara Quiche Salads Cajun and Tex-Mex food Salami Pork Thai and Chinese food Cold meats	Anything in tomato sauce, including shellfish Tomatoes Pizza Indian food Salads with sharp dressing Sushi Goat's cheese South-East Asian food Tex-Mex food Chinese Szechuan food	Creamy and buttery sauces Plain grilled white fish Grilled or roast chicken and turkey Smoked salmon Spaghetti carbonara Grilled or baked salmon and tuna	Grilled or baked salmon and tuna Creamy and buttery sauces Grilled or roast chicken and turkey Barbecues Pheasant or rabbit Spaghetti carbonara	Pizza Lasagne Tomato-based dishes Spaghetti Bolognese Cold meats and salamis Roast pork Garlicky and herby dishes	**Rosés** that are dry and fruity make excellent partners for a whole range of dishes from delicate fish to rich spicy food, but, as they're light, steer away from heavy meaty dishes. **Dry sparkling wines** are good all-rounders too, and particularly good with shellfish and smoked fish. Champagne with oysters is a classic luxury match, although non-vintage Champagne is more suitable than richer, more expensive vintage.
OK MATCH ✓	Tomato-based dishes Pizza Creamy and buttery sauces	Grilled or baked salmon and tuna Asparagus	Seafood in a white wine and cream sauce Pork Rabbit Pheasant or partridge	Seafood in a white wine and cream sauce Smoked fish Mildly spiced food	Roast or grilled red meats Grilled fish	**Tangy fortified wines** are good with nibbles such as olives and salted almonds, go well with soups and smoked fish and are the classic partner to tapas.
DISASTER WARNING ✗	Avoid pairing any dry white with sweet food, but otherwise you can't go wrong with these wines.	These wines work with all sorts of hard-to-match foods, but they don't suit simply cooked red meats.	For all their intensity, these are subtly flavoured wines, and spices will destroy all that subtlety.	Heavily oaked wines overwhelm delicate fish – but they won't stand up to too much spice or acidity.	Aromatics are great food wines, but they're better suited to complex dishes than simple ones.	**Warming fortified wines** suit cheese and chocolate. **Rich sweet wines** go with both sweet food and blue cheese.

wine and health

The image of wine as a healthy drink is both an ancient and a very modern one. Wine was once highly prized for its medicinal qualities, largely because it was more reliably hygienic than water. It made a reasonable antiseptic and a good base for medicines. Some doctors went further, and recommended particular wines for particular ailments. Scientists are constantly researching the links between wine and health, but remember it's not just wine – anything you eat and drink can have benefits or cause problems.

The damaging effects of alcohol have been known for a long time and the anti-alcohol lobby has tried for years to persuade us that all alcohol is bad for us. However, there's now a wealth of medical evidence to suggest that moderate consumption of alcohol, particularly wine, is actually better for most people's health than total abstinence.

Health benefits

The main research finding is that drinking wine in moderation reduces the likelihood of dying from a heart attack, stroke or other form of vascular disease. It does this by helping to prevent clogged arteries and blood clots. Some of the benefits are due to the alcohol in the wine. Alcohol acts as an anticoagulant, which eases blood flow and prevents clots forming. It boosts HDL – or 'good' cholesterol – which actually cleans fatty deposits out of our arteries, and reduces LDL, the 'bad' cholesterol that puts them there in the first place.

Wine has an extra trick up its sleeve in the form of powerful anti-oxidants, which reduce the amount of fatty LDL deposits that can stick to the walls of our arteries. This benefit was originally attributed only to red wines, but subsequent research has shown that white wines are also effective. It also appears that wine may reduce the risk of some cancers and aid mental alertness into old age. And of course, we don't need researchers to tell us about the relaxing effects of a glass or two at the end of the day.

A poster from 1937 advertising the joys of French wine, bringing its imbiber health, laughter and hope. If only it were so simple today.

Governments set guidelines for sensible drinking limits, but these aren't consistent worldwide, often depending on whether the country has a wine culture or not. Most are in the range of 28–40 grams of alcohol per day for men (equivalent to two to three 125ml (4-ounce) glasses of wine containing 13.5% alcohol), and half to two-thirds that amount for women.

Social drinking can sometimes get a bit out of hand. I drink a large glass of milk before a big evening and try to drink a glass of water between each glass of wine. None of us wants to spoil the party but most of us have to work the following day.

Moderate consumption

All advocates of wine as a healthy beverage stress that the benefits of wine come only with moderate, regular consumption. Excessive amounts of alcohol increase the likelihood of many health problems, including all those that moderate consumption can guard against. In addition, alcohol is not recommended for people suffering from certain diseases, and pregnant women in particular should take medical advice regarding alcohol.

Individuals should talk to their doctors and make up their own minds, but my feelings on the matter are simple. Drink water for your thirst and enjoy good wine for its flavour. If you're not drinking enough to harm yourself, then the pleasure and sense of wellbeing that wine adds to your life are benefits enough.

PART THREE
THE WORLD OF WINE

Once the only important places on the wine map of the world were

European nations with long traditions of winemaking.

Then, in the late 1970s, came the challenge from

the so-called New World countries with their

innovative ideas and bright, fresh, modern interpretations of the

classic wines of Europe. California and Australia led the way and

were joined by New Zealand and, more recently, Chile, Argentina and

South Africa. And now, there are more 'new' countries, eager to impress.

India, China, Uruguay and Brazil, Canada and the northern European

countries like England, Holland, Belgium and Denmark. But New World

and Old World are attitudes of mind as well as places, and tradition and

innovation now go hand in hand throughout the world of wine.

france

Ah, France. Say the words 'French wine' and everybody's got a response: it's the best, the worst, too expensive, cheap plonk... whatever you think about France, the opposite is probably just as true. But nobody can deny that France is at the very heart of the world of wine.

Facing page: The Jurançon vineyards in the deep south-west of France make some ravishing, peachy, dry and sweet white wines.

Right: The turreted Château Palmer in the Margaux appellation of Bordeaux makes magical red wine that can last for decades.

What thrills me is the range of flavours I can find here. For a start, so many international wine styles have their origin in France. The worldwide vogue for Cabernet Sauvignon sprang from the cedary, blackcurranty flavours of red Bordeaux. Burgundy inspired the worldwide love of Chardonnay and Pinot Noir. Champagne has spawned a thousand sparkling imitators across the globe.

But the influence of the New World is being felt here as much as anywhere, and flavours have become softer and richer than they used to be. All the same, you should still expect French wines to be less obviously fruity than their New World counterparts. More subtle, in some cases; more austere in others.

Bear in mind, too, that France's reputation as a producer of great wines is based on the very top layer of quality. Below that things have always been more mixed. And if you go for the very cheapest French wines – well, frankly, you could be getting better value and better flavours in a dozen other countries.

FRENCH CLASSIFICATIONS

France, like all European Union countries, has a tiered classification system. The higher the grade, the stricter the rules covering place of origin, grape variety, method of growing and method of making. But don't ever mistake the Appellation Contrôlée classification for a guarantee of quality: it's not. Instead it's a guarantee that the wine comes from the region stated on the label, and was made in accordance with the law – just that and no more.

Appellation d'Origine Contrôlée (AC or AOC) The top grade of French wine applies stringent rules. Producers may only grow certain grape varieties in each area, and yields per hectare are regulated. Producers may also use the term **Appellation d'Origine Protégée (AOP)**, in line with new European designations.

Indication Géographique Protégée (IGP) Previously called Vin de Pays. Relatively loosely regulated regions producing 'country wines' that are supposed to have the character of their region. Innovative winemakers love this category, because it allows them to do pretty well what they like. Most of the wines will have the grape variety on the label. You'd think that was just about the most helpful piece of information they could give, but, amazingly, most AC wines aren't allowed to mention the grape variety.

Vin de France The most basic wine, this used to be pretty rough, anonymous stuff, labelled vin de table. It can now display grape variety and vintage, and can be OK.

Bordeaux

If there is one single wine that for generations has carried the reputation of France, it is red Bordeaux. It is a benchmark wine throughout the world, and the origin of the intense, blackcurranty style of red, but there's one thing I want to make clear. The top wines represent only a small percentage of Bordeaux production. Most Bordeaux red veers between good, decent and poor, between blackcurrant, savoury and thin. There's now quite a bit of tasty stuff even at the lower end but wines from a single property – a château – are always better.

So when I talk about the flavours of red Bordeaux I mean good to very good wines. Those flavours are, at their best, a complex blend of blackcurrants and plums, cedarwood and cigar boxes, with perhaps a touch of violets, perhaps a touch of roast coffee beans. They come especially from the Cabernet Sauvignon grape, which is always blended here, usually with both Merlot and Cabernet Franc. Wines with a lot of Merlot in the blend taste softer and more generously fruity.

The finest estates produce sublime wine, of immense complexity and fascination. If you can afford these treasures, good for you. Top red Bordeaux is out of reach for most of us, except for the most special of special occasions. Thankfully, more and more good wines – still expensive, but not prohibitively so – become available every year.

Bordeaux also makes a fair bit of white wine, which can be sweet or dry. The most famous golden, sweet whites are those of Sauternes and its neighbour, Barsac, and there are various lesser regions that produce lighter versions of this style. Oddly (considering my strictures on the lesser red wines) these wines can be rather good buys.

Dry whites also come up with the goods at the cheaper end. Basic white Bordeaux is a good bet these days. At the very least it will be fresh and clean and have some attractive grassy fruit. These wines are simple, less pungent versions of the green, tangy style typified by New Zealand Sauvignon Blanc. The same grape variety grows here, too, and is sometimes blended with Sémillon, sometimes not. At the top end, creamy, nectariny dry whites from Pessac-Léognan can be some of the best in France.

Bordeaux Clairet is, depending on your point of view, a dark rosé or a very light red wine. Either way, it's a good-value dry wine with a refreshing taste of summer fruits.

Do regions matter?

The simple answer is yes. The basic distinction is between those regions that grow a lot of Cabernet Sauvignon (the Médoc, Haut-Médoc, Pessac-Léognan and Graves) and those that specialize in Merlot (St-Émilion and Pomerol). Cabernet Sauvignon-based wines have more tannin and a more austere flavour than the juicier Merlot-based wines, especially when young.

On the map you'll see some less illustrious regions marked, like Castillon, Fronsac, Côtes de Bourg and Blaye. All these places make red wine, and they're often good spots to look if you want simpler flavours and lower prices. Flavours are at best juicier and fruitier than those of top wines, but at worst leaner and more austere, and which you get depends as much on the producer as the region. If somebody points you towards a good one, try it. Lalande-de-Pomerol produces some goodies in the Pomerol mould of rich, plummy fruit, and since Pomerol is rare and expensive these wines make a useful substitute. St-Georges-St-Émilion and Puisseguin-

St-Émilion make simpler, earthier versions of St-Émilion and if they're a bit cheaper, especially if they come from a single property, then give them a go.

The very best dry white Bordeaux comes from Pessac-Léognan and Graves. Simpler wines come from Entre-Deux-Mers or may just be labelled Bordeaux Blanc.

Sauternes and Barsac are the top sweet wine areas, but others, including Loupiac, Cérons and Ste-Croix-du-Mont, have some pretty good wines. Curiously, Monbazillac, the region that comes closest to Sauternes in style, is actually just outside the borders of Bordeaux.

Do vintages matter?

Vintages matter more in Bordeaux than in most places. The weather here can be blissfully warm and sunny one year, and cool and wet the next, so the wines can vary from intense and deep-fruited to lean and underripe. See the Quick Guide on page 112. All good red Bordeaux needs to age for a few years, but some vintages mature faster than others.

The simplest whites are less susceptible to vintage variation, and in any case should be drunk young. With top whites, take care with the vintage, and give them some age. Vintages matter terrifically with Sauternes because the noble rot fungus, which gives the wines their sweetness and character, can't be relied upon to show up every year.

When do I drink them?

If you're going to open a really good bottle of red Bordeaux, then it's an event. There's an air of formality about good Bordeaux that demands respect. Keep it for when you've got time to appreciate it and cook something that will flatter the wine (roast lamb, just cooked pink, is ideal).

Sauternes is just as special. Do what the Bordelais do, and drink it with Roquefort cheese. Believe me, the

BORDEAUX HIERARCHIES

Bordeaux has three tiers of AC wines. The basic AC Bordeaux covers the whole region, which is subdivided into districts with their own appellations. Within these are a few small appellations based around **communes** with exceptionally good land, e.g. Pauillac.

But the château – the single estate – is the crucial quality indicator. Top districts have lists of top performers, known as **crus classés** or classed growths. The most famous classification (made in 1855) rates the top 61 red wine châteaux on the Left Bank of the Gironde from First Growth (Premier Cru) to Fifth (Cinquième Cru). Sauternes gives the top award of First Great Growth (Premier Grand Cru) followed by First and Second Growths. Graves simply picks out Crus Classés; St-Émilion has Premiers Grands Crus followed by Grands Crus.

Even the most flexible of these systems doesn't keep pace with changes in quality year by year, so it's rather refreshing that Pomerol doesn't bother with *crus* at all.

combination is sublime. The simple whites, however, have no social pretensions at all: take them on a picnic if you want, or drink them out of a tumbler. They won't mind.

Can I afford them?

Look, you've got to live a little. Once in your life fork out for a top bottle of red, or share the cost with friends. Treat it properly and it shouldn't disappoint. Good whites, dry and sweet, are expensive too, but the everyday whites are excellent value. I think you will have gathered by now what I think about most of the everyday reds, but Blaye and Castillon can give you some delightful – and affordable – surprises.

For 300 years, from 1152 to 1453, Bordeaux owed allegiance to the English crown. No wonder that England, and later on, the English-speaking world, developed such a taste for the wine. Some of it was known as **clairet** because of its light style compared to the gutsier wines of Spain or Portugal; and the name became Anglicized to **claret**. The name claret is still widely used in Britain, and applies to all red Bordeaux, while *clairet* is now the name for rosé-style wines from this region.

QUICK GUIDE ▷ *Bordeaux*

Location Bordeaux is situated on the Atlantic coast in South-West France.

Grapes Intense, blackcurrant reds are made from blends of varying proportions of Cabernet Sauvignon, Merlot and Cabernet Franc, with smaller amounts of Petit Verdot and Malbec. Sémillon and Sauvignon Blanc are the main white grapes for both dry and sweet wines.

Cabernet-dominated communes Listrac, Margaux, Moulis, Pauillac, St-Estèphe, St-Julien (all in the Haut-Médoc); Graves, Pessac-Léognan.

Merlot-dominated communes Pomerol, St-Émilion, Castillon.

Local jargon *Left Bank, Right Bank* – reds from the Médoc, Haut-Médoc, Graves and Pessac-Léognan, the appellations on the left bank of the Gironde, are colloquially known as Left Bank wines; those from St-Émilion, Pomerol and other regions on the river's right bank are called Right Bank wines. Left Bank wines are Cabernet-dominated; Right Bank wines major on Merlot. *Grand Vin* – this means that the bottle contains the main wine of a château; it doesn't refer to the quality of the wine. *Second*

wine – some châteaux produce a second wine from younger vines, or lesser parts of the vineyard than the Grand Vin. They can be a good buy. *Petit château* – a general term for the mass of unclassified châteaux in Bordeaux. Some are good, but some produce dross.

Vintages to look for (reds) 2010, 2009, 2008, 2006, 2005, 2004, 2001, 2000; (Sauternes) 2009, 2007, 2005, 2003 and 2001.

Vintages to avoid (Sauternes) 2008, 2006, 2004 and 2000.

Ten to try
RED
• **Château d'Angludet** Margaux ❹

• **Château des Annereaux** Lalande-de-Pomerol ❸
• **Château Balestard-la-Tonnelle** St-Émilion ❹
• **Château Léoville-Barton** St-Julien ❺
• **Château la Tour-de-By** Médoc ❸
DRY WHITE
• **Château Haut Bertinerie** Blaye-Côtes de Bordeaux ❷
• **Château Reynon** Sauvignon Blanc ❶
• **Château Smith-Haut-Lafitte** Péssac-Leognan ❺
SWEET WHITE
• **Château Lafaurie-Peyraguey** Sauternes ❺
• **Château La Rame** Ste-Croix-du-Mont ❸

Burgundy

Burgundy, like Bordeaux, is a classic region of France. The French name for the region, and the one you'll see on the label, is Bourgogne. It's home to three famous grape varieties, which make three benchmark styles of wine: silky, strawberryish Pinot Noir; intense, nutty Chardonnay; and juicy, fruity Gamay, the grape of Beaujolais.

Top Chardonnays and Pinot Noirs fetch millionaire prices, and are available in tiny quantities. Beaujolais is far less serious, and even at its best has no such aspirations. The first two have been imitated with great success elsewhere in the world, using the same grape varieties. Beaujolais has acted more as an inspiration – for juicy, fruity reds from a whole host of different grapes.

Pinot Noir is the most fascinating grape of all, the hardest to grow and the trickiest to vinify. Whereas Cabernet Sauvignon is robust and easy-going and seems to taste reliably Cabernet-like almost no matter what you do to it, Pinot Noir is light and subtle and will, at the least provocation, lose its freshness or its perfume or its ineffable silky quality. It takes a very good grower along with a very good winemaker to make good Pinot Noir.

To get a picture of red Burgundy you have to add to the truculent nature of the grape the complexities of vineyard ownership in Burgundy. While Bordeaux is composed of large estates with clear boundaries, a Burgundian estate may consist of tiny parcels of vines in perhaps 20 different vineyards. Likewise, each vineyard in Burgundy is divided between many different owners. It's due to the way the French inheritance laws work. Each estate will make a different wine from each block of vines. Each wine will have a different name, and (in theory) a

WINE TERMS
Growers and négociants

In Burgundy wine may be bottled and sold by the **grower** or by a **négociant** (merchant) who buys up grapes and wines from a number of growers to sell under his own name. In the past the received wisdom was that growers' wines were better and more characterful than *négociants'*; generally that's still the case, but now there are a number of excellent *négociants* producing quite large quantities of classy wine. It's no longer possible to say that one is always better than the other, but I'd still favour the grower.

The colourful glazed roof tiles of the Hospices de Beaune are typical of the region and give a clue to the wealth of medieval Burgundy.

different character. These facts alone make Burgundy far harder to grasp than Bordeaux. In Bordeaux the name of the vineyard and the name of the producer are identical and interchangeable; in Burgundy, you need to know the name of both the vineyard and the producer – more than anywhere else, it pays to seek knowledgeable advice. Buy from a bad producer and you'll wonder what all the fuss is about.

Chardonnay in Burgundy is easier to grow, easier to make and easier to buy than Pinot Noir. It's far more reliable, but it's in just as great demand, so prices are high. It comes in a number of styles. Chablis is as lean and minerally as Chardonnay gets, but ages to a nutty complexity after several years. In the Côte d'Or, the world-famous heart of the region, flavours range from the apple and nuts of the simpler wines to the long-lived buttered-toast, oatmeal and cream of the very best. The style is leaner again in the Côte Chalonnaise, but fatter and fruitier down in the Mâconnais. Chardonnay is also the grape of most sparkling Crémant de Bourgogne, a lean but honeyish fizz. There's also a

little crisp, lemony wine made from Aligoté, a white grape grown in small quantities but to good effect. It rarely attains the weight of a really good Chardonnay, and is usually best drunk young.

And Beaujolais? It's a region devoted to one red grape, Gamay, and offers several variations on a basic light and bright, juicy, fruity taste. Beaujolais-Villages has the juiciest flavours. Simple Beaujolais and Beaujolais Nouveau can be as good but often lack fruit. Drink them all young. A Beaujolais from one of the ten top villages, known as the Beaujolais *crus*, should have more character and depth. The most notable *crus* are light Chiroubles, fragrant Fleurie and heavier wines from Morgon and Moulin-à-Vent.

Do regions matter?

Absolutely. If you want Chardonnay, it is lean and minerally in Chablis, fuller and more complex on the Côte d'Or, more austere and chalky in the Côte Chalonnaise, fatter and softer in the Mâconnais. If you want Pinot Noir, the finest wines come from the Côte d'Or; wines from the Côte Chalonnaise are earthier. Within the Côte d'Or each village has its own style, and within each village there is a hierarchy of vineyards. If you want Gamay you have the choice between juicy, simple Beaujolais, the *cru* wines, which are more serious and will often age for a few years, or the mostly unexciting reds of the Mâconnais.

Do vintages matter?

Yes, but the name of the producer matters more. See the Quick Guide (right).

When do I drink them?

The best Burgundies are indulgent, hedonistic wines and I drink them with indulgent, hedonistic friends. I wouldn't waste them on people who take themselves too seriously. When I'm drinking good Bordeaux I feel I ought to be wearing a tie and sitting up straight. Give me a glass of good Burgundy and I'll take off my jacket and relax. Give me a good Beaujolais and I'll kick off my shoes as well.

Can I afford them?

Good Burgundy is expensive, but if you're clever (and get clever advice) you can find some wines that are reasonably good value. The trick for reds is to go for a good producer based in the Côte d'Or, but buy the less famous wines, like Bourgogne Rouge, Auxey-Duresses, Monthelie or Chorey-lès-Beaune. The price will be far less than that of grander appellations. You won't get the full weight and complexity, but you'll get the elegance and silkiness. The same goes for Chardonnay. The very top villages like Meursault and Puligny-Montrachet get more expensive every year. However, Chardonnay grows well in a leaner style in the Côte Chalonnaise and the number of good producers is increasing. The Mâconnais region is also seeing a resurgence of quality for fatter, fruitier styles.

As for Beaujolais: yes, you can afford it. It's probably overpriced for what is an everyday country wine, but it's uplifting and delicious when it's good.

QUICK GUIDE ▷ *Burgundy*

Location Burgundy's vineyards form a narrow belt of land stretching north-south through eastern France.

Grapes Pinot Noir for silky strawberryish reds; Gamay for fruity Beaujolais. Chardonnay makes intense, nutty whites but can also be bone dry and neutral in Chablis; Aligoté is crisp and lemony.

Local jargon *Climat* – individual vineyard site. *Clos* – walled vineyard. *Côte* – hillside. *Domaine* – estate. *Négociant* – merchant.

Vintages to look for 2010, 2009, 2008 (white), 2005, 2004 (Côte de Beaune white), 2002, 1999 (red), 1996 (red).

Vintages to avoid 2004 (except for Côte de Beaune white), 2001, 2000 (red).

Ten to try
RED
- **Joseph Drouhin** Chorey-lès-Beaune ❸
- **Georges Duboeuf** Fleurie la Madone (Beaujolais *cru*) ❷
- **Fourrier** Gevrey-Chambertin ❺
- **Jadot** Beaune Theurons ❹
- **Parent** Bourgogne Pinot Noir ❸
WHITE
- **Vignerons de Buxy** Montagny Premier Cru ❸
- **William Fèvre** Chablis ❷
- **Marc Morey** Chassagne-Montrachet ❹
- **Guy Roulot** Bourgogne Blanc ❸
- **Thévenet** Viré-Clessé ❸

Champagne

Champagne is the world's benchmark sparkling wine. Whenever quality producers in Australia, California, New Zealand – or England – set out to make the best fizz they can, Champagne is their role model, both in the way it's made and in the grapes they use: white Chardonnay and black Pinot Noir and Pinot Meunier. Black grapes can be used to make white Champagne because their juice is colourless.

The key to the flavour of good Champagne is that it doesn't taste obviously fruity. Instead it mingles fruit with biscuits or fresh bread or nuts or even chocolate, and it softens and mellows with age to a glorious nutty complexity. At least, that's the ideal. The method of production, which I've outlined on page 56, is what gives Champagne this flavour – as well as the bubbles.

Not all Champagne measures up; some can be lean and green and mean. Partly it depends on the weather – cold wet summers produce unripe-tasting Champagne – but mostly it depends on the producer. Happily most big names are reliable these days, though a bit more homogenized than before.

Champagne can benefit from bottle age, even after you've bought it. If you tuck a non-vintage Champagne away in a cupboard for six to twelve months it will gain extra roundness; and vintage Champagne isn't at its best until at least a decade after the vintage.

Do regions matter?

Only if you're visiting and have to find your way around. But with global warming, more single producers are starting to sell wine under their own label, and local variations in style will become more important.

CHAMPAGNE STYLES

Champagne comes in three tiers of quality and richness:

Non-vintage is the lightest. It's a blend of wines from several years, and can be drunk as soon as you buy it, though will benefit from a further six months' aging.

Vintage is only made in good years. It should be richer and more flavoursome than non-vintage, but needs to mature for a decade to taste its very best.

De luxe cuvées are mostly, but not all, vintage. They are the very top wines, sold in fancy bottles for huge prices. Dom Pérignon and Roederer Cristal are well-known examples. They should live for decades.

There are also levels of sweetness and it is worth knowing the term for the style you are seeking out as the descriptions on the label can be confusing. Most Champagne is sold as **brut** which is a dry but rarely bone-dry style. More extreme dry styles include **ultra brut, extra brut, brut nature, pas dosé, dosage zéro** and **brut zéro**. **Extra dry** is, bizarrely, slightly less dry than brut. **Sec** is off-dry, **demi-sec** is medium sweet and **doux (rich)** is sweeter still. **Rosé** Champagne is weightier than the white, with a more strawberryish, toasty flavour.

The finest Pinot Noir destined for Bollinger Champagne.

Do vintages matter?

Most Champagne is non-vintage, which means that it is a blend of several vintages. All houses keep stocks of older vintages so that they can blend to a consistent style year by year. Vintage Champagne, in which the vintage obviously does matter, is (in theory) only produced in the best years. You'll pay extra for vintage wines, and what you get for your money should be extra depth, extra character, extra weight – extra everything. Yet vintage Champagnes are not just bigger versions of non-vintage. There should be extra complexity, too, and the character of the year should show through. See the Quick Guide, page 118.

When do I drink it?

Any time, any place, anywhere. It's great to drink on the beach, in the bath, for breakfast, at smart parties – anywhere. Vintage Champagne is a more serious sort of wine than non-vintage and you probably ought to pay proper attention to it. Vintage Champagne goes well with food and non-vintage is the better choice for parties, if that's any help.

Can I afford it?

When you really want it, of course you can. Just give up something else. The cheapest Champagne can be pretty grim, but lots of good merchants have an excellent own-label Champagne at well below the big-brand prices.

QUICK GUIDE ▷ *Champagne*

Location The most northerly major wine region in France, situated east of Paris.

Grapes Chardonnay gives elegance to Champagne; Pinot Noir gives weight; and Pinot Meunier gives softness. Most Champagnes are a blend of all three grape varieties.

Local jargon *nv* – a commonly used abbreviation for non-vintage (see box, page 116). *Grand Cru* – wine made entirely from grapes from the region's very best vineyards. *Premier Cru* – wine made entirely from grapes from vineyards just one notch down from Grand Cru. *Blanc de Blancs* – white wine made entirely from white grapes: Chardonnay, in other words. Blanc de Blancs Champagne should be fresh, creamy and bright. *Blanc de Noirs* – white wine made entirely from the region's black grapes, Pinot Noir and Pinot Meunier. Blanc de Noirs Champagne should be weightier than other styles.

Vintages to look for 2009, 2008, 2002, 1999, 1996, 1995, 1990, 1989.

Twelve to try
All these producers make good vintage Champagne as well as non-vintage, but Charles Heidsieck's is particularly reliable.
• **Billecart-Salmon** ⑤
• **Bollinger** ⑤
• **Alfred Gratien** ⑤
• **Charles Heidsieck** ⑤
• **Henriot** ⑤
• **Jacquart** ⑤
• **Lanson** ⑤
• **Le Mesnil** ⑤
• **Louis Roederer** ⑤
• **Pol Roger** ⑤
• **Union Champagne (Avize)** ④
• **Veuve Clicquot** ⑤

Chalk is all important in the Champagne region both above ground and below. In the vineyards the chalky soil plays a vital role in drainage and in reflecting the sun's heat back onto the vines and the cool dark subterranean chalk pits originally excavated by the Romans are used by the Champagne houses to mature their wines. These cellars belong to the Champagne house Taittinger in Reims and are well worth a visit.

The Rhône Valley

If you want spicy, warm-hearted wines of remarkable depth and complexity, this is where you come. At least, this is where you come in France, because the Rhône Valley is the French home of the Syrah grape, which produces rich fruit flavours and the scent of herbs and smoke. The grape's other home is Australia, where it is known as Shiraz, so if you want to get a full picture of the grape's flavours, compare a good Rhône red with a softer, more obviously lush Barossa Valley Shiraz. It's the difference between Old World and New World styles encapsulated in a single grape variety.

There's a division in the Rhône, however, between north and south. On the map it's shaped a bit like an upturned funnel: narrow at the top, then abruptly widening at the base. Well, the narrow bit is the north, where Syrah is the only red grape planted. The wide bit is the south, and a whole range of grapes is planted here – 12 red varieties are allowed for the various appellations. Wines from the south don't have the minerally, smoky austerity of the northern wines. Instead they're broader and more generous – mostly because the soft, juicy Grenache grape is the heart of the blend. And there's far more wine made in the south. That has two effects for us: first, prices are generally higher in the north. Secondly, quality is more variable in the south.

That's the red wines. When it comes to whites, the Rhône starts springing surprises. With the Viognier grape it produces some of the most aromatic whites in the world, with a flavour of apricots mingled with spring flowers and the richness of crème fraîche. Viognier's traditional home is in a couple of tiny, high-priced appellations in the northern Rhône: Condrieu and Château-Grillet.

The good news is that growers in the southern Rhône have caught on to the fact that we all love Viognier, or would if we could afford it, and they're busy planting it, so some cheaper versions are appearing. They're not, I have to admit, quite as magical as a top Condrieu, but they do show the grape's astonishing flavours.

The other white grapes of the northern Rhône are Marsanne and Roussanne. This duo is responsible for the dry whites of Hermitage, Crozes-Hermitage, St-Joseph and St-Péray – and they go from austerely herbal, through floral to fat and unctuous. The dry whites of the south vary according to the cocktail of grapes used: Châteauneuf-du-Pape can be citrussy and mineral or broad and sensual, Côtes du Rhône can be soft and scented, often flecked with the perfume of wild herbs.

The south has one more trick to pull yet. It's the Muscat grape, making golden, sweet wines that pack a head-reeling punch of crunchy, grapy flavours, laced with rose petals and orange spice, and yet manage to be elegant with it. These wines pack quite a punch of alcohol too, because they're fortified with grape spirit. Muscat de Beaumes de Venise is the most famous and the best, but if you'll permit me to venture beyond the confines of the Rhône for a moment, I'll introduce you to some others scattered around the South of France – Muscat de Frontignan, Muscat de Mireval, Muscat de Rivesaltes and Muscat de St-Jean-de-Minervois.

Do regions matter?

There are differences between north and the south, but the reds are basically all spicy and warm-hearted and the whites, with the exception of aromatic Viognier, are honeysuckle or herb-scented wherever they come from.

Do vintages matter?

People talk about a given vintage being better in the north than in the south, or vice versa. But don't get too hung up on Rhône vintages – they're rarely bad. See the Quick Guide on page 121.

The view from the top of the famous Hermitage hill looking down towards the Rhône flowing southwards.

When do I drink them?

It's a question of mood, as well as food. The reds are cold-weather wines; they're a bit too robust for a summer's day. You can almost feel warmth flowing out of the bottle. They're happiest with strongly flavoured food: a rich casserole, a peppered steak or a slice of saucisson.

Viognier will go with some foods, but it's so hedonistic in flavour that you might enjoy it best on its own. As for the other dry whites, well, drink them for the sake of trying a flavour you won't find elsewhere. They're quite versatile partners for food. You can drink the sweet fortified Muscats as apéritifs – that's what the French do – but they're also a rare match for chocolaty puddings.

Can I afford them?

The top wines, like top wines everywhere, are expensive and rising. Hermitage and Côte-Rôtie in the north and Châteauneuf-du-Pape in the south are the priciest appellations for reds. Viognier from Condrieu and Château-Grillet is astronomically expensive. But there

Location The Rhône Valley is in south-east France. The vineyards are split into two regions with separate identities: the steep slopes of the north and the hot plains of the south.

Grapes Syrah is the red grape of the north, making smoky, minerally wines; southern reds are made from a cocktail of grapes, including Syrah and juicy Grenache, for softer, broader flavours. All Rhône reds are variants of the spicy, warm-hearted style. Viognier is a highly aromatic white grape, while Marsanne and Roussanne deliver herb and honeysuckle flavours. Muscat is used in the southern Rhône for fortified golden, sweet wines.

Syrah-dominated appellations (all in the north) Cornas, Côte-Rôtie, Crozes-Hermitage, Hermitage, St-Joseph.

Appellations where reds are mostly blends (all in the south) Châteauneuf-du-Pape, Costières de Nîmes, Côtes du Rhône, Côtes du Rhône-Villages, Gigondas, Grignan-les-Adhémar (the new name for Coteaux du Tricastin), Lirac, Lubéron, Vacqueyras, Ventoux.

Viognier appellations Château-Grillet, Condrieu.

Vintages to look for 2010, 2009, 2007, 2006, 2005, 2001.

Vintages to avoid 2008 and 2002.

Ten to try

RED
- **Allemand** Cornas ❺
- **Chapoutier** Côtes du Rhône-Villages ❷
- **Cuilleron** St-Joseph ❹
- **Graillot** Crozes-Hermitage ❸
- **Domaine du Grand Montmirail** Vacqueyras ❸
- **Domaine du Vieux Télégraphe** Châteauneuf-du-Pape, Télégramme ❺

WHITE
- **Domaine Grand Veneur** Côtes du Rhône Viognier ❷
- **Guigal** Côtes du Rhône ❷
- **Perret** Condrieu, Coteau de Chéry ❺

SWEET WHITE
- **Domaine de Durban** Muscat de Beaumes-de-Venise ❸

are lots of tasty wines at the middle and lower end which are very affordable. Crozes-Hermitage is the north's best-value appellation.

The south isn't uniform in quality – it's too big for that – and the all-inclusive Côtes du Rhône appellation covers everything from rich, concentrated wines to thin, dilute ones. So shun the very lowest priced examples and pay more for a single-domaine wine from a serious producer: you'll get far better flavours for your money. Côtes du Rhône-Villages and the village appellations of Gigondas and Vacqueyras, as well as Costières de Nîmes, are the best bets in the south.

The Loire Valley

The Loire Valley is the place for classically French flavours that have stayed true to their roots – elegant, restrained and very good with food. They are very popular as lunchtime wines in the restaurants of nearby Paris.

Internationally, the whites are far better known than the reds. There are four main grape varieties, two white, two red; the white Sauvignon Blanc and Chenin Blanc are the best known and most widely spread.

Sauvignon Blanc is the easier to get to grips with. You will probably have encountered the almost shockingly intense fruity Sauvignons from New Zealand or South Africa – well, the Loire Valley is where Sauvignon comes from. The flavours here aren't quite so vivid as in those New World examples, but that's no bad thing because, especially in Sancerre, Pouilly-Fumé and Touraine, they have a palate-tingling green apple, gooseberry and blackcurrant leaf taste that's as refreshing as a wine can get.

Chenin Blanc is less easy to understand because it comes in a whole range of styles, dry, medium, sweet and sparkling. And unless it is fully ripe it makes lean and sullen wines. All this changes when the sun shines and it then displays fascinating flavours. Dry styles run the gamut from steely and austere through to honeyed wines laced with quince and angelica. Vouvray and Savennières need several years' aging. Saumur and Anjou Blanc are better young.

Thrilling sweet Chenins come from grapes affected by noble rot – labelled Vouvray *moelleux*, Quarts de Chaume, Bonnezeaux and Coteaux du Layon. These need 10 to 20 years to transform their youthful high acidity and piercing sweetness into a marvellous mellow maturity of honeycomb and quince.

The other two major grapes are red – Pinot Noir (producing delicate reds and rosés, especially in the upper Loire and Sancerre) and Cabernet Franc (producing superb, tinglingly leafy-fresh, raspberry-rich reds in Saumur, Chinon and Bourgueil.) One more important grape is Muscadet, grown around Nantes at the mouth of the Loire and used for the neutral-tasting dry wine of the same name.

WINE TERMS
Know your Pouillys

Pouilly-Fumé is the Loire's famous crisp, refreshing wine made from Sauvignon Blanc. It has a slight smoky edge that earns it the 'Fumé' tag. Don't confuse this with **Pouilly-sur-Loire**, an unmemorable wine made in the same area from a grape called Chasselas. And don't mix it up with **Pouilly-Fuissé, Pouilly-Loché** or **Pouilly-Vinzelles**. These are rich, fruity Chardonnay wines and they come from Burgundy.

Location A large region stretching the length of the River Loire from central France to the west coast.

Grapes Sauvignon Blanc and Chenin Blanc make green, tangy whites; Chenin also makes sweet wine. Muscadet is bone dry and neutral. Cabernet Franc and Pinot Noir make crunchy raspberryish or mild strawberry-scented reds; Gamay is simple and light.

Sauvignon Blanc appellations Menetou-Salon, Quincy, Reuilly, Pouilly-Fumé, Sancerre, Touraine.

Dry Chenin Blanc appellations Anjou Blanc, Montlouis, Saumur Blanc, Savennières, Vouvray.

Sweet Chenin Blanc appellations Bonnezeaux, Coteaux de l'Aubance, Coteaux du Layon, Montlouis, Quarts de Chaume, Vouvray.

Local jargon *Sec* – dry. *Moelleux* – sweet. *Liquoreux* – very sweet. *Crémant* – traditional-method fizz. *Mousseux* – sparkling. *Sur lie* – aged on lees.

Vintages to look for (dry wines) 2010, 2009, 2008, 2007, 2006, 2005, 2003 (not Sancerre), 2002 (not Sancerre); (sweet wines) 2010, 2009, 2007, 2005, 2002, 1997, 1996, 1995, 1990.

Nantes Tours Loire

① Muscadet
② Anjou-Saumur
③ Touraine
④ Sancerre and Pouilly-Fumé

Ten to try
RED
- **Frédéric Mabileau** St-Nicolas-de-Bourgueil ③
- **Château de Villeneuve** Saumur-Champigny ③

DRY WHITE
- **Domaine des Aubuisières** Vouvray ③
- **Henri Bourgeois** Sancerre ③
- **André-Michel Brégeon** Muscadet de Sèvre-et-Maine Sur Lie ②
- **Jacky Marteau** Sauvignon de Touraine ②
- **Domaine Richou** Anjou Blanc ②

SWEET WHITE
- **Château de Fesles** Bonnezeaux ⑤
- **Huet** Vouvray Moelleux ⑤

SPARKLING WHITE
- **Langlois-Château** Crémant de Loire ②

Facing page: The river Loire meanders across open countryside at les Loges in the heart of the Pouilly-Fumé appellation, the Loire Valley's famous white wine from Sauvignon Blanc.

The Loire also produces fairly sharp sparkling wines made in the same way as Champagne. The whites have a more appley fruit than Champagne and there are a few strawberryish sparkling rosés, too. Ah, yes, rosé. The Loire rather lets itself down with sweetish, cloddish still Anjou Rosé, which is seldom much fun. Cabernet d'Anjou is usually drier, tastier and much more refreshing.

Do regions matter?

Different regions grow different grapes, so yes. Sancerre and Pouilly-Fumé in the east grow Sauvignon Blanc and Pinot Noir; Anjou and Touraine in the middle grow mostly Chenin Blanc and Cabernet Franc, though the best Touraine whites are Sauvignon Blanc; and the Pays Nantais in the west grows Muscadet.

Do vintages matter?

They do, and it's a complicated picture. Chenin Blanc and the red grapes do best in the warmest years; but if it's too warm the Sauvignon Blanc gets flabby. The great sweet wines are only made in years when noble rot (see page 57) occurs. See the Quick Guide (left).

When do I drink them?

Sauvignon is delicious enough to enjoy anytime, with or without food, but Chenin Blanc and the reds really cry out for it – their balance, their subtlety are brilliant as part of a meal. The reds, in particular, are perfect for drinking in the summer, slightly chilled if you like, but they're good enough for quite grand dinner parties too. Muscadet comes into its own with a plate of seafood.

Can I afford them?

Chenin Blanc is great value, the reds are good value and Sancerre and Pouilly-Fumé are on the pricy side: other wines made from Sauvignon Blanc are cheaper. Muscadet makes fairly priced, refreshing drinking.

Alsace

When it comes to aromatic white wines, no region in the world can match Alsace. These wines all share a rich, dry spiciness, a fatness quite unlike anything from the rest of France, or anywhere else in the world.

Gewurztraminer is the spiciest, most fragrant grape of the lot – it's the benchmark for the aromatic white wine style – but even a grape like Pinot Blanc, which everywhere else makes a rather well-behaved, sober sort of wine, can become lush in Alsace. Sylvaner, too, normally a light, dry and rather earthy individual, here has a touch of spice. Even lean, citrussy Riesling, which takes on a limy, toasty character in Australia, and in Germany is minerally or smoky and peachy, often runs to a bit of spice here. And Pinot Gris is second only to Gewurztraminer in its richness, though it tends to be

smoky, earthy and honeyed rather than rose- and lychee-scented like Gewurz.

The exception to the rich, spicy rule is the tiny amount of dry Muscat made in Alsace, but it wins through with a heavenly floral, grapy aroma which, in its own way, is almost as intense as that of Gewurztraminer.

And these wines are all dry. Well, dryish at least; that spiciness makes them seem richer. That means they go well with food, particularly spicy foods, or foods that mix sweet and savoury flavours.

There are sweet whites, too. The richest are made from noble-rotted grapes, but they're rare and expensive. The locals drink them with foie gras. There's also some light red, made from Pinot Noir, but it's

Alsace is a wine tourist's and gourmet's paradise. This is the medieval town of Riquewihr.

Grapes left on the vine beyond the usual harvest time develop extra ripeness if bad weather holds off. Alsace wines made from these grapes are called **Vendange Tardive** (literally 'late harvest'), and they are full-bodied and alcoholic, ranging in sweetness from richly dry to dessert-sweet. Luscious sweet wines produced from the rarer grapes affected by **noble rot** are called **Sélection de Grains Nobles**. All these wines can age for ten years or even longer.

generally little more than dark rosé – attractively perfumed, but not up to the quality of the whites.

Do regions matter?

No, all the wines are in the uniquely Alsatian style.

Do vintages matter?

The wonderful sweet wines are made only in the best years, and the reds need warm summers. But otherwise don't worry too much about vintages.

When do I drink them?

At any time. They're good restaurant choices because they'll go with a whole range of different foods around the table, and I've never met anyone who didn't like them. They're also unusual enough to impress at special occasions. Riesling is the best all-round food wine; Gewurztraminer and Pinot Gris are especially good with Chinese and other Asian foods. They are delicious on their own, too, and Muscat is a pure delight by itself.

Can I afford them?

Yes, certainly. They're never the cheapest wines in any shop, and the best ones are pretty pricy, but they can be bought with confidence at every level. Even the simplest wines will be good buys.

Location In north-eastern France in a rain shadow between the Vosges Mountains and the River Rhine along the German border.

Grapes The white grapes, in ascending order of spiciness and intensity, are: Sylvaner, Pinot Blanc, Riesling, Pinot Gris, Muscat (floral rather than spicy) and Gewurztraminer. There's also Pinot Noir for light reds. Unlike most other French wines Alsace wines are labelled by the grape name.

Local jargon *Grand Cru* – the official classification of the 51 best vineyards. *Edelzwicker* – a lightweight blend of several grapes, generally not very thrilling. *Special reserve* – this and similar terms have no legal weight. Producers use them to distinguish one wine from another, but they are not a quality guarantee.

Vintages to look for 2010, 2009, 2007, 2005, 2004, 2002, 2001; (sweet wines) 2007, 2005, 2001, 1998, 1997, 1996, 1995, 1990.

Vintages to avoid 2003.

Ten to try
WHITE
- **Blanck** Riesling, Schlossberg Grand Cru ❹
- **Josmeyer** Pinot Blanc, Mise du Printemps ❷
- **Albert Mann** Riesling ❷
- **Ostertag** Sylvaner, Vieilles Vignes ❷
- **Cave de Pfaffenheim** Pinot Gris ❷
- **Rolly Gassmann** Muscat, Moenchreben ❸
- **Schoffit** Riesling Grand Cru Rangen ❺
- **Cave de Turckheim** Gewurztraminer ❷
- **Domaine Weinbach** Pinot Gris, Cuvée Ste-Catherine ❺
- **Zind-Humbrecht** Gewurztraminer, Clos Windsbuhl ❺

Southern France

This is where the excitement is in France right now. It all began when Australian and Australian-trained winemakers looked at the vast unfulfilled potential of southern France – the biggest vineyard area in the world – and thought that a bit of New World know-how could transform the area's vast ocean of feeble plonk into a great source of juicy, tasty, affordable reds, pinks and whites, especially if they planted internationally popular grapes like Cabernet, Merlot, Syrah/Shiraz and Chardonnay to supplement the local varieties. This gave an enormous kick up the backside to the whole area and revived local pride in the ancient wine types of the region. The Pays d'Oc (Languedoc-Roussillon) is now a thrilling mix of New World style wines labelled according to grape variety and a richly satisfying array of less well-known but highly individual wines from specific zones (Appellation Contrôlée wines).

This influence is being felt in South-West France and Provence as well as in Languedoc-Roussillon. More and more producers are using improved techniques to get the best out of the many local grape varieties found throughout these regions, although the wines, particularly in the South-West, still taste resolutely Old World. Flavours in much of the South-West are influenced by Bordeaux. But as you get further from Bordeaux you'll find highly individual wines that are often robust and wildly herby, but which are increasingly showing the benefits of modern freshness.

Do regions matter?

Yes, very much, because of the division between Old World and New World styles. In Bergerac and Côtes de Duras in the South-West you get red and white Bordeaux lookalikes. A little further from Bordeaux, you'll find wild, spicy, brawny and tannic reds in Cahors and Madiran.

In Languedoc-Roussillon the traditional reds are spicy and often herb-scented, sometimes with a dry austerity as well. You'll find these flavours in the wines of Fitou, Minervois, Corbières, Faugères, St-Chinian, Coteaux du Languedoc and Côtes du Roussillon.

Provence, with appellations such as Bandol and Coteaux d'Aix en Provence, makes both spicy, warm-hearted and intense, blackcurranty reds, plus a great many good rosés. The dominant grape often determines the style: Cinsaut makes the palest rosé; Syrah the tastiest rosé and red.

IGP 'country wines' from Pays d'Oc and elsewhere in the south should be juicier, more directly fruity interpretations of these red and rosé styles; the white wines are ripe, nutty and/or aromatic.

Traditional whites range from bone dry and neutral to those with a tang of wild herbs; Jurançon, dry or sweet, can be delightfully perfumed. Sparkling Blanquette de Limoux is sharp, refreshing and appley. There are some sweet, golden fortified Muscats, too, from Frontignan, Mireval, Rivesaltes and St-Jean-de-Minervois, and in Bergerac, next door to Bordeaux, the sweet Sauternes-lookalikes of Monbazillac.

Do vintages matter?

Not really, but even here there are occasional aces.

When do I drink them?

Whenever you feel like it. The reds can be a bit assertive for hot weather, but the whites and rosés are perfect.

Can I afford them?

With the exception of a few cult wines, yes.

Facing page: The village of Caramany is one of several in the northern Roussillon producing exciting reds from mountainous vineyards.

QUICK GUIDE ▷ Southern France

Location The vineyards are in three regions: the South-West, Languedoc-Roussillon and Provence.

Grapes In the South-West Cabernet Sauvignon, Cabernet Franc and Merlot are widely grown reds. Malbec has its moment of glory in Cahors. Tannat and Négrette are intriguing local varieties. Whites are often Sémillon and Sauvignon Blanc, but there is also a host of local grapes. Carignan is the traditional Languedoc-Roussillon red, but the better-quality Rhône grapes, Grenache, Syrah, Mourvèdre and Cinsaut, are widely grown, too. International favourites, both white and red, are commonly found. Provence has the same red varieties; its best white is Rolle.

Ten to try
RED
- **Jean-Michel Alquier** Faugères ❸
- **Château Camplazens** Coteaux du Languedoc La Clape ❸
- **Château de Pibarnon** Bandol ❹
- **Domaine Gauby** Côtes du Roussillon-Villages ❹
- **Prieuré de St-Jean-de-Bébian** Coteaux du Languedoc ❹
- **Château Ste-Eulalie** Minervois ❷
- **Château La Voulte-Gasparets** Corbières ❸

DRY WHITE
- **Domaine de Cauhapé** Jurançon ❸
- **Tariquet** Côtes de Gascogne ❶

SWEET WHITE
- **Domaine Cazes** Muscat de Rivesaltes ❸

① Bergerac
② Cahors
③ Minervois
④ Corbières
⑤ Fitou
⑥ Bandol

• Lyon

• Bordeaux
Dordogne

SOUTH-WEST

Rhône

Durance

Garonne

LANGUEDOC-ROUSSILLON

Hérault

PROVENCE

Aude

Marseille •

• Perpignan

N

0 km   100   200

0 miles   100

italy

Italy has its own grape varieties and its own way of doing things; and it's now doing them better than ever. Famous names like Soave, Valpolicella and Chianti are restoring the shine to their tarnished reputations, while the south is re-establishing itself with inexpensive wines, brimful of character, that every wine shop wants on its shelves.

Facing page: Vineyards near the town of Montalcino in southern Tuscany. The powerful wine from here, Brunello di Montalcino, is now one of Italy's most famous reds.

Below: I can tell you from experience that grape-picking is really hard, messy work but these pickers in Campania, southern Italy, still seem remarkably cheerful.

Italy doesn't really make the sorts of wines that other countries do. Even when Italian producers use international grapes like Cabernet or Chardonnay or modern techniques like aging the wine in new oak, they give the wines a distinctive Italian twist. So when do you opt for a bit of Italian style? When you're staring at a plate of food, that's when. The reds are full of sweet-sour cherryish fruit that sets your mouth watering, and the bone-dry, neutral, but increasingly herb-scented whites are so well behaved they'll accompany even the most delicate dish. The whites make terrific apéritifs, but the reds need food.

ITALIAN CLASSIFICATIONS

The Italian system is loosely based on the French model. DOC is the equivalent of France's AC.

Denominazione di Origine Controllata e Garantita (DOCG) In theory the classic wines, limited to a few regions and with tight restrictions on yields and production methods. But it's still a completely mixed bag.

Denominazione di Origine Controllata or **Protetta (DOC/DOP)** These are the major appellations, similar to the AC regions of France. Grape varieties, yields, vineyard sites and production methods are all regulated.

Indicazione Geografica Tipica or **Protetta (IGT/IGP)** Wines with a regional identity, similar to the French IGP. This classification is also widely used by producers of high-quality wines that do not comply with the DOC or DOCG regulations.

Vino da tavola In general the most basic wines, with little regulation and no information on the label about where the wine was made or the vintage. Once used for maverick high-quality wines, but most of these have now converted to IGT (above).

Piedmont and the North-West

If you like powerful, scented reds that mature majestically, this is your region. Nebbiolo is the grape and Barolo, if you're feeling rich, is the summit of your ambition. The colour is rarely dark, but the flavours are impressive.

Barolo is a blockbuster of a red wine. Think of the scents of chocolate and cherries, of prunes and tobacco, of tar and of roses. Whirl them all together and you've got an idea of what mature Barolo tastes like. It used to be a wine that took years and years to age, but a new generation of modernizing producers is making wines that are approachable far younger, and are less tannic and forbidding. But Nebbiolo *is* a tannic grape and Barolo, ancient or modern, is a tannic wine. Barbaresco is similar but lighter. Other Nebbiolo wines – Langhe, Nebbiolo d'Alba, Carema and Gattinara – range from ripe and juicy to rough and ready.

But Nebbiolo doesn't dominate the vineyards. That role is left to Barbera, which crops up everywhere. Mouthwatering high acidity and low tannin are its keynotes, together with flavours of slightly unripe plums and raisins; the best age well, but most can be drunk young. The third main red grape is Dolcetto, which is juicier and fruitier than the other two, but still has that typical Italian sweet-sour tang, and often a good streak of tannin as well.

Whites are not a big deal round here, with the exception of deliciously grapy, sweet Asti and other sparkling wines made from the Muscat, or Moscato, grape. There's some aromatic Arneis and refreshing and improving Gavi, made from the citrussy Cortese grape.

Do regions matter?

Yes, because styles vary. Barolo is the biggest, grandest Nebbiolo, followed by Barbaresco, followed by the others I mentioned above. Dolcetto d'Asti and Dolcetto d'Acqui tend to be lighter than Dolcetto d'Alba. Barbera d'Alba and Barbera d'Asti are the best Barbera wines.

Do vintages matter?

Yes, for the better reds. See the Quick Guide (right).

When do I drink them?

With food. In the case of the reds, they simply demand food like almost no other wines. They're powerful, expressive, impressive, but not easy to understand. Asti and the other sweet Moscato whites are perfect for summer drinking, or with rich desserts.

Can I afford them?

Top Barolo and Barbaresco are fantastically expensive. Go for a fairly simple Nebbiolo from a good producer – though it still won't be cheap. Barbera and Dolcetto are less costly; Asti is inexpensive and fun.

Location Piedmont is the most significant wine region of north-west Italy.

Grapes Nebbiolo, Barbera and Dolcetto make reds in the mouthwatering sweet-sour style, with Nebbiolo being the weightiest and most perfumed. Of the whites, Arneis is fairly aromatic; Moscato (the Italian name for Muscat) is very aromatic and used for sweet and sparkling wines; and Cortese is dry and lean.

Nebbiolo-dominated regions Barbaresco, Barolo, Carema, Gattinara, Langhe, Nebbiolo d'Alba.

Barbera-dominated regions Barbera is grown everywhere in north-west Italy. DOCs include Barbera d'Alba and Barbera d'Asti where the top estates can produce stunning wines.

Dolcetto-dominated regions DOCs include Dolcetto d'Acqui, Dolcetto d'Alba and Dolcetto d'Asti.

Local jargon *Bricco* – a prime hilltop vineyard. *Sorì* – a south-facing hillside vineyard (i.e. one that catches the best of the sun). *Riserva* – wine given extra aging before it goes on sale. *Spanna* – a nickname for Nebbiolo. *Spumante* – sparkling.

① Barolo and Barbaresco
② Asti

Vintages to look for 2009, 2008, 2007, 2006, 2004, 2001, 1999, 1996.

Vintages to avoid 2002.

Ten to try
RED
- **Elio Altare** Dolcetto d'Alba ②
- **Domenico Clerico** Barolo, Ciabot Mentin Ginestra ⑤
- **Aldo Conterno** Barbera d'Alba, Conca Tre Pile ⑤
- **Pio Cesare** Barbaresco ⑤
- **Albino Rocca** Dolcetto d'Alba ③
- **Vajra** Langhe ③
- **Vietti** Barbera d'Asti ⑤
- **Voerzio** Barolo Brunate ⑤

WHITE
- **Bruno Giacosa** Roero Arneis ③
- **La Spinetta** Moscato d'Asti ②

Facing page: Truffle hunting with dogs is a serious activity in the hills around Alba in Piedmont.

Right: Vineyards of Barolo, one of the most famous names in Italian wine.

North-east Italy

This is mostly white wine country. The wines range in style from light and mountain-fresh up in the high Alto Adige to riper and fuller further south and east in the Veneto and Friuli. But bear in mind that Italian penchant for neutrality in white wines. Even with aromatic grapes like Sauvignon Blanc, you won't find anything like the pungency that you'll get from New Zealand. Pinot Grigio is generally light and dry: quite different from Pinot Gris in Alsace. Gewürztraminer is floral but delicate. Sparkling Prosecco is fresh, bouncy and light. Many wines are made from single grape varieties, and named by the grape, which makes it easy to guess the flavour. Soave is the major exception. It's made from Garganega and Trebbiano grapes and is a typically Italian bone-dry, neutral white. Some is pretty classy, with an ability to age, but most are merely light, uncomplicated and, so long as you buy Soave Classico from the heartland of the region, enjoyable. The wines of Alto Adige, Trentino and Friuli will usually offer more flavour and personality.

Reds, including Valpolicella and Bardolino from the Veneto, are mostly light, but can have an attractive bitter-cherry twist. International grapes like Merlot are almost always much lighter than versions from other countries. However, if you see a Valpolicella labelled Recioto, it will be sweet, rich and probably wonderful. Buy it. (There's a white Recioto from Soave, too, which is just as good.) Amarone della Valpolicella is another masterpiece: it's a fascinating, bitter-sour, heavyweight dry red.

Do regions matter?

Yes, hugely, since each region has its own style. Alto Adige makes the lightest, tangiest wines; Trentino's are slightly fuller; Friuli's the most intense. Valpolicella, Bardolino and Soave from the Veneto are the most famous. Quality here has been compromised by overproduction, but plenty of producers make the kind of wine that earned these regions their fame in the first place. Stick to wines labelled Classico and you are less likely to be disappointed.

Facing page: Alto Adige is a spectacular mountain region.

Above: Drying grapes for Valpolicella Amarone, one of the greatest but most unusual red wines in the world.

Do vintages matter?

They do vary, but they're not worth worrying about unless you're buying Reciotos and Amarones or the most expensive whites. See the Quick Guide, right.

When do I drink them?

The whites are good as apéritifs, or as partners for light food. The light reds are for simple meals like pizza and pasta. Reciotos and Amarones are for feasts. The latter demand aging in bottle – up to ten years if you can wait.

Can I afford them?

Not all the wines are brilliant value. Friuli is expensive for the quality; Alto Adige relatively so. The Veneto, if you choose well, is not so expensive, especially for Valpolicella, Soave Classico and lemony white Lugana.

QUICK GUIDE ▷ *North-east Italy*

Location The Veneto and Friuli-Venezia Giulia are located around Venice. Valpolicella and Soave are near Verona. Trentino-Alto Adige extends north into the Austrian Alps.

Grapes Garganega and Trebbiano are the grapes of Soave. Red Corvina is the main grape of Valpolicella and Bardolino. Alto Adige, Trentino and Friuli have a number of local varieties, such as white Friulano and red Teroldego, but are dominated by international grapes. Whites include Pinot Bianco, Pinot Grigio, Gewürztraminer, Chardonnay and Sauvignon Blanc; reds include Merlot, Pinot Noir and Cabernet Sauvignon.

Local jargon *Classico* – the central heartland, and therefore the best part, of a region. *Amarone* – made from semi-dried grapes fermented out to dryness. *Recioto* – sweet Soave or Valpolicella made from semi-dried grapes. *Ripasso* – wine passed over the lees of Amarone to add a bitter-sweet flavour and increase the alcohol level.

Vintages to look for
(Amarone) 2010, 2008, 2006, 2004, 2003, 2000.

Vintages to avoid
(Amarone) 2007, 2005, 2002.

① Bardolino
② Valpolicella
③ Soave

Ten to try
RED
- **Allegrini** Amarone della Valpolicella Classico ⑤
- **Foradori** Teroldego Rotaliano ③
- **Tedeschi** Valpolicella Classico Superiore ①
- **Villa Russiz** Collio Merlot, Graf de la Tour ⑤
- **Zenato** Valpolicella Superiore Ripasso ③

WHITE
- **Andriano** Alto Adige Gewürztraminer ③
- **Anselmi** I Capitelli ⑤
- **Pieropan** Soave Classico ③
- **Schiopetto** Collio Tocai Friulano ③

SPARKLING
- **Villa Sandi** Prosecco di Valdobbiadene ②

Tuscany and central Italy

Chianti is far and away the most famous wine of this part of Italy – in fact it's probably the most famous wine of Italy, period. It's the essence of the sweet-sour cherryish style that dominates Italian reds, but there's a twist of tea leaves in there as well, if you're lucky – a tomato savouriness if you're less lucky – a whiff of violets, and a good backbone of tannin. And quality, you'll be glad to hear, has been surging upwards since the late 1990s.

The key to most of the reds in this part of Italy, including Chianti, is the Sangiovese grape. It's at its lightest in the inexpensive vini da tavola you'll find in every Tuscan supermarket, and at its richest and most expensive in two DOCGs, Brunello di Montalcino and Vino Nobile di Montepulciano. Both these wines need some serious aging to allow their acidity and tannin to soften, but there are sort of 'junior' versions, Rosso di Montalcino and Rosso di Montepulciano, which are fruitier and can be drunk younger. Morellino di Scansano and the other wines from the Tuscan coastal area called the Maremma are riper and juicier in style, although Bolgheri is home to some dark, dense superstars like Sassicaia. Carmignano near Florence is austere but good.

Apple-fresh, plum-rich Montepulciano (the grape, not the town that makes Vino Nobile mentioned above) is the other major red variety and is the main player on the east side of the Apennines. Montepulciano d'Abruzzo is good, gutsy stuff at its best. Tasty Rosso Piceno and Conero from Marche blend it with Sangiovese.

Whites are light, dry and generally neutral: Vernaccia di San Gimignano, Verdicchio, Frascati and Orvieto are the best known. They can all be very attractive, but apart from the top wines, you can treat them interchangeably. Lambrusco is light, fizzy white or red. The best is purple and dry with a lipsmacking sharp bite, but most exported Lambrusco is sweetened, and pretty insipid.

Do regions matter?

With the exception of the Super-Tuscans and 'designer' wines (see right), Tuscany has one basic style of red. There is a theoretical hierarchy of regions, with Brunello di Montalcino as top dog, but it would be snobbish to insist on it. Vino Nobile di Montepulciano and the best Chianti Classicos are serious contenders. Other Chiantis are less serious (and dare I say easier to enjoy), while Bolgheri and

A tranquil scene near Panzano in the heart of the Chianti Classico area.

WINE TERMS **Vin santo**

Traditionally a Tuscan speciality but made all over Italy, **vin santo** (holy wine) is produced from dried Trebbiano, Malvasia and other grapes. It can be dry or sweet, depending on whether it is intended as an apéritif or a dessert wine. The best truly are divine – sweet wines with a taste of nuts, dried apricots and crystallized orange peel.

WINE TERMS **Super-Tuscans and modern 'designer' wines**

There was once an Italian wine law which, among other absurdities, forced Tuscan producers to add white grapes to their Chianti. Top producers couldn't stand it and they started a rebellion. They made no effort to comply with the rules and instead experimented with grape varieties that were forbidden for DOC wines, like Cabernet Sauvignon, and techniques like aging wine in new oak barrels, which was also forbidden. They classified the wines as simple vini da tavola, gave them fancy names, like Sassicaia or Tignanello, and charged a fortune for them. The wines became known as **Super-Tuscans** or **Super Vini da Tavola**. Now, the law has changed and most of them have become DOC or, more commonly, IGT. But those top producers have never stopped experimenting and are famed for both traditional wines like Chianti and highly fashionable ones made from international grapes, including Cabernet, Syrah, Merlot, Pinot Noir, Chardonnay and Viognier.

Scansano in the Maremma region are making increasingly exciting wines. Montepulciano-based reds taste different: richer, but coarser with it. The whites are mostly neutral, with some shining exceptions among Verdicchios and Orvietos.

Do vintages matter?
Yes, for the better reds. See the Quick Guide, right.

When do I drink them?
Whites are best as everyday wines. Drink the reds with robust food – it's what they were made for. Really good reds demand a few years' bottle age.

Can I afford them?
Yes and no. Top quality reds hit the investment market. Less expensive wines are good value.

QUICK GUIDE ▷ *Central Italy*

Location These are the wine regions forming the calf and knee of Italy's boot shape. Tuscany is the most significant.

Grapes Principally Sangiovese for the reds. Montepulciano is grown in Marche and Abruzzo. Trebbiano, Verdicchio and Vernaccia are the main whites. Cabernet Sauvignon and Chardonnay are well established international varieties and producers are experimenting with others such as Sauvignon.

Local jargon *Riserva* – wine with extra aging before release. *Classico* – the central, best part of a region. *Rufina* – the best Chianti sub-zone after Chianti Classico. Other Chianti zones are Colli Aretini, Colli Fiorentini, Colli Senesi, Colline Pisane, Montalbano, Montespertoli.

Vintages to look for 2009, 2008, 2007, 2006, 2004, 2001 and 1999.

Vintages to avoid 2002.

① Chianti
② Verdicchio
③ Orvieto

Ten to try
RED
- **Antinori** Brunello di Montalcino, Pian delle Vigne ❺
- **Avignonesi** Vino Nobile di Montepulciano ❹
- **Casanova di Neri** Rosso di Montalcino ❹
- **Isole e Olena** Cepparello ❺
- **Marramiero** Montepulciano d'Abruzzo ❺
- **Selvapiana** Chianti Rufina ❷
- **Umani Ronchi** Conero, Cúmaro ❹
- **Villa Cafaggio** Chianti Classico Riserva ❸

WHITE
- **Barberani** Orvieto Classico Secco ❷
- **La Monacesca** Verdicchio di Matelica ❷

Location Campania, Molise,
Puglia, Basilicata and Calabria,
which make up the toe and
heel of Italy's boot, plus the
islands of Sicily, Sardinia,
Pantelleria and Lipari.

Grapes Almondy Aglianico,
dark, glowering Negroamaro
and scented Nero d'Avola are
the most exciting reds,
followed by burly, peppery
Primitivo. Cannonau is a
Sardinian relative of
Grenache. Local whites
include Greco, Fiano,
Falanghina, Nuragus,
Vermentino, Vernaccia,
Grillo and Catarratto.
Muscat produces delicious
sweet wines.

Fortified wines Marsala,
Moscato di Pantelleria.

Ten to try
RED
• **Caggiano** Taurasi ⑤
• **Candido** Salice Salentino ③
• **D'Angelo** Aglianico del
  Vulture ③
• **Felline** Primitivo di
  Manduria ②
• **Feudo di Santa Tresa**
  Cerasuolo di Vittoria ②
• **Planeta** Santa Cecilia ④
• **Santadi** Antigua,
  Monica di Sardegna ②

WHITE
• **De Bartoli** Vecchio
  Samperi ⑤
• **Feudi di San Gregorio**
  Fiano di Avellino ③
• **Sella e Mosca** Vermentino
  di Sardegna, La Cala ②

① Fiano di Avellino
② Taurasi
③ Aglianico del
   Vulture
④ Primitivo di
   Manduria
⑤ Salice Salentino
⑥ Copertino
⑦ Marsala

Southern Italy

I think I love this part of Italy most of all. The wines are just
so good. They're stuffed with flavour, unrestrained and
slightly wild. They couldn't taste more Italian if they tried.
In other words, it's an up-and-coming region, and it's
coming up so fast I can hardly keep pace with it. Mostly it's
the reds that excite me: sturdy, spicy and chocolaty, with
a touch of prunes and raisins and roast coffee beans.
Puglia led the way with Salice Salentino and Copertino
but now Sicily and Campania are striding ahead with
some brilliant wines and Sardinia is racing to catch up.

Southern Italy has loads of exciting and individual
red grape varieties, like Aglianico, Negroamaro, Nero
d'Avola, Nerello Mascalese and Frappato. Puglia is the

home of Primitivo, the grape that is generally agreed to be the European ancestor of California's Zinfandel. In some places there are terrific whites, too: Puglia generally makes them from international grapes like Chardonnay, but especially in Campania and Sicily you'll find fascinating fragrant, herb-scented native varieties such as Fiano, Falanghina, Catarratto, Grillo, Greco and Vermentino. I'm also fond of fortified Marsala, for its brown-sugar sweetness and its tingling acidity, but dry versions are even tastier.

Do regions matter?

Well, the regions *are* different. Campania is particularly good for whites, Puglia for big reds and Sicily for sensuous reds and whites.

Do vintages matter?

Not a lot.

When do I drink them?

These are relaxed, informal wines, but they still repay attention. It's a waste to knock them back too carelessly. Cook some good rustic Italian food for them.

Can I afford them?

Yes, yes, yes. There are loads of brilliant-value budget wines, and the expensive ones are seriously classy.

Along with Puglia and Sicily, the mountainous region of Campania is leading the wine revolution in Italy's south.

spain

Spain could now justifiably claim to be Europe's trendiest country when it comes to eating and drinking. Spanish cuisine is buzzing with imagination and irresistible raw materials. And Spanish wine has leapt to the fore with a whole array of flavours and styles, ancient and modern. I love the freshness, the brightness that modern methods and ideas have brought to wine. But I'd hate to lose the great traditional flavours of wines like Rioja or sherry – and luckily, in Spain, the old and the new exist successfully side by side.

Above: The Spaniards always know how to throw a good party. This is Jerez's Festival of the Grape in the far south of Andalucia.

Rioja, sherry and Cava fizz used to be pretty much the only Spanish wines you'd see under their own names. That's all changed. Areas that used to simply despatch their wines to vast blending vats around the world – La Mancha, Valdepeñas, Valencia, Campo de Borja, Jumilla – are all discovering what they do best, and offering us very individual flavours at very fair prices, with their names on the

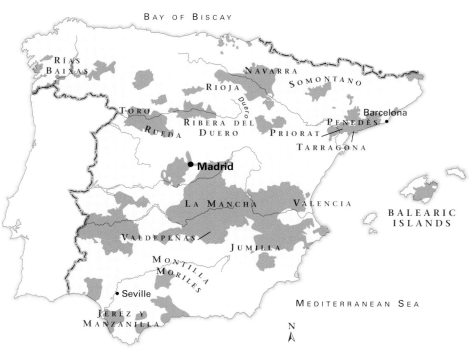

label. Old vineyards, modern methods – that's the key here – resulting in easy-drinking reds packed with the flavours of strawberries and damsons and scented with the swish of herbs, dry, gutsy pink wines and light, refreshing, citrussy whites.

The more serious flavours haven't disappeared – indeed there are more spicy, warm-hearted vanilla-scented reds aged in oak barrels than ever before. There are still creamy, oak-aged whites. And the flavours of great sherry haven't changed for generations.

Cava

All Spanish fizz made by creating a second fermentation in the bottle – this is how they do it in Champagne – is called Cava. Nearly all of it comes from Penedès, near Barcelona. Cavas used to be recognizable for their rustic, earthy flavours, but since they were cheap, no one worried too much.

Nowadays the vineyards and production methods have greatly improved, and most Cava is fresh, lemony, clean and invigorating. The grapes normally used are Parellada, Macabeo and Xarel-lo – all quite neutral – but you will often find some Chardonnay added to give a creamy sheen to the wine.

For some spectacular scenery head inland from Barcelona to the region of Priorat, where rugged mountains form a backdrop to the small terraced vineyards interspersed with olive and almond trees.

SPANISH CLASSIFICATIONS

The Spanish system, like all EU systems, has layers of quality. And like Italy, Spain has an extra, top tier.

Denominación de Origen Calificada (DOCa) This is the top category reserved for wines with a long tradition of high quality. So far only Rioja and Priorat have been awarded the accolade.

Denominación de Origen (DO) or **Denominación de Origen Protegida (DOP)** The standard designation for quality wine, with fairly strict regulations regarding grape varieties, yields and the like.

Vino de pago A category for single-estate DO wines. There are about a dozen of these.

Vino de la tierra These 'country' regions may be labelled **Indicación Geográfica Protegida (IGP)** – for wines that should have regional character. Many have ambitions to be promoted to DO status.

Vino de mesa As in other European countries the most basic wines are known as table wine – or simply **vino**.

North-west Spain

A very diverse offering, with wines ranging from light, fresh whites to Spain's biggest, burliest dry reds. The most famous – and most expensive – is Ribera del Duero (see page 141) – but there are lots of more affordable wines to try. Let's look at whites first.

Rueda, south of Valladolid, is one of Spain's leading white wine regions. Flavours are green and tangy; quality reliable. You might think, from a quick taste, that they're all made from Sauvignon Blanc. No, it's the Sauvignon lookalike Verdejo (there is some Sauvignon too). Some are aged in oak for a butter-and-toast flavour.

Rías Baixas, in the wet, cool, northwestern corner of the country, is Spain's other leading candidate for the title of most refreshing white. These aromatic, citrussy wines generally come from the Albariño grape. They get better every year as vineyards and winemaking improve – but they're expensive. Similar wines from Valdeorras, Ribeiro and Ribeira Sacra can be cheaper and more fragrant, with the perfumed Godello grape at work.

For red wines, the leading contender after Ribera del Duero is Toro. Toro – the flavours reflect the name: big, aggressive, hoof-stomping, not to be mucked around with, but if you're in the mood for a gobfull of palate-blasting red, Toro will do it. Toro is quite good value, though prices have risen.

There are lighter, fresh reds in Ribeiro and Ribeira Sacra, and the wines get fuller further inland with warmer, drier conditions in Valdeorras and, especially, Bierzo where the local Mencía grape is producing exciting modern reds. Cigales is famous for *rosado* (pink), but is making increasingly good reds.

Do regions matter?
Sure they do – see above.

Do vintages matter?
In almost all cases, drink the youngest. Toro reds have significant aging potential.

When do I drink them?
Pinks and whites make lovely apéritifs and Rías Baixas is excellent with fish and seafood. Toro needs red meat.

Can I afford them?
Rueda is affordable, Rías Baixas just a bit more expensive. Toro is getting more expensive, as is Bierzo.

QUICK GUIDE ▷ *North-west Spain*

Location The cool, wet, northwestern corner of Spain and warmer, drier vineyards along the River Duero.

Grapes Reds – Tempranillo (Tinta de Toro), Mencía; whites – Albariño, Godello, Sauvignon Blanc, Verdejo.

Local jargon Red wines with extra aging before release may be labelled *Reserva*.

Ten to try

RED
- Descendientes de José Palacios Bierzo, Pétalos ③
- **Frutos Villar** Toro, Muruve ①
- **Luna Beberide** Bierzo, Mencía ②
- **Elias Mora** Toro ③
- **Fariña** Toro, Gran Colegiata ③

WHITE
- **Adegas Galegas** Rías Baixas ③
- **Belondrade y Lurton** Rueda ④
- **Godeval** Valdeorras ③
- **Marqués de Riscal** Rueda ②
- **Pazo de Señorans** Rías Baixas ③

BAY OF BISCAY

① Rías Baixas
② Ribeiro
③ Ribeira Sacra
④ Valdeorras
⑤ Bierzo
⑥ Toro
⑦ Cigales
⑧ Rueda
⑨ Ribera del Duero

Valladolid

Ribera del Duero

If I were the king of Spain I'd expect to be able to get my hands on pretty much any Spanish wine I wanted at the flick of my fingers. I'd pay, of course, but what's the point of being king if you're told, you'll have to wait your turn, just like everybody else. Well, that's allegedly what happened when King Juan Carlos tried to buy some Vega Sicilia red without getting on the waiting list. At the time – in the early 1990s – Vega Sicilia, from Ribera del Duero, was Spain's most famous single wine. Although Vega Sicilia has been going since 1864, Ribera del Duero only began to receive recognition – and then adoration and obsession – in the 1980s.

The grape used is a version of Tempranillo (Rioja's grape), which they call Tinto del País or Tinto Fino, and growers can also use non-Spanish grapes such as Cabernet Sauvignon and Merlot. The remarkably focused flavours of black fruit, especially blackcurrant, are possible because of limestone-dominated vineyards on the slopes of the Duero Valley that are sometimes so white they seem to be coated in snow.

Well, they might be, because these vineyards are very high – up to 850 metres. This is dangerous – only 125 days frost-free days a year – but the short summer period brings very high daytime and very low nighttime temperatures. That temperature difference, with the limestone, creates the gorgeous pinging black fruit of Ribera del Duero. When the wine is aged – but not for too long – in oak barrels, the result is sublimely good. But these wines have become the darlings of wealthy wine lovers the world over, and prices are high.

Do regions matter?
The region stretches east to west for 100km, with correspondingly different conditions, but the Ribera del Duero DO covers the entire zone.

Do vintages matter?
Yes. Sometimes the autumn rains come early, as do frosts. But in less good years the cheaper/younger *joven* or *crianza* wines can be very good because no top end *Reservas* are made – all the grapes are blended together.

When do I drink them?
These are impressive wines, often oaky, often tannic, but with a magnificent core of dark sweet fruit. Drink them with your best cuts of lamb or beef.

Can I afford them?
They're never cheap, but the *crianza* and non-*crianza* wines (less special grapes, less oak aging) should be affordable and sometimes easier to enjoy. Top examples are some of Spain's most expensive wines.

Rioja

Rioja is an area in transition and all the better for it. If you like the traditional flavours of Spain – the soft vanilla and strawberries, the leathery maturity of the reds and the powerfully dry and nutty whites – you can still find them here. But there are plenty of juicy, unoaked or lightly oaked young reds being made in Rioja, too, and there's been an upsurge in oaky, dark and dense single-estate wines, too. Many producers now make white Rioja in a modern tangy, lemon-zesty style. The best examples become nutty and creamy, not unlike mature white Burgundy, but with a fascinating, pungent, citrussy sour-cream finish.

Muga is the only bodega in Rioja still using oak for every stage of their red winemaking.

Do regions matter?
Rioja Alta and Rioja Alavesa are the best sub-regions, but most wines are a blend of grapes from all over Rioja.

Do vintages matter?
They do for the top wines. But don't worry about vintages for the young wines.

When do I drink them?
They're tasty enough for any occasion, though the finer red Riojas deserve good food and a reflective mood. The light young *joven* reds are great for summer glugging. Really top traditional sour-creamy white Rioja might come as a shock the first time you try it. Persevere.

Can I afford them?
Usually, although the top wines (often labelled Gran Reserva or with a fancy title from a single estate) will be pretty expensive. Simple young Riojas no longer offer the same value as reds from elsewhere in Spain, but the lightly oaked styles (reds and whites) can be very tasty. Young rosés are usually dry, appetizing and affordable.

QUICK GUIDE ▷ *Rioja*

Location The region stretches for more than 100km and grapes may be blended from all over Rioja.

Grapes Red Rioja is traditionally a blend of Tempranillo and Garnacha (the Spanish for Grenache), increasingly with a little Graciano and Mazuelo. Rioja's traditional white grapes are Viura and Malvasía.

Local jargon *Joven* ('young') – often less than a year old. *Sin crianza* ('without aging') – usually one to two years old. *Crianza* – with at least two years' aging. *Reserva* – at least three years' aging in barrel and bottle. *Gran Reserva* – at least five years' aging. White Reservas and Gran Reservas have less aging than the reds.

Vintages to look for 2010, 2009, 2005, 2004, 2001.

Ebro
Haro • ②• Logroño
① ③

① Rioja Alta ③ Rioja Baja
② Rioja Alavesa

Five to try
RED
• **Artadi** Viñas de Gain ❹
• **Baron de Ley** Reserva ❷
• **Contino** Reserva ❹
WHITE
• **López de Heredia** Viña Gravonia ❸
• **Muga** Blanco ❷

North-east Spain

There could hardly be a better overview than this of what's been happening to Spanish wine in recent years. Navarra, once Rioja's understudy, is a hotbed of experimentation and there's no one single style. There are young juicy, fruity reds and oak-aged, mature wines; there are varietal wines and there are blends; there are traditional Spanish grapes like Garnacha and Tempranillo, and international ones like Cabernet and Chardonnay. There are plenty of crisp whites and strawberryish *rosados* (the Spanish term for rosé), too.

Penedès was the first region in Spain to plant international varieties like Chardonnay and Cabernet Sauvignon. Whites come in both the ripe and toasty, and green and tangy styles; reds are intense and blackcurranty or spicy and brawny. Some are varietals; others are blends of international and Spanish grapes. Penedès, like Navarra, has struggled to create an identity outside Cataluña, but there is a different reason here. Torres. This great family company is so well-known throughout the world that its name overshadows that of the region. Its enormous fame may be a mixed blessing, but Miguel Torres has done more to modernize Spanish wine practices and flavours than anyone else.

If Navarra and Penedès have led the modernizing wave, two smaller areas have taken full advantage. Somontano, squeezed up against the Pyrenees foothills, is a cool green oasis that produces delightful fresh, sometimes aromatic, whites and lean but tasty reds. Costers del Segre, inland from Penedès, makes modern reds and whites. Coastal Alella produces attractive fresh whites, most of which go to satisfy local thirsts. And in Mallorca, it is, at last, worth sampling the local wines.

The most fashionable area of the North-East is Priorat, a wild, mountainous region where tiny yields of mostly black grapes (95%) produce dense, raisined, sun-drenched reds that I sometimes find a bit much, but which have developed cult status in Spain and the USA. The neighbouring area of Montsant produces milder examples at a much lower price.

Relatively unfashionable are the inland areas of Campo de Borja, Calatayud and Cariñena, near Zaragoza. Vast plantations of old bush vines – mostly Garnacha, backed up by Tempranillo – produce juicy, herb-strewn reds, some of Spain's best-value wines.

QUICK GUIDE ▷ *North-east Spain*

Location Navarra is Rioja's neighbour (see page 142). Somontano is cooler, the regions to the south – Campo de Borja, Cariñena and Calatayud – are warmer. Penedès and Priorat are the best-known wine regions of Cataluña in the east.

Grapes For the reds, Tempranillo (under various names, such as Ull de Llebre in Penedès) and Garnacha (some from very old vines), as well as Cariñena (Spanish for Carignan), and international varieties such as Cabernet Sauvignon. For the whites you'll find Moscatel (Muscat), Parellada, Xarel-lo (aka Pansa Blanca) and Macabeo (aka Viura), plus international varieties such as Chardonnay and Gewurztraminer.

Vintages to look for (Priorat) 2010, 2009, 2008, 2007, 2005, 2004, 2001, 2000.

Ten to try

RED

- **Artadi** Navarra, Artazuri ❶
- **Borsao** Campo de Borja ❷
- **Capçanes** Montsant, Mas Collet ❷
- **Chivite** Navarra, Gran Feudo Crianza ❷
- **Joan d'Anguera** Montsant, Finca L'Argatà ❸
- **Tomàs Cusiné** Costers del Segre, Vilosell ❷

WHITE

- **Marqués de Alella** Alella ❷
- **Pirineos** Somontano, Mesache Blanco ❶
- **Torres** Penedès, Fransola ❸
- **Torres** Penedès, Viña Sol ❶

BAY OF BISCAY

MEDITERRANEAN SEA

Barcelona

① Rioja
② Navarra
③ Campo de Borja
④ Calatayud
⑤ Cariñena
⑥ Somontano
⑦ Alella
⑧ Penedès
⑨ Priorat

Do regions matter?

Yes they do – see above.

Do vintages matter?

Not a lot for fizz and whites, but Navarra reds differ quite a bit and Priorats reflect vintage conditions.

When do I drink them?

I wouldn't choose the cult wines of Priorat unless I was being treated to dinner by a well-heeled enthusiast. Otherwise these are wines for pretty well any occasion.

Can I afford them?

Definitely. However, top Penedès and Navarra wines are expensive, and as for the top Priorats, well, I expect you've got the message by now: they're not cheap, and Montsant wines give you most of the flavour for a lot less money.

Central & South-east Spain

The different regions here are at last making a name for themselves, either for good quality at a low price or, in some cases, for very high quality at a high price (as in Manchuela). The vast vineyard region south of Madrid is the home of fresh, bright – and cheap – reds, pinks and whites, led by La Mancha and Valdepeñas. The Levant, the hot but fertile strip along the Mediterranean, is famous for its fruit and veg, but Valencia, Utiel-Requena, Alicante, Yecla and especially Jumilla are now producing good-quality red, pink and white wines at low prices.

Do regions matter?

Less than usual.

Do vintages matter?

Rarely. It's very hot every year.

When do I drink them?

Mostly easy-going everyday wines, though the red wines from the Levant can be pretty beefy.

Can I afford them?

Easily. Except for the occasional boutique winery in Manchuela and Dominio de Valdepusa near Toledo.

QUICK GUIDE ▷ *Central & South-east Spain*

Location The vast central region of Castilla-La Mancha lies to the west of the Levant.

Grapes Monastrell (aka Mourvèdre), Tempranillo (aka Cencibel), alone or blended with Syrah or Cabernet Sauvignon; Bobal for rosés and reds. Airén for neutral but increasingly modern whites. Sweet whites – either light or rich – from Moscatel (aka Muscat).

Ten to try

RED
- **Casa de la Ermita** Jumilla, Monastrell ❷
- **Casa de la Viña** Vino de la Tierra de Castilla, Tempranillo ❷
- **Finca Antigua** La Mancha, Syrah ❷
- **Juan Gil** Jumilla ❷
- **Mustiguillo** Mestizaje ❷
- **Piqueras** Almansa, Valcanto ❷
- **Ponce** Manchuela, Clos Lojen ❷

WHITE
- **Ercavio** Blanco ❶

SWEET WHITE
- **Gutiérrez de la Vega** Casta Diva Cosecha Miel ❹
- **Vicente Gandia** Valencia, Fusta Nova ❷

① La Mancha ⑤ Valencia
② Valdepeñas ⑥ Alicante
③ Manchuela ⑦ Yecla
④ Utiel- ⑧ Jumilla
　 Requena

Sherry

If I tell you that good sherry is one of the greatest wines in the world, don't clamour for me to be locked up. It's a spectacular bargain, and you can get stupendous flavours, based on wines that might be 20, 40, 50 years old. But they *are* different. They're not mainstream.

For a start, almost all great sherries are bone dry. *Finos* and *manzanillas* are pale, austere, smelling of bread yeast and apple cores and the sea breeze. *Amontillados* – real ones, not cheap imitations – and *olorosos* taste of nuts and prunes, coffee and toast and generations of experience.

Good sweet sherries do exist. The Pedro Ximénez grape makes intensely grapy, scented wine that is almost black in colour. The Spanish drink this with dessert, or pour it over ice cream – so do I. Seeing words like *muy dulce* ('very sweet') or *muy viejo* ('very old') on the label is a good sign: they indicate that the same wine is sold on the Spanish market.

Nearby Montilla makes wine similar in style and flavour, though it seldom has the bite of good sherry.

Málaga is a sweet fortified wine and the best are intensely nutty, raisiny and caramelly.

Do regions matter?

Not a lot. But *manzanilla* – from the seaside – is saltier and lighter than *fino* from Jerez inland.

Do vintages matter?

Virtually all sherry is non-vintage. It is produced by the solera system, which basically means that you have a series of barrels of wine at different stages of maturity. You bottle wine from the most mature barrel, but you take only a proportion of the barrel. You top up the barrel from the next most mature barrel, and so on until you reach the youngest, which you top up with new

QUICK GUIDE ▷ *Sherry*

Location In the far south of Spain. The region's official name is Jerez y Manzanilla. See the map on page 138.

Grapes Most sherry is made from Palomino, which makes incredibly boring unfortified wine. But turned into sherry it's fabulous. The other grape (and the main one in Montilla) is Pedro Ximénez (or PX), which makes wonderfully grapy sweet sherry.

Local jargon *Dulce* – sweet. *Muy dulce* – very sweet. *Muy viejo* – very old. *Seco* – dry. *Almacenista* – small-scale producer with just a few barrels of high-quality sherry. The company of Emilio Lustau makes a speciality of bottling these.

Ten to try

FINO AND MANZANILLA
- **Barbadillo** Solear ②
- **Gonzalez Byass** Tio Pepe ②
- **Hidalgo** La Gitana ②
- **Valdespino** Inocente ②

AMONTILLADO
- **Barbadillo** Principe ④
- **Hidalgo** Napoleon ③

OLOROSO
- **Williams & Humbert** Dos Cortados ④
- **Lustau** East India (sweet) ③
- **Valdespino** Don Gonzalo ④

PEDRO XIMÉNEZ
- **Harveys** Pedro Ximénez VORS ④

wine. Every bottle of sherry is therefore a blend of wine of almost all ages.

When do I drink it?

Fino and *manzanilla* are perfect apéritifs, and ideal with tapas. Dry *amontillado* makes a good winter apéritif, when it seems a bit dark and cold for *fino*. Intense, dry *olorosos* are wonderful winter warmers before or after a meal, and really good sweet sherries are excellent after dinner. *Fino* needs to be fresh: ideally, buy half bottles and polish them off in one go.

Can I afford them?

Good sherry is terrifically cheap for the quality.

portugal

Portugal is just discovering itself, in wine terms. Yes, port and Madeira are among the world's great sweet fortified wines, but the table wines, red and white, are only now finding their feet. And they have flavours, especially in the reds, that you'll find nowhere else: of chocolate, cherries, damson and vanilla; soft and juicy, yet slightly sour.

Below: Port is Portugal's most famous wine, but is drunk much more outside Portugal than in it. There are several styles of port, but my favourite has to be a glass of the vintage stuff – dark, powerful and serious with a good few years of aging. You really should age it for 20 years, and ideally more. I've had stuff from the 19th century which was absolutely astonishing.

Right: Inland from Lisbon the huge Alentejo region is now producing some of Portugal's most exciting modern red wines.

Table wines

Good reds are now being made in Portugal, from the far north to the deep sandy south of the Algarve. Red Vinho Verde is an acquired taste in the north, sharp and pungent. A little further south, the home of port, along the Douro river, is now making some of Portugal's best and most expensive reds. Deciding whether to use their top grapes for Douro table wine or for port has become much harder for the producers. Bairrada, Beiras and Dão make austere but increasingly good wines while the Lisboa region, the Tejo, Alentejo and even the Algarve make numerous juicy, sun-ripened reds.

Portugal has less of a white wine tradition. White Vinho Verde can be excellent if it's the real thing – snappy, sharp, tasting of laurel and apricot skins – but much of the exported wine is sweetened up. There are serious whites made in all Portugal's wine areas – sometimes from international grapes such as Chardonnay, but more often from Portugal's own honeyed, lanoliny varieties. And pink Portuguese isn't just Mateus. There's lots of tasty dry stuff as well.

Do regions matter?
Northern regions like Douro, Dão and Bairrada are noticeably different from the southern regions of Tejo and Alentejo.

Do vintages matter?
Only rarely, and mostly in the north. Most Douro vintages are good but Dão and Bairrada vary a lot.

When do I drink them?
The reds mostly need food – they're full of flavour and reasonably assertive. White Vinho Verde is excellent with seafood and lovely as a tangy apéritif. The dry rosés are anytime quaffers.

The Baga grape is one of Portugal's many wonderful, unique varieties, making dark tannic wines in the Bairrada region.

Can I afford them?
Yes, yes, yes. Most Portuguese wines are cheap for the quality they offer. Their unfamiliarity keeps the prices down, but the lack of demand fuels a determination to succeed among the producers. Unfamiliar names and grape varieties also help the price/quality ratio. Douro table wines can be pricier but the quality can be superb.

PORTUGUESE CLASSIFICATIONS

The top tier of quality, the equivalent of France's Appellation Contrôlée, is **Denominação de Origem Controlada/Protegida (DOC/DOP)**. Below that is **vinho regional** or **Indicação Geográfica Protegida (IGP)** – 'country wines', where winemakers have a freer rein. The lowest level is simply labelled **vinho**.

Port and Madeira

Both these famous wines are fortified, but they are totally different. Port is sweet and heady, and vintage port is full of black fruits, pepper and spice; Madeira is tangy and pungent with a dry finish, even when it's sweet.

Port styles are basically divided between vintage and non-vintage. **Vintage** port comes from a single harvest, and only in the best years do the producers 'declare' a vintage. The wines are bottled after two years and should be matured in bottle for ten or 15 years before being opened. **Single-quinta vintage** ports are a variation on this theme: they come from the best estate owned by the producer, but are made in the second-best years. They are ready to drink at about ten years old. **LBV**, or **Late-Bottled Vintage**, is rather different. Yes, it's wine from a single year, but bottled after four to six years. 'Traditional' unfiltered LBV is a lovely, perfumed drink that can be enjoyed as soon as you buy it, or kept.

Crusted is a non-vintage blend that is usually an excellent budget substitute for vintage port; **vintage character** is mostly undistinguished. **Tawny** is the most wonderful of the non-vintage styles. 10-Year-Old tawny is russet-coloured, sweet and fruity; 20-Year-Old is nuttier and smoother; and 40-Year-Old is very nutty, smooth and rare. **Ruby** is the simplest and youngest of ports, and at its best is bursting with young, peppery fruit. **Reserve** is a slightly older Ruby. **White** port should be dry and nutty but most is coarse and alcoholic.

Madeira is classified quite differently. Here levels of sweetness are the key. **Sercial** is the lightest and driest; **Verdelho** is slightly weightier and off-dry. **Bual** is fairly sweet and rich, and **Malmsey** is very sweet. All get their pungent, smoky tang from they way they are aged, sometimes being artificially heated, sometimes just stored very warm, so that the wine gently oxidizes. It's not a flavour you'd welcome in other wines, but in Madeira it's essential.

Do regions matter?

No.

Do vintages matter?

Only for vintage port. Most Madeira is non-vintage.

When do I drink them?

At the end of the day, unless you want to fall asleep.
The Portuguese drink tawny as an apéritif; dry Madeira
is also a good apéritif. Vintage port deserves serious
treatment, not to mention a lie-in the next morning.

Can I afford them?

Good ports and Madeiras aren't cheap, and poor ones
aren't worth the hangover. Having said that, if you are
looking for a classic mature wine to celebrate a birthday
or anniversary, there are still examples around and they
are much cheaper than an equivalent Bordeaux or
Burgundy and much more likely to be a lovely drink.

QUICK GUIDE ▷ *Portugal*

Location Vinho Verde, port,
Douro, Dão and Bairrada are
from the north; the upcoming
regions are further south in
Lisboa, Tejo and Alentejo.
Madeira is a Portuguese island
west of Morocco.

Grapes Portugal has an
abundance of indigenous
grapes found nowhere
else. Few of their names
appear on labels, but Touriga
Nacional, Baga and Aragonez
or Tinta Roriz (the latter two
are Portuguese names for
Tempranillo) are good red
grapes whose names you
might see. The main Madeira
grapes are Sercial, Verdelho,
Bual and Malmsey: each of
the different styles is made
from the grape of that name.

Local jargon *Quinta* –
estate. *5/10/20/40-Year-Old* –
Age statements refer to the
average age of the wine in
the blend, not to any
particular vintage. The age is
an indicator of style for tawny
port. Only buy Madeira with
an age statement, preferably
10-Year-Old, or you won't get
the full character.

Vintages to look for (port)
2010, 2009, 2008, 2007,
2005, 2004, 2003, 2000,
1997, 1994, 1985, 1983,
1980.

Ten to try
RED
- **Bacalhôa** Alentejo, Tinto da
  Anfora ❷
- **Quinta do Crasto** Douro ❷
- **Luís Pato** Beiras, Vinha Pan ❺
- **Casa Santos Lima** Alenquer,
  Quinta das Setencostas ❷
- **Tagus Creek** Tejo ❷
WHITE
- **Quinta de Azevedo** Vinho
  Verde ❷

PORT
- **Ramos Pinto** Quinta de
  Ervamoira 10-Year-Old Tawny
  ❹
- **Taylor** Quinta de Vargellas
  (single-quinta vintage) ❺
MADEIRA
- **Blandy's** 10-Year-Old
  Verdelho (dry) ❹
- **Henriques & Henriques** 10-
  Year-Old Malmsey (sweet) ❹

*Facing page: The vines for port are planted on steep terraces
along the Douro Valley.*

*Left: The grapes for the finest vintage port are sometimes still
trodden in shallow tanks or* lagares *in the traditional way.
(That's me, second left.)*

germany

Tell me your attitude to German wine, and I'll tell you whether you're a wine snob or not.

Seriously. You see, Germany produces some sensationally good white wines – some of the best in the world. They have elegance, refinement, concentration and they live for decades, maturing to a fascinating honeyed richness. But these vinous wonders have been horribly overshadowed by the fact that Germany also makes some of the worst wines in the world. They're cheap, sugary and the worst of it is, they are made in a style that apes that of the very best wines.

The river Mosel twists and turns as it makes its way from Luxembourg to Koblenz on the Rhine and I never tire of its great beauty. This view is at Trittenheim.

Anybody who has tasted good German wine and fallen in love with it – and the two processes are usually simultaneous – could not possibly mistake the two styles. But several generations of wine drinkers have been brought up to despise German wines because all they've ever tasted is the dross.

The fact that you're reading this chapter indicates that you're prepared to look beyond the received opinions of wine snobs. Read a bit further and I'll tell you how to find those sensationally good wines.

Riesling

The best and simplest guide to quality is the word Riesling on the label. Riesling is the classic white grape of Germany, and it's too costly to grow to be used for the worst wines. Riesling is *never* used for sugared-up cheap wines like Liebfraumilch. Riesling's characteristic flavour in Germany is tangy, though not particularly green; grapy and flowery, sometimes peachy, sometimes appley, sometimes smoky when young, and there's usually some sweetness in the wine to balance the grape's high acidity. That's important, because these are light wines with low levels of alcohol, and the acidity has to be balanced by something.

Looking at it the other way round, don't be put off by a touch of sweetness in a good Riesling: the acidity makes it delicious rather than cloying. That's the basic flavour. The picture is complicated by the German system of classification, which grades wines according to the ripeness and natural sweetness of the grapes. The highest grades of wines are invariably very sweet. The lower grades can be dry or off-dry. Most of the wines drunk in Germany itself are made dry, but in good examples a little perfumed fruitiness always peeps out.

Certain regions, mostly in the south, are producing increasing amounts of red wine, and as global warming kicks in they can be surprisingly ripe and good; but, to me, Germany is still fundamentally a white-wine country.

Do regions matter?
They do, very much, but above all stick to good grape varieties. The best wines usually come from the Mosel (lighter, tangier, slatier wines); the Rheingau (weightier, riper); the Rheinhessen (softer, and with only a small proportion of its vineyards dedicated to good quality); and the Pfalz (big ripe wines, often from Pinot Blanc, Pinot Noir and others as well as Riesling). Baden wines, white or red, should be good – the Pinot family is more important here than Riesling – and Franken has impressive dry Silvaner, Riesling and Müller-Thurgau.

Do vintages matter?
Yes and no. There is certainly great vintage variation, but the system of classification of wines by grape ripeness means that the better grades are only produced when the grapes are ripe enough – so in poor vintages only simple wines will be made, but they're often delightful, since the grapes from the best vineyards will end up in the cheaper wine.

When do I drink them?
The lighter wines – QbAs (see page 152), Kabinetts, Spätleses – make lovely apéritifs, but also go well with foods like trout or salmon or crab, with pâté, or with gently spicy Chinese or South-East Asian food. Keep the very sweet wines for puddings or preferably for drinking on their own after dinner. But remember that Riesling needs bottle age. Even a light Kabinett will improve for four years or so after the vintage, and the higher grades need longer.

Can I afford them?
Luckily, yes. Prices for top producers are high because demand is high in Germany, but it's still possible to buy a very good quality Kabinett or Spätlese from a less trendy producer or village for a much lower price than you would pay for a comparable wine from many other countries. And you'll often find good merchants selling mature Kabinetts or Spätleses for surprisingly low prices – because nobody wanted them.

German red wines

Most people think of Germany as a white wine country. Well, it is – just. About 60 per cent of the wines are white, but that leaves a remarkable 40 per cent that are red. I say 'remarkable' because Germany is the coolest, the furthest north of all Europe's great wine countries, and all its most famous wines over the centuries have been white and usually sweet. Global warming and an ambitious bunch of young winemakers are changing all that.

Yet the area with the greatest percentage of red vines has traditionally been the Ahr Valley – most northerly of the vineyards clustered along the Rhine Valley, and only beaten in the latitude stakes by the old East German areas of Sachsen and Saale-Unstrut, almost on the 52nd parallel – that's nearly as far north as London. Even they have 20 per cent red varieties.

The Mosel Valley actually used to ban red varieties but now has 10 per cent, including, amazingly, some Cabernet Sauvignon. The areas along the Rhine have always made some red wine, especially at Assmannshausen near Rüdesheim, but as we follow the river south past Mainz and down towards Switzerland and the Bodensee, more and more red vines are planted. The Pfalz has 40 per cent red grapes and is a hotbed of experimentation. Baden has even more with 44 per cent and Württemberg a whopping 70 per cent. Much of this is Pinot Noir (also called Spätburgunder) and some of it is outstanding. There are modern, 'created' varieties like Dornfelder and Regent, but Cabernet and Merlot also crop up, and I wouldn't be surprised to be tasting German Syrah some time soon. After all, the Swiss have been making Syrah for years.

Assmannshausen's beautiful vineyards sloping down to the river Rhine are unusual for the Rheingau region in that they are best known for their excellent red wines from Pinot Noir.

GERMAN CLASSIFICATIONS

Germany's classification system is based on the ripeness of the grapes and therefore their potential alcohol level.

Deutscher Wein and **Landwein** are the most basic and not worth bothering with. **Qualitätswein bestimmter Anbaugebiete (QbA)** wines come from one of 13 wine regions. They can be OK – and there's some good QbA Chardonnay and Pinot Noir – but the infamous Liebfraumilch is a QbA, so beware. The next grade up and the one to look for is **Prädikatswein** and there are six levels, in ascending order of ripeness: Kabinett, Spätlese, Auslese, Beerenauslese, Eiswein and Trockenbeerenauslese.

Typically a good wine is also labelled by village and vineyard. For example, Bernkasteler Doktor is from the Doktor vineyard in the village of Bernkastel. Some villages are better than others and there are some clearly superior vineyard sites. Single vineyards, or **Einzellagen**, are generally the best, but many estates now use single-vineyard names only for their top wines. The second-best wines are sold under the village name, the estate name or sometimes just as Riesling.

Grosslagen are bigger areas without the same specific character. Grosslagen are difficult to spot on labels, because they have names that sound just like single vineyards. For example, Niersteiner Gutes Domtal is a Grosslage and Niersteiner Pettenthal is a top vineyard. A **Bereich** is larger than a Grosslage, but again it can be confusing. For example, Bernkastel is a top village and produces excellent wine, but the Bereich Bernkastel extends much further and includes some decidedly inferior vineyards.

QUICK GUIDE ▷ *Germany*

Location The wine regions are mostly in the south-west of the country, gathered around the river Rhine and its tributaries.

Grapes Riesling makes the best wines, in a tangy though not green style; Scheurebe is fragrant and grapefruity; Pinot Blanc (or Weissburgunder) is less tangy and more nutty; Pinot Gris (Grauburgunder or Ruländer) is honeyed and smoky; Silvaner is dry and neutral. Traminer (Gewürztraminer) is floral. Müller-Thurgau is generally undistinguished. The best red is Pinot Noir (Spätburgunder).

Local jargon *Trocken* – dry. *Halbtrocken* – off-dry. *Sekt* – sparkling wine. *VDP* – an organization of quality wine estates.

Vintages to look for 2011, 2009, 2007, 2005, 2004, 2002, 2001.

Ten to try
All these producers make a range of wines from various individual estates in their region. Prices begin at ❷ for a Kabinett wine, ❸ for a Spätlese. The best and rarest wines are ❺.

• **Dönnhoff** Nahe
• **Gunderloch** Rheinhessen
• **Fritz Haag** Mosel
• **Karl H Johner** Baden
• **Toni Jost** Mittelrhein
• **Juliusspital** Franken
• **Franz Künstler** Rheingau
• **J Leitz** Rheingau
• **Dr Loosen** Mosel
• **Müller-Catoir** Pfalz

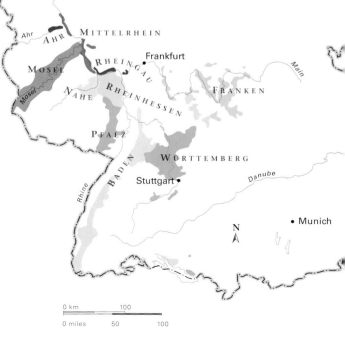

austria

I can't think of a European nation where the wine culture has changed so dramatically over a generation as it has in Austria. Austria still makes great sweet wines, but a new order based on medium- and full-bodied dry whites and increasingly fine reds has emerged.

Above: Lake Neusiedl on the border with Hungary is a paradise for water birds, holiday makers and noble rot, a type of fungus that attacks the grapes at harvest time and concentrates their sweetness.

Facing page: In the Wachau region west of Vienna the vineyards rising up above the Danube produce some of Austria's top dry Rieslings.

Austria may classify its wines in much the same way as Germany (with one or two differences), but the basic style of Austrian wine is not the same. Many wines in Germany are light and low in alcohol, and may be dry or medium depending on the producer. Austrian wines are basically dry, but riper and weightier, and noticeably higher in alcohol. Whites can be neutral, green and tangy, or intense and nutty; the peppery, bay-leaf scented Grüner Veltliner is a fascinating speciality. Reds are mostly juicy and peppery, though the more serious of them discard that instant juiciness in favour of greater structure concealed beneath velvet fruit. And when Austria makes wines sweet, they are very sweet: rich, honeyed, complex and concentrated.

All of Austria's vineyards lie along the warmer and drier eastern edge of the country, from the border with the Czech Republic and Slovakia in the

AUSTRIAN CLASSIFICATIONS

Wine categories are similar to those in Germany, beginning with **Wein** and **Landwein** (country wine). **Qualitätswein** wines must come from a named wine region. Like German wines, Austrian **Prädikat** or quality wines may additionally have a special category (in ascending order of ripeness, sweetness and price): Spätlese, Auslese, Beerenauslese, Ausbruch, Trockenbeerenauslese, Eiswein and Strohwein. Most Austrian wines are either dry or nobly sweet.

Recently Austria has developed an additional geographic appellation system, called DAC, but it hasn't made much impact yet.

QUICK GUIDE ▷ *Austria*

Location The wine regions are all in the far east of the country, running north and south of Vienna.

Grapes Riesling makes the best white wines, more in the style of Alsace than Germany. Grüner Veltliner is Austria's speciality, making very individual dry whites with a peppery tang. Reds are mainly Blauer Portugieser, Zweigelt, St Laurent and Blaufränkisch.

Local jargon *Trocken* – dry. *Halbtrocken* – off-dry. In the Wachau, Steinfeder wines are made for early drinking,

Federspiel wines can last for three years or so and the most powerful wines are known as Smaragd.

Vintages to look for
There hasn't really been a bad vintage since 1999, though 2003 is atypical.

Five to try
- **Bründlmayer** Riesling Alte Reben ❺
- **Franz Hirtzberger** Grüner Veltliner ❹
- **Alois Kracher** Grande Cuvée (sweet) ❺
- **Franz X Pichler** Riesling ❹
- **Umathum** Zweigelt (red) ❸

north, running past Vienna, south to Slovenia and Hungary. The climate here makes viticulture pretty easy and only in the Wachau and Kremstal is the benign influence of the river Danube really necessary.

Different regions have different styles. The best, fruitiest, most velvety reds, as well as the darkest and oakiest, come from Burgenland and the Neusiedlersee on the border with Hungary, as do the intense sweet wines, some of which are truly world class. The best areas for dry whites are either on or near the river Danube in the Niederösterreich region to the west of Vienna. Greatest of these areas is the Wachau, home of superlative Rieslings and fine Grüner Veltliners. Almost as good are the Kremstal and Kamptal areas where Grüner Veltliner is transformed into spectacular savoury yet rich whites as good as any in Europe. The Weinviertel, in the north-east, produces large quantities of decent reds and Grüner Veltliner whites. The Steiermark region in the far south makes pale and steely whites, especially from Chardonnay, Pinot Gris and Sauvignon, which have achieved cult status in the country.

other european countries

This is where we get into unfamiliar grape varieties, and flavours which, without being strident, manage to be quite unlike any others. Vineyards crop up across the continent from the eastern border of Germany right across to the shores of the Black Sea and well beyond. And to the north, an increasing number of spots in England and Wales have what it takes to grow excellent grapes.

England and Wales

This is a great time to be an English wine enthusiast. A mixture of global warming, talented winemakers and some business-savvy owners has brought English wine to a place in the sun. Vineyards are now flourishing as far north as Yorkshire and west into Wales and Cornwall, though most are still in the south. Kent, East and West Sussex are the most heavily planted areas, and hundreds of acres of brand new vineyards are now taking advantage of growing conditions on the chalky Downs that are extremely similar to those in Champagne (just across the Channel). Sparkling wines have made huge strides in the last decade and the best, led by Nyetimber, Ridgeview and Camel Valley, can easily stand up to French competition. White wines have developed a delightful delicate elderflower-scented style based on Bacchus and Siegerrebe. Rondo and Regent are producing gutsy dark reds while Pinot Noir and Dornfelder make lighter reds and gorgeous pinks.

QUICK GUIDE ▷ England and Wales

Location Most of the vineyards lie in a swathe across the south of England, from Cornwall in the far west to Kent in the east.

Grapes Producers have learnt which varieties do well – Bacchus, Siegerrebe and Seyval Blanc for whites; Rondo, Regent, Dornfelder and Pinot Noir for reds, and increasingly the Champagne grapes of Chardonnay, Pinot Noir and Pinot Meunier for sparklers.

Six to try
RED
• **Three Choirs** Ravens Hill ❷
WHITE
• **Chapel Down** Bacchus ❷
• **Stopham Estate** Pinot Blanc ❷
SPARKLING
• **Camel Valley** Pinot Noir rosé ❹
• **Nyetimber** Classic Cuvée ❹
• **Ridgeview** Bloomsbury ❹

Facing page far left: Vineyards in Kent, the 'garden of England'.

Facing page left: The Valais is the most important wine region in Switzerland.

Switzerland

There are three basic styles of Swiss wine: French, German and Italian. The best wines are nearly all French-style, made in the French-speaking cantons. The main white grape is the neutral Chasselas; reds are mostly light, jammy Gamay or Pinot Noir, or often a blend of the two, such as Dôle. They don't taste as good as Burgundy or Beaujolais, but they cost as much.

Well, Chasselas whites can be tasty and zesty if drunk young. Or, try to find some of Switzerland's speciality grapes, such as Petite Arvine, Amigne and Humagne Blanc. These produce rich, dry wines – sometimes sweet ones, too. The beautiful Valais region also manages some good Chardonnay and Syrah. Whites from German-speaking Switzerland are mostly made from the dull Müller-Thurgau (Riesling-Sylvaner). The southern Italian-speaking canton of Ticino makes light, easy-going Merlots, but a new wave of producers is now making deep, ripe, oaky reds of real interest.

QUICK GUIDE ▷ Switzerland

Location Three-quarters of the vineyards are in the western, French-speaking cantons. Most of the rest are in the northern parts of the German cantons, on warmer sites near the many lakes. Ticino, the Italian canton, is in the far south.

Grapes Switzerland is the only country to make a speciality of Chasselas, also known as Fendant in the Valais where it is used for spritzy, neutral whites. Pinot Noir is the red speciality of the Valais. The traditional varieties (such as Amigne and Petite Arvine) are undergoing a revival. German cantons use Müller-Thurgau (Riesling-Sylvaner) for whites and Pinot Noir (Spätburgunder) for reds and rosés. Ticino specializes in Merlot.

Five to try
Few Swiss wines are exported.
RED
• **Daniel Gantenbein** Pinot Noir ❺
• **Gialdi** Merlot ❺
WHITE
• **Henri Badoux** Aigle, Les Murailles ❹
• **Louis Bovard** Dézaley, Médinette ❺
• **Adrian Mathier** Petite Arvine ❸

Greece

Greece has grape varieties grown nowhere else. And many are pretty good: you'll see names like Assyrtiko, Robola and Moschofilero on the labels of the whites; Xynomavro, Limnio or Agiorgitiko on the reds. The whites are green and tangy, with a crisp lemony flavour and good acidity and weight, though Moschofilero and Malagousia are aromatic and Muscat is usually sweet. The reds are spicy, sometimes herby, full-bodied and assertive, often unnervingly but satisfyingly dry.

Above right: Bottles of Tokaji aging in the cellars. Don't worry about that mould – it's been in the Tokaj cellars for centuries and never done any harm. In fact, it protects the wine, if anything.

QUICK GUIDE ▷ *Greece*

Location Greek vineyards are scattered from Makedonia in the north to the islands of Rhodes and Crete in the south.

Grapes Many of the best Greek wines today successfully combine traditional native varieties such as the red Agiorgitiko, Limnio and Xynomavro, and white Assyrtiko, Malagousia, Moschofilero, Robola and Roditis with international varieties such as Cabernet, Chardonnay and Semillon. Muscat is used for the famous sweet whites of Samos and Patras.

Five to try
RED
• **Gaia** Nemea Agiorgitiko ❸
WHITE
• **Biblia Chora** Ovilos Semillon-Assyrtiko ❹
• **Domaine Costa Lazaridi** Amethystos white ❷
• **Domaine Gerovassiliou** Malagousia ❸
• **Samos co-op** Anthemis (sweet) ❷

Eastern Europe

It's now a generation since the fall of Communism, but progress in Eastern Europe has been far slower than I'd hoped, as political and socio-economic necessities took precedence over improved winemaking. The Communist-era attitude to wine often favoured volume over quality and conservatism over innovation. But at last there are real signs of a new quality-led wine world blossoming in Hungary, Slovenia and Croatia. Bulgaria and Romania, which used to be the most impressive producers, are struggling to stay in touch, despite a few courageous ventures, often led by investors from overseas – French-owned Enira is a good newcomer in Bulgaria.

Bulgaria's success in the 1980s was based on cheap, tasty versions of Cabernet Sauvignon, Merlot and Chardonnay; they are still made, but they no longer stand out. There are also some indigenous grapes like the red Mavrud, Gamza and Melnik.

Romania has some of Eastern Europe's finest vineyards, although few reds and whites have so far been better than pleasant. But the Tămîioasă grape makes deep, syrupy sweet wines.

Hungary is most famous for Tokaji, a fabulous sweet wine, renowned for centuries. There is also very good Sauvignon, Chardonnay and Pinot Gris as well as

WINE TERMS **Tokaji**

Hungary's delicious sweet wine is uniquely tangy and smoky. It is made using grapes with a high level of natural sugar (usually the result of noble rot, the fungus that concentrates the sugar in grapes) which are known as **Aszú**. These wines are labelled **Tokaji Aszú** and the sweetness is measured in **puttonyos**. A 3-puttonyos Tokaji is sweet, 6-puttonyos is concentrated and rich. **Aszú Eszencia** is sweeter still and very intense. **Szamorodni** contains only a small proportion of Aszú grapes and ranges from dry to medium-sweet.

indigenous scented white Irsai Olivér, lean Furmint and tasty red Kadarka and Kékfrankos.

Slovenia was always the best white wine region of the old Yugoslavia and has made a considerable reputation for whites – and a few reds. Croatia makes fragrant, light reds and whites in Istria, big burly reds in Dalmatia and full-bodied reds and whites on the Danube and Drava rivers to the east.

Moldova has enormous potential and some fine reds. Slovakia and the Czech Republic make good, light, tangy whites and reds. First sightings in Ukraine are promising.

Do regions matter?
They will do as things improve, because there are big differences.

Do vintages matter?
Generally, each year things improve: choose the youngest.

When do I drink them?
Mostly at mealtimes. Tokaji is for special occasions.

Can I afford them?
Good Tokaji is expensive. Prices are relatively high in Slovenia; elsewhere they're very affordable.

QUICK GUIDE ▷ *Eastern Europe*

Location Bulgaria, Hungary and Romania are the main exporters. Slovenia, Croatia, Moldova, the Czech Republic and Slovakia also have good wine.

Grapes Bulgaria has lots of Cabernet Sauvignon, Merlot, Gamza, Mavrud and Melnik for reds, and a fair bit of Chardonnay. Hungary has white Furmint, Hárslevelü and Irsai Olivér, red Kékfrankos, Kadarka and Kékoporto as well as international grapes. Romania has Pinot Noir, Chardonnay and others, plus the indigenous Fetească and Tămîioasă. Slovenia has Laski Rizling, Pinot Blanc, Sauvignon Blanc and others. Croatia has white Malvasia and Grasevina, red Plavac Mali (related to Zinfandel) and Frankovka, plus international grapes.

Ten to try
BULGARIAN RED
- **Bessa Valley** Enira red ❷
- **Telish** Cabernet Sauvignon ❷

CROATIAN WHITE
- **Vina Laguna** Malvasia ❷

HUNGARIAN RED
- **Weninger & Gere** Cabernet Franc ❺

HUNGARIAN WHITE
- **Hilltop Neszmély** Irsai Olivér ❷
- **Royal Tokaji Wine Company** Tokaji Aszú, 5 Puttonyos (sweet) ❹
- **Istvan Szepsy** Tokaji Aszú, 6 Puttonyos (sweet) ❺

ROMANIAN WHITE
- **Cotnari** Grasa (sweet) ❶

SLOVENIAN WHITE
- **Movia** Veliko Bianco ❹
- **Verus** Furmint ❸

united states

We all now expect to be able to drink clean, fresh, fruity-flavoured wine from all over the world at affordable prices. But this is a relatively new experience in the world of wine. Attractive, readily available, inexpensive wine is only possible because of a wine revolution that began in the 1970s and 80s in California, where the climate is reliably warm and a new generation of winemakers were eager to say, Move over, the New Wave is here.

Since then, California has adopted many European traditions, but the modern revolution begun in the Golden West has completely transformed Europe. California dominates American wine in terms of both volume and international renown, but many other states grow good grapes and make tasty wine, especially Washington, Oregon, New York and Virginia.

California

The wines here are generally big, ripe and ultra-modern in style. They can be simple and mass-produced, or rich, complex and made in artisan quantities. Well-made, interesting wines abound in all but the cheapest price brackets, but they are generally more expensive than an equivalent from Chile or Australia. And be aware that by forking out for the most expensive cult reds you may be paying as much for the ego of the winemaker as for the quality of the wine: California is a place where you can produce a supposedly world-class super-premium wine simply by saying you will, and by charging a world-class, super-premium price. For wines that are genuinely world-class (and affordable) – and California has plenty – start by looking for a track record of quality.

Cabernet Sauvignon, Merlot and California's speciality grape, Zinfandel, rule for reds, often in the intense, blackcurrant or spicy, warm-hearted styles, with Napa and Sonoma the most important areas. But Pinot Noir is a cult grape, making fine, silky, strawberryish wines in cooler spots such as the Russian River Valley, Sonoma Coast, Carneros, Monterey, Santa Maria and Santa Rita Hills. Ripe, toasty Chardonnay accounts for most of the best whites; Riesling and Sauvignon Blanc are also widely grown, though they tend to be less tangy than their counterparts elsewhere. Oak-aged Sauvignon may be labelled Fumé Blanc.

The range of flavours is continually expanding, as more and more producers become interested in the grapes of Italy and the Rhône Valley: Sangiovese is spreading, as are Syrah, Grenache, Mourvèdre, Petite Sirah and others. These are big spicy, attention-grabbing reds. The aromatic Rhône white variety Viognier is increasingly popular. Sparkling wines have fallen strongly under the influence of Champagne, partly because so many Champagne houses have set up shop here, and the best match Champagne for quality. A few Sauternes-style sweet Sémillons and sweet fortified Muscats have ultra-ripe fruity flavours.

Zinfandel deserves special consideration because it is thought of as California's own grape. In fact, it is the same as Primitivo from southern Italy. But Zinfandel has achieved renown in a way that Primitivo never did. At its best it makes warming, heavyweight, berry-flavoured reds with soft, ripe tannins; but it is the most amenable of grapes and can make any style you fancy, from soft, juicy gluggers to sweetish pink wine that is usually labelled as 'blush' or White Zinfandel, right up to the burliest of beefy reds and even heady 'port' styles.

US CLASSIFICATIONS

The first **American Viticultural Areas (AVAs)** were introduced in 1983 to impose some degree of classification on the rapidly developing US wine industry. They indicate only the area of origin of a wine and impose no regulations on its quality. They also require honest labelling of grape varieties. In general, the name of the producer is a surer guide to both style and quality when you are buying wine.

Do regions matter?

AVAs (American Viticultural Areas) on the whole don't matter in the way French AC or Italian DOC regions do. AVAs are delimited appellations, but often based on political boundaries rathern than soil or climate. They don't tell you what grapes you can grow, or what style of wine you must make. This is winemaker heaven: you can make what you want, where you want – just as long as nature will let you and you reckon you can sell it.

Nevertheless, some places are particularly well suited to individual grapes or styles. Napa Valley is California's most famous area. It's where many of the most renowned wineries are based and its red wines, in particular its Cabernet Sauvignons and Merlots, have long been regarded as California classics. Stags Leap, Oakville and Rutherford are outstanding subregions for Cabernet Sauvignon.

Sonoma County is right next to Napa and is home to excellent whites and reds. The reds are generally a little softer and rounder than those from Napa. Two subregions – Dry Creek Valley and Russian River Valley – produce exciting Chardonnay and inspired Zinfandel and Pinot Noir. Sonoma Coast is proving inspirational for Pinot Noir. To the south of Napa and Sonoma, straddling both regions, is Carneros, a cool, foggy region famous for Chardonnay, Pinot Noir and sparkling wine.

South of San Francisco there are vineyard regions sprinkled right down the coast to Los Angeles. Most important of these are Monterey, Paso Robles – home to rich, ripe reds – in San Luis Obispo County, and Santa Barbara, including Santa Maria and Santa Rita Hills, where some of California's finest Pinot Noir and Chardonnay are grown.

Further inland, the Sierra Foothills produce tub-thumping Zinfandel while the Central Valley is a vast

Autumnal vineyards in northern Sonoma near Healdsburg.

agro-industrial area making the bulk of California's everyday wine, but with the good subregions of Lodi and Clarksburg. If the label says North Coast, it means the general region north of San Francisco right up to Mendocino. Central Coast wines come from south of San Francisco.

Do vintages matter?

Only really for the finest wines and the coolest areas. Vintage variation is never as drastic as in, say, Bordeaux.

When do I drink them?

Nearly all California wines can be drunk young: only the very best need age. Since the very best are startlingly expensive, treat them with the respect due to a hefty outlay of cash and save them for a special occasion.

Can I afford them?

They're not cheap, compared to what's available from some other countries, particularly at the lower level. There's upwards pressure on price at the premium level, with producers seemingly competing to make the most expensive Cabernet or Chardonnay. Pinot Noir is about the price of its Burgundian equivalent; top Cabernet does not aim to be cheaper than top Bordeaux.

WINE TERMS **Meritage**

California producers introduced this marketing term to describe wines made from the same grape varieties as the classic wines of Bordeaux in France. It can apply to both red wines blended from **Cabernet Sauvignon, Merlot** and **Cabernet Franc** and to white **Sauvignon Blanc-Semillon** blends. However, it's rare to see the term on the wine label: as most meritage wines are sold instead under a suitably dignified proprietary name. If a California wine is called anything like Tapestry, Anthology, Elevage, Hommage or Affinity, chances are it's a meritage blend.

QUICK GUIDE ▷ *California*

Location The West Coast of the US.

Grapes Intense, blackcurranty reds come from Cabernet Sauvignon, sometimes blended with Merlot, or from Merlot on its own. There's good Pinot Noir in the cool spots. Zinfandel comes in many styles: the best are spicy and rumbustious. The spicy style also belongs to blends of Syrah, Mourvèdre, Petite Sirah and Grenache. Italian grapes tend to be spicy, too. Whites are most often ripe and toasty, from Chardonnay and Viognier; Sauvignon Blanc and Riesling tend to be soft rather than tangy.

Vintages to look for 2009, 2007 and 2006 – but most are good.

Twenty to try
RED
- **Au Bon Climat** Santa Barbara County Pinot Noir ❸
- **Bonny Doon** Le Cigare Volant ❹
- **Cline Cellars** Bridgehead Zinfandel ❹
- **Laurel Glen** Cabernet Sauvignon ❺
- **Long Meadow Ranch** Cabernet Sauvignon ❺
- **Ravenswood** Sonoma County Zinfandel ❸
- **Ridge** Zinfandel ❹
- **Saintsbury** Pinot Noir ❺
- **Shafer Vineyards** One Point Five Cabernet Sauvignon ❺
- **Spottswoode** Cabernet Sauvignon ❺
- **Sean Thackrey** Orion ❺
- **Truchard** Syrah ❹
- **Viader** Cabernet Sauvignon ❺

WHITE
- **Calera** Viognier ❸
- **Marimar Estate** Chardonnay ❺
- **Newton** Unfiltered Chardonnay ❺
- **Ramey** Chardonnay ❺

SPARKLING
- **Roederer Estate** Anderson Valley Brut ❸
- **Schramsberg** ❹

SWEET FORTIFIED
- **Quady** Elysium Black Muscat ❷

Ten for starters
Exciting California wine is expensive. These less costly wines give an idea of the styles, but don't expect the thrills of the main selection.
RED
- **Eberle** Syrah ❸
- **Hahn** Monterey Pinot Noir ❷
- **Kenwood** Russian River Valley Pinot Noir ❷
- **Pedroncelli** Dry Creek Valley Zinfandel ❷
- **Ravenswood** Lodi Zinfandel ❷

WHITE
- **Beringer** Knights Valley Alluvium ❸
- **Dry Creek** Dry Creek Valley Sauvignon Blanc ❷
- **Edna Valley** Chardonnay, Paragon ❷
- **McManis** Viognier ❷
- **St-Supéry** Sauvignon Blanc ❷

Right: Ballooning above the Napa Valley. These early morning fogs blanket the valley floor and play a crucial part in cooling the vineyards.

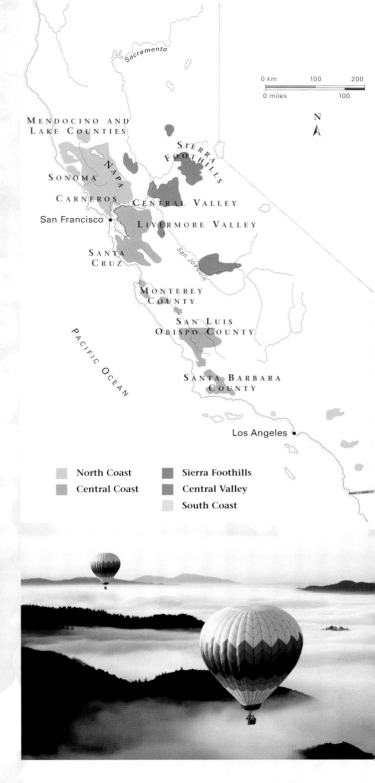

■ North Coast
■ Central Coast
■ Sierra Foothills
■ Central Valley
■ South Coast

Washington

The states of Washington, Oregon and Idaho are known collectively as the Pacific Northwest. They are newer wine regions than California, but have gained a reputation precisely because they make wines in a non-Californian style.

Most of Washington's vineyards are in the Columbia Valley, east of the Cascade Mountains, in what are virtually desert conditions. It's very sunny, very dry, but there's plenty of water for irrigation. Subregions within the Columbia Valley include Walla Walla, Red Mountain, Wahluke Slope, Horse Heaven Hills and Yakima Valley.

The most popular red wines are intense, blackcurranty Cabernet Sauvignon and Merlot and good, warming Syrah. Riesling – in a range of styles, from dry to sweet – and Chardonnay – usually ripe and toasty – vie for position as most widely planted white grape. Semillon and fairly tangy Sauvignon Blanc are worth a look, too. And whereas Oregon has some real stars and a lot of wannabes, Washington State is more reliably good all round.

Do regions matter?
Not really. Most vineyards are in the Columbia Valley or one of its subregions.

Do vintages matter?
Not really.

When do I drink them?
Any time. Washington reds are good food wines.

Can I afford them?
Washington can produce great flavours at a fair price. However, some of the top producers' wines are almost impossible to get hold of – at any price.

QUICK GUIDE ▷ *Washington*

Location Most of Washington's vineyards are east of the Cascade Mountains, in the dry Columbia Valley region.

Grapes Cabernet Sauvignon, Merlot and Syrah are the main Washington reds; white grapes are Chardonnay, Riesling, Semillon and Sauvignon Blanc.

Vintages to look for
The vineyards in eastern Washington enjoy modest weather fluctuations and the reds are consistently good.

Ten to try
With a few exceptions, Washington wines are difficult to find outside the US.
RED
• **Chateau Ste Michelle** Indian Wells Cabernet Sauvignon ❷
• **Col Solare** ❺
• **Columbia Crest** H3 Horse Heaven Hills Merlot ❷
• **Hedges** CMS ❷
• **K Vintners** Syrah ❺

① Columbia Valley
② Yakima Valley
③ Red Mountain
④ Walla Walla Valley

• **Long Shadows** reds (Pedestal Merlot, Sequel Syrah, Feather Cabernet Sauvignon) ❺
WHITE
• **Eroica** Riesling ❸
• **L'Ecole No 41** Semillon ❸
• **Chateau Ste Michelle** Columbia Valley Chardonnay ❷
• **Pacific Rim** Riesling ❷

Above: Mount Rainier looms over the Yakima Valley in eastern Washington State.

Oregon

Oregon Pinot Noir gained international recognition in the early 1980s thanks to the stunning wines made by a handful of pioneering winemakers who planted vines in the Willamette Valley in the late 1960s and early 1970s. This long, wide valley lies between the Cascade Mountains to the east and the Coast Range to the west; it's cooler and wetter than California, but has an extra hour of sunlight a day, and there is a huge difference in temperature between the warm days and cool nights, all of which go to produce wines with bright fresh fruit flavours. That's the theory, anyway. Oregon wines are generally light, with Pinot Noir in the silky, strawberryish style, understated, nutty Chardonnay, spicy Pinot Gris and the odd good Riesling.

Oregon's wine industry is mainly in the hands of small, family-run wineries that focus on quality over quantity, so the wines tend to be expensive.

Do regions matter?

Not to most wine-drinkers. The Dundee Hills (a sub-region of the Willamette Valley with ancient red volcanic soils) is usually considered to be the star region, but Willamette winemakers are exploring the many different types of soil in the valley.

Do vintages matter?

They matter most for Pinot Noir (see Quick Guide).

When do I drink them?

Any time. Oregon Pinot Noirs and Chardonnays are food-friendly wines.

Can I afford them?

Oregon wines can never be cheap – conditions just aren't conducive to bulk production.

QUICK GUIDE ▷ *Oregon*

Location Most wineries are in the Willamette Valley, extending from Portland to Eugene. Further south, the Umpqua and Rogue Valleys are drier and hotter.

Grapes Pinot Noir for reds; Pinot Gris, Pinot Blanc, Chardonnay and Riesling for whites.

Vintages to look for
Oregon can experience severe swings in rainfall levels from year to year. (Pinot Noir) 2009, 2008, 2006.

① Columbia Valley
② Willamette Valley
③ Dundee Hills

Vintages to avoid (Pinot Noir) 2010, 2007.

Ten to try
Oregon wines are pretty difficult to find outside the US.
RED
• **Cristom** Pinot Noir ❹
• **Domaine Drouhin** Pinot Noir ❹
• **Elk Cove** Willamette Valley Pinot Noir ❸
• **Shea Wine Cellars** Pinot Noir ❺
• **WillaKenzie Estate** Pinot Noir ❹
WHITE
• **Adelsheim** Chardonnay ❸
• **Elk Cove** Pinot Blanc ❷
• **Ponzi** Pinot Gris ❷
• **Willamette Valley Vineyards** Riesling ❷
SPARKLING WINE
• **Argyle** Brut ❸

Below: Oregon's reputation was made on Pinot Noir from the cool Willamette Valley.

① Finger Lakes   ② Long Island

Location New York State is the leading East Coast state for wine production.

Grapes The best European vines are Merlot and Pinot Noir for reds; Chardonnay and Riesling for whites. American or hybrid vines have very different flavours. They include Concord, Baco Noir, Chambourcin, Norton, Seyval Blanc and Vidal.

Vintages to look for
Nearly all the wines are made to be drunk young.

Ten to try
New York wines are difficult to find outside the state.

RED
• **Bedell** Merlot ❺
• **Paumanok** Assemblage ❺
• **Pellegrini** Cabernet Franc ❸
• **Wölffer** Merlot ❸

WHITE
• **Fox Run** Reserve Chardonnay ❷
• **Dr Konstantin Frank** Dry Riesling ❸
• **Glenora** Chardonnay ❸
• **Heron Hill** Reserve Riesling ❸
• **Lamoreaux Landing** Dry Riesling ❷
• **Hermann J Wiemer** Dry Riesling ❸

New York State

The best wines come from European vines like Merlot, Pinot Noir, Chardonnay and Riesling, but New York State has a long history of making wines using native vines and hybrids (crosses between American and European varieties), which can cope better with the harsh climate. The native vines belong to a different vine species from European varieties and have quite different flavours: strawberryish, with an intense floral perfume. Quality from the European vines is pretty good, and improving. Chardonnay is quite light and toasty; Finger Lakes Riesling is citrussy and flowery, and Gewürztraminer fragrant. Finger Lakes Pinot Noir can be succulent and silky. Long Island makes the ripest reds. Merlot and Cabernet Franc are earthy, leafy and Bordeaux-like.

Do regions matter?
The Finger Lakes region is the largest and the most important; Riesling is particularly good. Long Island grows good reds, especially on the North Fork, and savoury, balanced whites. The Hudson River Region and the shores of Lake Erie have several good producers.

Do vintages matter?
The erratic weather patterns of the East Coast mean that there is vintage variation between the regions.

When do I drink them?
Ideally, when holidaying in the Hamptons or in the beautiful Finger Lakes. Failing that, anytime will do.

Can I afford them?
Yes, but don't expect them to be bargain basement wines. Top wines are pricy and rare.

The Finger Lakes is New York State's most important wine region.

Other East Coast states

Virginia and Pennsylvania each have well over 100 wineries, and the wines are improving year by year. Wines made from European grapes are beginning to make their mark, especially in Virginia, where Cabernet Franc and Bordeaux-style red blends and Chardonnay and Viognier whites are rapidly establishing Virginia's identity among 'serious' wine enthusiasts. Italian varieties such as Sangiovese and Pinot Grigio thrive in south-eastern Pennsylvania. Native American vines such as Virginia's Norton, and hybrids such as Chambourcin, can make pretty nice wine, and the white hybrid Seyval Blanc makes a delicious accompaniment to the East Coast's famous seafood. Maryland has fewer wineries than its larger neighbours, but all three states offer a very wide range of wines, including good sparkling.

North Carolina has a subtropical climate, but has wineries throughout the state. Maine, farther north than Montreal, *can* ripen grapes, although its handful of wineries are best known for their fruit wines.

QUICK GUIDE ▷ *Other East Coast states*

Location There are pockets of vineyards throughout the states of Pennsylvania, Maryland, Virginia, Delaware and North Carolina – climate conditions and wine quality vary enormously.

Grapes The best European vines are Cabernet Franc, Merlot, Cabernet Sauvignon, Pinot Noir and Sangiovese for reds; Viognier, Chardonnay, Pinot Grigio, Riesling and Gewürztraminer for whites. Hardy native American and hybrid vines are widely planted but have very different flavours. They include Chambourcin, Norton, Seyval Blanc and Vidal.

Seven to try

Virginia's wines are making a tentative debut on the world stage; otherwise, few of these wines are seen outside their home state.

RED
- **Allegro** Merlot, Pennsylvania ❸
- **Barboursville** Cabernet Franc Reserve, Virginia ❸

WHITE
- **Boordy** Chardonnay, Maryland ❷
- **Breaux** Viognier, Virginia ❸
- **Chaddsford** Pinot Grigio, Pennsylvania ❷
- **Horton** Viognier, Virginia ❸
- **Williamsburg** Chardonnay, Virginia ❷

Below: In the heart of Virginia wine country near the Blue Ridge Mountains, Barboursville Vineyards has links with Thomas Jefferson who designed the original estate mansion.

Midwest

The Midwest has a history of growing grapes and making wine dating back to the 1850s; in the late 19th century Ohio and Missouri rivalled California and New York as the major wine-producing states, but Prohibition brought this to an abrupt end. Freezing winters and hot summers are best suited to hardy native American grapes such as Catawba, Concord and Norton, as well as newer hybrids such as Vidal, Vignoles and Seyval Blanc for white wines, Chambourcin and Foch for reds; these grapes are also ideal for the semi-sweet and sweet wines preferred by many Midwesterners.

Classic European grape varieties are gaining ground in Ohio. One of the most promising regions is along the southern shore of Lake Erie, in the north of the state, which is producing a diverse range of wines; whites such as Chardonnay, Pinot Grigio, Gewürztraminer and Riesling are successful here, along with reds from Cabernet Sauvignon, Cabernet Franc and Pinot Noir. Icewines are another speciality.

Missouri's leading grape variety is Norton, for red wines ranging from dry to sweetish. Whites from hybrid grapes are also popular. Cold, snowy, old Michigan is positively throbbing with vineyards and wineries. Old Mission Peninsula and Leelanau Peninsula that jut out into Lake Michigan near Traverse City benefit from warm air from the lake and produce bright fresh Riesling, Gewürztraminer, Pinot Grigio, Pinot Blanc and good sparkling wine. Wisconsin's revival began in the 1970s; it has been most successful with the hybrid Foch, for red wine in a variety of styles. Illinois' fast-growing wine industry is based on hybrids such as Chambourcin (red) and Chardonel (white).

Left: Hermann is a historic town in the heart of Missouri wine country.

QUICK GUIDE ▷ *Midwest*

Location The Midwestern states of Ohio, Missouri and Michigan produce only a tiny percentage of US wines, but winemaking is undergoing a revival and there are now nearly 100 wineries in each of these states.

Grapes The best European vines are Cabernet Sauvignon, Cabernet Franc and Pinot Noir for reds; Chardonnay, Riesling, Pinot Grigio and Gewürztraminer for whites. Native American and hybrid vines have very different flavours. They include Chambourcin, Concord, Foch and Norton for red wines, Seyval Blanc and Vidal for whites.

Five to try

Few of these wines are sold outside their home state.

RED
- **Debonné Vineyards** Cabernet Franc, Ohio ❷
- **Stone Hill** Norton, Missouri ❸
- **Wollersheim** Domaine du Sac, Wisconsin ❷

WHITE
- **Firelands** Gewürztraminer, Ohio ❷

SPARKLING
- **L Mawby** Blanc de Blancs, Michigan ❸

Texas

Texas took its first steps into the modern world of wine in the late 1970s, with the usual suspects – Cabernet Sauvignon and Merlot – but grapes better suited to the Texan heat, such as Sangiovese, Syrah, Tempranillo, Grenache and Viognier, have gradually risen in favour. Unfortunately for Texan winemakers, no grape variety can withstand the occasional devastating hailstorms, which can destroy crops within minutes. Storms permitting, vintages are fairly consistent.

Since 2000 the number of wineries has increased dramatically, from 40 to more than 180, but many of these are small producers. Texas can't grow enough grapes to meet demand, so grapes are often bought in from California and elsewhere.

Other US wine regions

It's when I find that North and South Dakota have vineyards and a handful of wineries; that Minnesota has over 150 acres of vines and that even Alaska and Hawaii have wineries that I realize I need to get out and about more. Many of these states make their wines from native American grape varieties like Concord, which gives floral-scented wines, or newer French-American hybrids such as Minnesota's Frontenac or Hawaii's Symphony, bred to cope with challenging conditions. But wherever they can, winemakers are using the classic varieties – Riesling, Chardonnay, Cabernet, Merlot and Pinot Noir. Colorado, in particular, is making some top Merlot, Syrah, Riesling and Chardonnay wines from high-altitude vineyards in the west of the state.

Most of these wines never leave their state, some hardly make it to their nearest town – but if you're visiting, well, there isn't a single state now that can't offer a glass of something proudly homegrown.

QUICK GUIDE ▷ *Texas and other US wine regions*

Location Every state in the Union now boasts wineries, and with the gradual loosening of inter-state shipping regulations there has been a huge explosion in the last decade or so. California produces over 90% of US wine, followed far behind by Washington, New York and Oregon. States such as Texas are becoming serious players, too.

Grapes In Texas there are reds from Cabernet Sauvignon, Syrah, Sangiovese and Tempranillo, plus whites from Sauvignon Blanc, Chenin and Chardonnay. Elsewhere it's a mixed bag: some states are too cold, too wet, too dry or too humid to grow anything but hybrid varieties – although many have a go with Chardonnay and/or Riesling for whites and Cabernet Sauvignon for reds.

Five to try
Few of these wines are sold outside their home state.
RED
• **Boulder Creek** Syrah, Colorado ❸
• **Flat Creek** Super Texan, Texas ❸
• **McPherson** Tre Coloré, Texas ❶
WHITE
• **Llano Estacado** Chardonnay Cellar Reserve, Texas ❸
SPARKLING
• **Gruet** Gilbert Grande Reserve, New Mexico ❺

Above: Barren moonscape cliffs tower over the vineyards in western Colorado.

canada

Icewine is the wine that made Canada famous – sweet white made from grapes picked when the temperature plummets and freezes them on the vines. They are picked and pressed before they defrost, with the result that the water content stays behind in the press, and just the stickily sweet juice oozes out. It's a remarkable wine, made in tiny quantities from Riesling or Vidal grapes.

The Okanagan Valley is British Columbia's most important wine region. The large lakes help moderate the climate and also provide a spectacular backdrop for the tourists.

But of course it's not a wine you can drink every day. To make up for that, Canadian producers have been busy improving the quality of their dry wines, and they're now producing light, elegant and sometimes positively intense flavours from classic cool-climate grapes. Pinot Noir and Merlot make pleasant, juicy reds; Chardonnays are savoury and nutty, Pinot Gris mild but spicy and Riesling crisp and citrussy. There are plenty of hybrid vines grown as well, for simple, perfumed, jammy reds and off-dry whites, but the best wines come from European vines.

Do regions matter?

British Columbia and Ontario produce 98 per cent of Canada's premium wine. The two major regions are the Niagara Peninsula in southern Ontario and Okanagan in British Columbia. Québec and Nova Scotia both have a small but keen wine industry. One enthusiast in Prince Edward Island produces wine from grapes grown under glass; and the remaining provinces make fruit wines.

With its long sunny days and ice-cold nights Okanagan looks set to become a region of considerable diversity, suited to delicate whites in the north and some substantial Syrah and Cabernet-Merlot blends in the south down by Lake Osoyoos on the US border. Here the weather can get so dry you need to irrigate the vines. Ontario's vineyards rely on being between two vast bodies of water – the cool Lake Ontario and the warmer Lake Erie – which moderates what would otherwise be a very harsh climate and allows excellent ripening of whites like Riesling and Chardonnay, but also Pinot Noir, Merlot, Cabernet and Syrah, in particular on the limestone slopes and benches above Lake Ontario.

Do vintages matter?

They vary, but the wines are made to be drunk young. Red grapes don't always ripen; white grapes usually do.

When do I drink them?

The dry wines are good, light, all-purpose wines. Icewine should be savoured more slowly.

Can I afford them?

None of these wines are cheap and the best are snapped up by Vancouver and Toronto locals for high prices; icewines are expensive but luscious.

Picking grapes for icewine, Canada's speciality and a perfect example of how to turn a difficult climate to good effect.

QUICK GUIDE ▷ *Canada*

Location The vineyards are in the south, hugging the shores of the Great Lakes in Ontario, near the Atlantic Coast in Quebec and Nova Scotia, and near the Pacific Coast in British Columbia. See the map on page 160.

Grapes Pinot Noir, Merlot, Cabernet and Syrah for reds; Chardonnay, Pinot Gris, Riesling and Gewürztraminer for whites; Riesling and Vidal for whites and icewine.

Local jargon *VQA* – the letters stand for *Vintners Quality Alliance*, an organization which enforces high quality standards.

Ten to try
Apart from icewine, Canadian wines are difficult to find outside the country.
WHITE
- **Burrowing Owl** Pinot Gris ❸
- **Jackson-Triggs** Chardonnay ❷
- **Mission Hill** Chardonnay ❷
- **Southbrook** Chardonnay ❸
- **Sumac Ridge** Gewürztraminer ❷
- **Thirty Bench** Riesling ❷
ICEWINE
- **Inniskillin** ❺
RED
- **Cedar Creek** Syrah ❸
- **Henry of Pelham** Cabernet-Merlot ❷
- **Quails' Gate** Pinot Noir ❸

south america

The great revolution in wine – the emergence of ripe, fruity reds and whites at prices everyone could afford – began in California in the 1970s and really took hold in Australia in the 1980s. But as the 20th century galloped to a close, South America had begun to mount a very serious challenge and was laying claim to becoming the most consumer-friendly region of the wine-producing world. The reasons were simple: fruit, flavour and value.

South American wine is the epitome of the modern New World style: flavours are soft and juicy for reds; clean, tangy or toasty for whites. Experimentation is the order of the day in the two major wine-exporting countries, Chile and Argentina, and some extremely serious wines are emerging alongside the excellent everyday bottles. Brazil can produce some lovely fizz, decent whites and reds and together with Uruguay and its beefy, throbbing Tannat reds could yet provide a South American second division, but right now, for flavour and value, Chile and Argentina are a wine drinker's new best friends.

The Vale do São Francisco in northern Brazil is hot and arid and produces two harvests of grapes a year.

Brazil

Brazil is South America's major wine producer after Argentina and Chile (see pages 174–177). Traditionally most vineyards have been in the very beautiful and verdant Rio Grande do Sul, where high humidity and summer rains make ripening reds difficult. However, several new areas are now being developed in the drier conditions towards Uruguay and in the sub-equatorial north at São Francisco Valley where the vines produce two vintages a year. Reds have improved recently and there is a refreshing lack of oak and lowish alcohol in many of them, but sparkling, both dry and grapily sweet, are Brazil's best wines so far.

Mexico

This Central American country suffers dry and fierce heat and has more a beer and brandy than a wine culture. With the aid of irrigation Baja California in the north and high-altitude vineyards further south make good sites for heat-loving red grapes: varieties like Petite Sirah, Zinfandel, Nebbiolo and Cabernet do well. Whites struggle for freshness.

Uruguay

Most of the vineyards are on clay soils spread around the capital, Montevideo. Cooled and dampened by the Atlantic gales, ripening isn't easy, and the Tannat grape, from South-West France – a traditional late ripener – struggles a bit. But it is the national grape and can make good, tough but scented reds. The 'international' reds and whites make up most of the rest of the vines. Dry hot vineyards on the Brazilian border show promise.

Peru and **Bolivia** make Pisco brandy from most of their grapes, but there are a few wines made in other countries, for example in **Venezuela**.

The vineyards of Chile and Argentina are some of the most spectacular in the world: these ones are in Chile's Aconcagua Valley just north of Santiago.

Chile

This is a country on the fast track to stardom. Chile has the good fortune to possess vast disease-free vineyards, stuffed full of classic grape varieties and blessed with endless sunshine due to the rain shadow of the Andes – and endless supplies of irrigation water from these mountains. Add all that to new-found political and economic stability and the 1990s were ripe for Chilean wine to burst onto the international stage.

Soft, juicy Merlot, Cabernet Sauvignon and Carmenère are what Chile is best known for in red wine, and toasty, tropically fruited Chardonnay and crisp, tangy Sauvignon Blanc in whites. But all sorts of other grape varieties are popping up, too. Reds share a basic style of ripe fruit and lots of it; whites are fresh and generally have good acidity, while aromatic grapes like Gewürztraminer and Viognier can be very highly perfumed. There's also dark rosé, with a strong, strawberryish taste. Quality is reliable. A few mega-priced reds have been launched: some are genuinely excellent, while others rely more on smart marketing.

So let's take a look at this pencil-thin country that stretches for 4300 kilometres/2700 miles from the Atacama desert (the world's driest place) in the north to the frozen wastes of Patagonia in the south. There are some amazing wines coming from the far north, from the valleys of Elqui, Limarí and Choapa in Coquimbo. It should be too hot up there, but there is an icy off-shore ocean current called the Humboldt Current which runs up from the Antarctic. Each day as the sun rises in the wide sky, bone-chilling cold winds get dragged up these river valleys from the sea. Brilliant sunshine and ice-cold winds create fantastic conditions for the grapes, resulting in full, fruity ripeness balanced by refreshing acidity. These valleys produce some of Chile's best and

The Maipo Valley south of Santiago.

newest reds from Carmenère and Syrah and whites from Chardonnay and Sauvignon.

The Humboldt Current continues to exercise its chilly charm further south. You'll find increasing numbers of wines – particularly whites, with Sauvignon in the lead – sporting the names Aconcagua, Casablanca and Leyda, all very sunny spots cooled by icy blasts off the ocean.

Chile's traditional vineyard areas are further inland in the Central Valley. Maipo, just south of Santiago, is famous for reds, particularly Cabernet. Cachapoal and Colchagua make round, smooth reds and whites, though the Apalta subregion is known for dark dense reds. Curicó and Maule are fairly warm and produce much of Chile's cheaper stuff, often labelled Valle Central, but Maule also boasts Chile's oldest vines and some increasingly exciting reds.

In the far south, things turn cool again and, frequently, damp, but lovely, fragrant wines are coming from the regions of Itata, Bío Bío and Malleco, with Pinot Noir, Riesling and Gewürztraminer leading the way.

Do regions matter?
Yes. Styles are very different from north to south. Cheaper wines may be labelled Valle Central or Central Valley.

Do vintages matter?
Not much. There are vintage variations, but the wines are never less than good.

When do I drink them?
Chilean reds and whites are great all-rounders, with enough bright fruit to drink by themselves, yet enough weight and structure to accompany all foods.

Can I afford them?
Yes, 99 per cent of the time. There are a few absurdly priced 'icon' wines – but you don't have to buy them.

QUICK GUIDE ▷ *Chile*

Location The vineyards are mainly in the Central Valley and its subregions Maipo, Rapel, Curicó and Maule. To the west of Santiago are the important Casablanca Valley and San Antonio, with its cool sub-zone of Leyda. To the north is Aconcagua and the exciting cool regions of Limarí and Elqui. To the south, below Maule, are the cool, damp Itata and Bío-Bío sub-regions.

Grapes Chile grows the whole range of international grapes. Merlot, Cabernet Sauvignon, Carmenère and Syrah are the main reds; Chardonnay and Sauvignon Blanc the major whites. More than half of what was thought to be Merlot in Chile turned out to be Carmenère, a fantastic traditional Bordeaux grape variety thought to be extinct, which gives rich yet savoury wines in its own right and blends brilliantly with Merlot and Cabernet.

Twelve to try
RED
- **Emiliana** Coyam ❸
- **Errázuriz** Merlot ❷
- **Falernia** Carmenère ❷
- **Viña Leyda** Pinot Noir ❷
- **Loma Larga** Pinot Noir ❸
- **Montes** Alpha Syrah ❷
- **Peñalolén** Cabernet Sauvignon ❷
- **Tabalí** Limarí Syrah ❷

WHITE
- **Concha y Toro** Amelia Chardonnay ❸
- **O Fournier** Centauri Sauvignon Blanc ❷
- **Luis Felipe Edwards** Leyda Sauvignon Blanc ❷

ROSÉ
- **Torres** Santa Digna Cabernet Sauvignon ❷

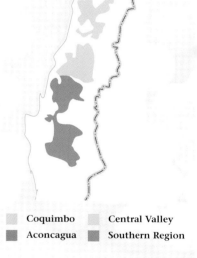

Santiago

▪ Coquimbo	▪ Central Valley
▪ Aconcagua	▪ Southern Region

Argentina

Both Chile and Argentina manage to make wines with a real national identity which are nonetheless international in their appeal. As yet Chile's offerings are a bit more focused and individual, but that is partly because she has found it much easier to identify and develop her cooler-than-average vineyards along the chilly Pacific coast.

Argentina's main vineyard area is Mendoza, tucked up against the Andes and a very long way from any cooling sea breezes. Ah, but the Andes have foothills and valleys and it is up there that the vineyards are climbing. The higher the vineyard, the cooler the conditions, yet the sun shines relentlessly, so Argentina's general style is always going to be rich and round and ripe. This is fine for the reds, especially the Malbec – which is Argentina's calling card and excellent for rich, juicy flavours – as well as Cabernet, Syrah, Merlot and another Argentine speciality, Bonarda. Whites are not so good, but the local Torrontés grape provides delightful, musky flavours, Chardonnay is quite chubby and Sauvignon only occasionally works.

There has been an influx of investment and enthusiasm both from Europe and the Americas. Most of the incomers have focused on Mendoza, and this has created a far greater awareness of the subregions of this vast vineyard area. South of the city of Mendoza, altitudes rise from about 850 metres to 1060m and the higher vineyards do give a fresher, juicier quality, especially to Malbec. Look for names of top zones like Las Compuertas, Luján de Cuyo, Perdriel, Agrelo and Ugarteche on the label. The Uco Valley, climbing up into the Andes, has long been identified as having the best cool conditions in Mendoza, but there are big differences in the valley between Tupungato, at an altitude of up to 1500 metres, whose reds and whites are precise and mouthwatering, and San Carlos, whose warmer vineyards are nearer 900m high.

North of Mendoza, the areas of San Juan, La Rioja and Catamarca used to be dismissed as hot, dusty, bulk wine regions, but all are now showing some style and even producing fragrant whites. Argentina's most

Luján de Cuyo's high-altitude vineyards produce beefy red wines, primarily from well-established Malbec vines.

perfumed whites come from Cafayate, even further north, in Salta, where the Torrontés grape balances succulence with heady floral scent. Altitudes of over 1700 metres and clear skies create perfect conditions for intense reds and whites. One winery, Colomé, has planted vines at 3100 metres – the highest in the world.

There's also a load of wine activity way south of Mendoza in Patagonia. At present most of the action is along the fast-flowing Río Negro, the black river, so called because it runs deep and clear while most of Argentina's Andean rivers look more like milky tea. The Río Negro region is well-established, while the Neuquén region is newer. Both offer reds and whites of intensity and focused flavours. And there are even a few hardy souls planting vines a good deal farther south.

Do regions matter?
Yes. They're very different, north to south. And within Mendoza and the Uco Valley, subregions give quite distinct flavours.

Do vintages matter?
Argentina has very few bad vintages – too much sun is more likely to be the problem. Vintages are more important in the south and the north.

When do I drink them?
Reds are mostly fairly full and ripe, but young ones can be fresh and fruity. They mostly demand sturdy food. Scented Torrontés white can be a delight on its own.

Can I afford them?
Yes, although there are some pricey 'boutique' estates and 'icon' wines, particularly reds.

Right: Summer hailstorms are a real problem for Argentina's grape growers. The hailstones can be as big as golf balls and wreak havoc in the vineyards. This is the high Uco Valley.

Location Mendoza in central Argentina has by far the largest wine production. Salta in the extreme north and Rio Negro in the south are both upcoming quality wine regions. Other regions are San Juan, Catamarca and La Rioja in the north, and Neuquén in the south.

Grapes Red Malbec and white Torrontés are the main ones, but you'll also find Spain's red Tempranillo, the Italian red varieties Sangiovese, Barbera and Bonarda, and international favourites like Cabernet, Syrah and Chardonnay.

Ten to try
RED
- **Colonia las Liebres** Bonarda ❷
- **Doña Paula** Selección Malbec ❺
- **Fabre Montmayou** Cabernet Sauvignon ❷
- **Humberto Canale** Malbec ❷
- **Viñalba** Reserva Malbec ❷
- **Zorzal** Pinot Noir ❷
- **Familia Zuccardi** Tempranillo ❸

WHITE
- **Catena** Alta Chardonnay ❸
- **Colomé** Torrontés ❷
- **Etchart** Torrontés ❷

① Salta
② Catamarca
③ La Rioja
④ San Juan
⑤ Mendoza
⑥ Neuquén
⑦ Río Negro

australia

Australia, as you might expect from a land built by pioneers, is a wine pioneer as well. A nation that has had to make its own rules from the word go was never likely to be happy conforming to the norms of classic wine styles. And so it invented its own: upfront fruit, opulent texture and new oak – all at an affordable price. And it works equally well for reds and whites. European wines were the starting point, and the grapes (since Australia has no indigenous vines) are mainly the classic ones of Cabernet Sauvignon, Shiraz (France's Syrah), Chardonnay, Semillon and Riesling. Nowadays, many of Australia's wine styles are copied around the world, and Australian winemakers and vineyard experts have influenced wine production on every continent.

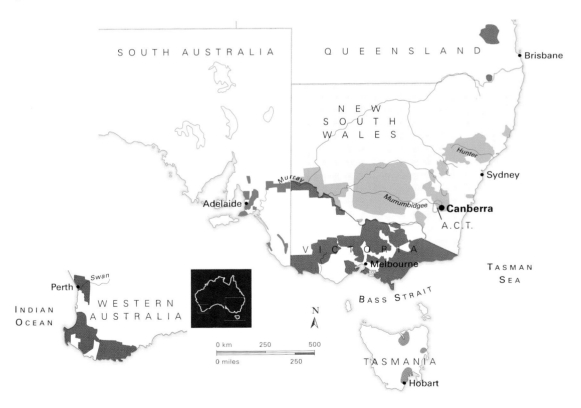

Australia has a **Labelling Integrity Program** which ensures that labels are honest about the region of production, the vintage and the grape varieties used. A system of **Geographical Indications** defines the source of Australian wines in varying levels of detail. **Produce of Australia** is the most basic, followed by **South-Eastern Australia**, a widely seen designation for popular blends. **State of Origin** is the next level and each state contains a number of **zones**. **Regions** are smaller still and some of these are broken up into sub-regions.

fruity wine in even the hottest, driest, most unpromising conditions – the sort of conditions that in Europe would in the past have been written off as incapable of making wine worth drinking. Australia changed all that with the introduction of refrigerated fermentation, for both whites and reds – the 20th century's single most important advance in winemaking technology. Arguably the world leader now in technology, it's almost impossible to overstate Australia's influence on the flavour of the wine we drink.

These sweet-looking roos are a real menace for the growers as they nibble the juicy ripe grapes just before harvest time.

Because Australia is so different from Europe in the way it organizes its wine industry, let's take a few moments to look at how it works. For one thing, every winemaking state in Australia makes almost every wine style. If you want a cool climate you go up into the hills, and further south; if you want a warm climate you go north, and stay nearer the plain. That way you can control whether your wines taste ripe, very ripe, or very ripe indeed. There's an increasing move to cool climates and more subtle wines; but Aussie wines never lose that ripeness. It's the single most important key to the national style.

Wines can come from a single vineyard, or they can be blended from every state in the country – or anything in between. Look at the distance involved – and then think of grapes being trucked perhaps from the Hunter Valley north of Sydney to the Barossa Valley near Adelaide, and arriving in perfect condition, ready to be made into ripe, fresh-tasting wines. That's the sort of technical know-how that Australia takes for granted. Its winemakers are trained to produce tasty, clean,

South Australia

South Australia produces huge quantities of wine. It makes more than any other Australian state – everything from light wines to lush ones, from everyday cheapies to seriously expensive reds and whites, and even ports. How to generalize? Impossible. Pick a style: chances are somebody's making it. Yes, there's the ubiquitous toasty Chardonnay, but South Australia has classic, unique styles, as well.

Barossa Valley Shiraz – often from very old vines, even a century or more old – can be extraordinarily dense, spicy wine, oozing sun-baked fruit: you'll taste ripe tannins and flavours redolent of old leather, spices, earth, blackberries. McLaren Vale Shiraz is similar. And Grenache, again from very old vines, can be a riot of herbal scent and rich strawberry fruit.

Rieslings from the Clare and Eden Valleys have established a new benchmark style. They're not a bit like either German or Alsace Rieslings: instead, they start lean and citrussy then develop an amazing taste of toast and limes. You can't believe it until you try it.

Coonawarra Cabernet is probably what all Cabernet Sauvignon would taste like if it could: intense and blackcurranty, yes, but with a vivid brightness of fruit that is hard to find elsewhere, and a glorious minty edge. These are just the main areas, but from the Limestone Coast in the south, to Langhorne Creek, Fleurieu and Adelaide Hills near Adelaide, right up to the baking Flinders Ranges in the north, you'll find people producing wine packed with individuality.

Do regions matter?
They do, but it's a complex picture since there are subtle and not so subtle differences inside all the regions. Wines from the Adelaide Hills are generally cool-climate and pinging with fruit; Barossa wines are bigger and beefier;

The Barossa Valley in South Australia is one of my favourite Australian landscapes, the green vines and gums standing like oases in the middle of the parched acres.

and Coonawarra, Clare and Eden go for intensity without brawn. Other regions, including bulk-producer Riverland, usually deliver big, ultra-ripe flavours.

Do vintages matter?
In Adelaide Hills, yes; in Coonawarra, yes; otherwise, not really. Poor in South Australia would be good elsewhere.

When do I drink them?
Drink Coonawarra Cabernets with lamb roasted with garlic and rosemary. Hefty Barossa Shiraz is more of a winter evening wine. Clare and Eden Rieslings are ideal for quenching your thirst as the sun goes down. As for the Grenache, drink it to put you in wild party mood.

Can I afford them?
Absolutely. There are lots of inexpensive, tasty wines. The best aren't cheap, but they are classics. Drink them once in a while to remind yourself how amazing wine can be.

Location High-quality wines come from Barossa, Eden and Clare Valleys, Adelaide Hills, McLaren Vale, Coonawarra and Limestone Coast. Riverland is the bulk-wine region.

Grapes Anything and everything. Classics are Shiraz, Cabernet Sauvignon, Chardonnay and Riesling.

Local jargon Don't confuse South Australia with the more general South-Eastern Australia appellation.

① Clare Valley
② Barossa & Eden Valleys
③ Riverland
④ McLaren Vale
⑤ Coonawarra

Twenty to try

RED

- **Tim Adams** Shiraz ③
- **Balnaves** Cabernet Sauvignon ④
- **Jim Barry** The Lodge Hill Shiraz ②
- **Coriole** Sangiovese ③
- **D'Arenberg** The Custodian Grenache ②
- **Henschke** Mount Edelstone Shiraz ⑤
- **Majella** The Musician Cabernet Sauvignon-Shiraz ②
- **S C Pannell** Shiraz-Grenache ⑤
- **Primo Estate** Joseph Cabernet Sauvignon-Merlot Moda ⑤
- **Rockford** Basket Press Shiraz ⑤
- **Skillogalee** Shiraz ③
- **Yalumba** The Cigar ②

WHITE

- **Tim Adams** Semillon ②
- **Grosset** Polish Hill Riesling ④
- **Jacob's Creek** Reeves Point Chardonnay ③
- **Peter Lehmann** Eden Valley Riesling ②
- **Mount Horrocks** Watervale Riesling ③
- **Petaluma** Chardonnay ③
- **Shaw & Smith** Sauvignon Blanc ③
- **Yalumba** Eden Valley Viognier ②

The Murray river is the lifeline for New South Wales, Victoria and especially South Australia, providing essential irrigation and, in Adelaide's case, largely keeping the city watered. Years of overuse and national drought have brought this great river to its knees, reducing water flow by up to 90%. Though the drought has broken, many of Australia's bulk producing vineyards may have to go out of business if, as is likely, it returns.

Victoria

Victoria has more small isolated wine regions than any other state, some boasting only a couple of wineries, some up and coming, some old and just hanging on. Styles range from pale and delicate to pungent and impressive, red, white and sparkling. Many are world class, but there are two styles that no one in the world does better – the fortified Liqueur Muscats and Tokays (now called Topaque) of North-East Victoria. These are explosively sweet, with a concentrated grapiness and an intense perfume of coffee and toffee, raisins and nuts, and sometimes rose petals, that is almost shocking in its richness.

Victoria does cool-climate wines, too. Some of Australia's tastiest Pinot Noirs and Chardonnays come from Yarra Valley and Mornington Peninsula. The best are a match for good Burgundy. Yarra Valley fizz is excellent.

Other wines range from the inexpensive bulk wines from Murray Darling up to elegant reds and whites with well-defined flavours from the cooler areas near the coast or special little pockets inland. There are a few big, fat wines, but not as many as in South Australia.

Do regions matter?

Yarra Valley has elegant wines with finely focused flavours: Chardonnay from here is more intense and nutty than rich and toasty. There are various small regions scattered around Melbourne. Mornington Peninsula and Geelong are fairly cool, but the climate gets warmer as you head north and the wines are correspondingly richer and beefier in the Goulburn Valley, Bendigo, Beechworth or Heathcote. Rutherglen and Glenrowan are the places for the fortified wines.

Do vintages matter?

In the Yarra and around Melbourne, yes. Elsewhere, not that much. See the Quick Guide, above.

Location Yarra Valley, Mornington Peninsula, Bendigo and Heathcote, Rutherglen and Glenrowan are significant for quality, Murray Darling for quantity.

Grapes The stars are sweet fortified Muscat and Muscadelle (Tokay/Topaque), subtle Pinot Noir, scented Shiraz and Chardonnay.

Local jargon Rutherglen Muscats come in four quality grades. In ascending order, they are: Rutherglen, Classic, Grand and Rare.

Vintages to look for (Yarra) 2010, 2008, 2006, 2005, 2004.

Ten to try
RED
• **De Bortoli** Pinot Noir ③
• **Kooyong** Pinot Noir ④
• **Mount Langi Ghiran** Billi Billi Shiraz ②
• **Tyrrell's** Rufus Stone Shiraz ③

① Bendigo
② Heathcote
③ Rutherglen and Glenrowan
④ Yarra Valley
⑤ Mornington Peninsula

WHITE
• **Coldstream Hills** Chardonnay ③
• **Stonier** Chardonnay ③
• **Tahbilk** Marsanne ②

SPARKLING
• **Green Point** ③
• **Seppelt** Show Sparkling Shiraz (red) ③

FORTIFIED
• **Chambers** Grand Rutherglen Muscat ⑤

When do I drink them?

Premium Yarra Valley reds and whites deserve a special occasion. The fortified Muscats are a match for chocolate and Christmas pudding, but you could also put them with – or on – ice cream, or just tuck into them on their own.

Can I afford them?

The best Yarra Valley and Mornington Peninsula wines are pretty expensive and suffer from vintage variations just as Burgundies, their European counterparts, do. Fortified Muscats are quite expensive, especially the oldest ones, but they're certainly not overpriced.

New South Wales

Well, this is where I started in Australia. There was a time when I thought virtually the whole world of wine revolved around the Hunter Valley, two hours' drive north of Sydney (or rather more if you stopped off at Wollombi for a snifter of Dr Jurd's Jungle Juice).

The rich, ripe, utterly un-European flavours were a revelation then – and Hunter Valley reds and whites are still some of Australia's most individual: Chardonnay is fat and full of tropical fruit and toast, tasting reassuringly old-fashioned; Shiraz is rich, berried and leathery-tasting – spicy and warm-hearted on a big scale from the top Hunter vineyards; and Semillon, usually unoaked, can be tart and raw when young but ages to a wonderful toastiness, allied to waxy, leathery, lanolin richness and a flicker of custardy sweetness – one of the wine world's greatest and most unexpected transformations.

Nearby, the small region of Mudgee, with marginally cooler temperatures, makes good blackcurranty reds and Cowra is famous for rich, fat Chardonnay. If you see Orange, Hilltops, Tumbarumba or Canberra District on the label, the wine will be from high, cool vineyards and should have a thrilling, if lean, intensity of fruit. Riverina is New South Wales's bulk wine area. Flavours here are generally simple, ripe and juicy, but there are oakier, more concentrated wines as well, and several world-class golden, super-sweet ones.

Do regions matter?

They do, but the producer usually matters more. Even so, Hunter Valley wines are quite unlike any others in Australia, coming from virtually subtropical vineyards and with a tricky climate. The regions of Orange, Hilltops and Canberra are quite different – the vineyards here are high altitude and cool.

Do vintages matter?

They matter a lot in the Hunter Valley where rainstorms often occur just before harvest – reds and whites can often have totally different results.

When do I drink them?

Hunter Valley wines for whenever you feel like fat, lush flavours. They can nearly all be drunk young; unoaked Semillon needs to age. Cool-climate wines are ready to drink when bottled, but they will age too.

Can I afford them?

Given that Sydney is near by, most wines are quite expensive, though Riverina is better value.

QUICK GUIDE ▷ *New South Wales*

Location The major quality regions are Hunter Valley, Cowra, Mudgee, Orange, Hilltops and Canberra. The largest regions are Riverina and Murray Darling, Swan Hill and Perricoota on the Murray River.

Grapes Semillon and ripe, toasty Chardonnay are the main whites; leading reds are spicy, full-on Shiraz and blackcurranty Cabernet.

Ten to try
RED
• **Brokenwood** Graveyard Shiraz ❺
• **Clonakilla** Shiraz-Viognier ❺
• **Hope Estate** Shiraz ❷
• **Tyrrell's** Vat 9 Shiraz ❹
WHITE
• **Allandale** Chardonnay ❷
• **Brokenwood** Semillon ❸
• **McWilliam's** Mount Pleasant Semillon ❷

• **Philip Shaw** No 19 Sauvignon Blanc ❸
• **Tyrrell's** Vat 47 Chardonnay ❹
SWEET WHITE
• **De Bortoli** Noble One Botrytis Semillon ❺

① Riverina   ④ Mudgee
② Cowra   ⑤ Hunter Valley
③ Orange

Western Australia

The thing is, Western Australia is so far away from the rest of Australia. It's about 4000 kilometres west–east from Perth to Sydney and most of that's desert. Basically 'Australia' has come to mean the states of the east and south-east and Western Australia was left to develop as best as it could an awful long way from the rest of the country. But with global warming threatening much of South Eastern Australia, the whole south-western corner of Western Australia where it's very cool and mostly undeveloped could be in a for a further bonanza as the world turns away from super-ripe styles of wine.

By far the most important area is Margaret River, a knob of land butting out into the sea just where the warm Indian Ocean and the cold Southern Ocean meet. This creates breezes that cool the vines down and give beautiful, tangy fresh whites and deep-flavoured serious reds that really do match the French classics of red and white Bordeaux and white Burgundy. Sauvignon, Semillon (often blended as in Bordeaux) and Chardonnay are the best whites; Cabernet, Merlot (again often blended as in Bordeaux) and Shiraz are the best reds. South of Margaret River the Manjimup and Pemberton both produce good cool-climate flavours, and the large Great Southern area right down near the Southern Ocean is brilliant for tangy whites and tasty reds. North of Margaret River there are good vineyards in Geographe, Peel and Perth Hills while the original area of Swan Valley is still well planted with vines. But it's hot here and the wines are rich and round. It would make wonderful Aussie 'ports' and 'sherries' but no one seems to want them nowadays.

Do regions matter?
Yes, there are big variations in style.

Do vintages matter?
Yes, the wines are always good, but cooler areas may not fully ripen their grapes in wet or cold vintages.

When do I drink them?
Great Southern whites, especially Riesling, are lovely just by themselves, as are Margaret River Semillon-Sauvignons. The reds are brilliant food wines.

Can I afford them?
Only Swan Valley wines are cheap. But Great Southern isn't expensive, and Margaret River, while never cheap, has lots of affordable labels.

The gums in Western Australia are some of the tallest and most beautiful in the nation.

QUICK GUIDE ▷ *Western Australia*

Location The best regions are Margaret River, Great Southern and Pemberton. Swan District near Perth is the bulk region.

Grapes Cabernet Sauvignon and Shiraz for the reds; whites from Chardonnay, Riesling and Sauvignon Blanc, plus Chenin Blanc and Verdelho.

Five to try
RED
- **Cullen** Cabernet-Merlot ⑤
- **Plantagenet** Shiraz ⑤
- **Voyager Estate** Cabernet-Merlot ⑤

WHITE
- **Cape Mentelle** Semillon-Sauvignon Blanc ③
- **Pierro** Chardonnay ⑤

Tasmania

The island state of Tasmania sits well south of the bottom tip of Victoria across the cold and stormy Bass Strait and for most of its history experts have said it's too cold for vines: why not grow apples? Well, most of Tassie *is* too cold or wet, but there are sheltered stretches of land often huddled together on river banks or along estuaries where the winds die and warmth is reflected off the water, where brilliant flavours can be created. Cool conditions are also exactly what you want for sparkling wine and Tasmania provides the fruit for most of Australia's best fizz.

In the north the vineyards are mostly on the Tamar Valley above Launceston or Pipers River. The East Coast is surprisingly warm and can make lush Pinot Noir and Chardonnay. And in the south, along the Coal, Derwent and Huon Valleys near Hobart you may sometimes lose most of your crop to frost, but some delicious wines are made. When choosing wines the producer's name is more important than the region or vintage. They won't be cheap but they should be good.

Queensland

On the face of it Queensland would seem to be getting too hot for growing quality wine grapes, let alone for producing some pretty classy reds and whites – even in the cooler far south along the border with New South Wales there is subtropical rain forest. But when the sun shines mercilessly the only way to get real consistent quality is to head up into the hills as the higher you go the cooler it gets, especially at night.

In Queensland this means the Granite Belt region, especially the vineyards around Stanthorpe on the border with New South Wales. Most of the best grapes either come from here or from South Burnett, north of Brisbane.

QUICK GUIDE ▷ *Tasmania*

Location Tasmania is the centre of cool-climate grape-growing in Australia, but has several diverse growing regions. See the map on page 178.

Grapes Intense, nutty Chardonnay, scented Pinot Gris and fine Riesling whites; silky, strawberryish Pinot Noir reds – but the real star is fabulous premium fizz.

Five to try
Apart from fizz, the wines are hard to find outside Australia.
RED
• **Tamar Ridge** Devil's Corner Pinot Noir ❷
WHITE
• **Freycinet** Chardonnay ❹
• **Pipers Brook** Riesling ❸
SPARKLING
• **Arras** ❺
• **Jansz** ❸

QUICK GUIDE ▷ *Queensland*

Location Most vineyards are in the south-eastern corner. See the map on page 178.

Grapes Shiraz is the principal grape. Cabernet Sauvignon, Chardonnay, Viognier and Verdelho also do well.

Five to try
A few larger producers export, but most wines are sold at the cellar door.
RED
• **Boireann** Shiraz-Viognier ❺
• **Clovely Estate** Shiraz Reserve ❹
• **Symphony Hill** Cabernet Sauvignon Reserve ❺
WHITE
• **Robert Channon** Verdelho ❹
• **Sirromet** Seven Scenes Chardonnay ❸

Below: Albert River in the Gold Coast hinterland is one of Australia's great wine tourism destinations.

new zealand

This is the home of benchmark New World Sauvignon Blanc, the archetypal green, tangy wine. And it's a pretty recent benchmark, too, because the first Sauvignon Blanc was planted in Marlborough – now a classic region for the grape – in 1973. It became clear almost instantly that this is what Sauvignon Blanc should taste like. Until then the only benchmark for the grape had been Sancerre and the other Sauvignons of the Loire Valley in France. New Zealand Sauvignon is more aggressive, more gooseberryish, more pungent, whereas Sancerre is rounder, more subtle – and more unreliable. Sauvignon Blanc in New Zealand, at whatever level of quality, has that hallmark gooseberry and lime zest fruit that makes it almost irresistibly mouthwatering.

New Zealand is not all Sauvignon Blanc from Marlborough – Sauvignon Blanc does well in other regions, too. In fact, New Zealand grows a variety of grapes as well as any other country in the southern hemisphere – and its reputation as a white-wine-only place is rapidly changing because of its recent successes with red grapes like Pinot Noir, Merlot and Syrah.

Generally speaking, New Zealand makes cool-climate New World styles that are lighter and more fragrant than Australian wines. It is good at grapes Australia finds more difficult, in particular subtle, mellow Pinot Noir, where New Zealand can be world class and the different regions all show encouragingly different styles. It's the same with Chardonnay. There are superb examples made all the way from up near Auckland, right down to Central Otago in the far south. Riesling is generally floral but can be sharp and thrilling in the deep south. Sparkling wine follows the Champagne model and often equals it in quality. Of the other red grapes, Cabernet Sauvignon struggles to ripen, but can be brilliant in Hawkes Bay and on Waiheke Island.

Merlot is outstanding in Hawkes Bay. Syrah, on Waiheke Island and a part of Hawkes Bay called Gimblett Gravels, is a cool, fragrant revelation.

Do regions matter?

Yes, very much. New Zealand's two islands are very different. Basically the North Island is virtually tropical in the north but cool enough for Pinot Noir at the southern end. The South Island was considered too cold for grapes until the 1970s but is now the centre of the wine industry and boasts wonderful vineyards all the way down to Central Otago in the snowfields of the south. There are some vines north of Auckland but the conditions are warm and humid, as they are around Auckland itself, though Waiheke Island out in the bay opposite Auckland is an outstanding Cabernet and Merlot producer. There are splashes of vineyard as we head south, but things don't really kick off until we get

How magical is this moonrise over the vineyards of Marlborough? How tranquil can a vineyard seem? But come daylight Marlborough is transformed into the engine-room of New Zealand's wine industry.

to Gisborne on the east coast, famous for Chardonnay and Gewürztraminer. Further south, Napier is the main city of Hawkes Bay, with its outstanding subregion of Gimblett Gravels, where Syrah, Merlot and Cabernet Sauvignon excel. Down by Wellington, Wairarapa, especially the area around the town of Martinborough, produces positively Burgundian Pinot Noirs.

Facing Wellington at the tip of South Island is Marlborough, now New Zealand's biggest wine region by far. It's centred in the Wairau Valley but spreads down the east coast through and beyond the Awatere Valley. Famous for Sauvignon, it does other whites very well, and is increasingly good at fizz and Pinot Noir. Nelson, north-west of Marlborough, is another excellent cool region, as is Waipara, heading south to Christchurch and the Canterbury Plains. It's getting very cool by now but Central Otago, in the mountains near Queenstown, provides one more brilliant vineyard region – extreme, continental, desert-like in summer and snow-covered in winter. The Pinot Noirs, Chardonnays and Rieslings reflect the extreme conditions.

Do vintages matter?

They do, but few wines need aging. Buy wines from a recent year and drink them young.

When do I drink them?

Anytime. Cult Sauvignon Blancs like Cloudy Bay will impress your wine buff friends, but you can buy equally good wine for half the price.

Can I afford them?

The wines are never going to be the cheapest to make, and most producers, realizing this, go for quality. It's worth spending a bit more for something extra good. Don't buy suspiciously cheap New Zealand wines.

Location The most southerly of the southern hemisphere wine countries.

Grapes Sauvignon Blanc, Chardonnay, Riesling (sweet and dry), Pinot Grigio and Gewürztraminer are the grapes for the best whites. Pinot Noir, the Cabernets, Merlot and Syrah are the reds. Styles vary from north to south. Hawkes Bay Sauvignon Blanc is softer than the tangy Marlborough style. Chardonnay is richer in the north. Pinot Noir likes cool Martinborough, Canterbury and Otago, but Cabernet and Merlot are happier in the north, especially Hawkes Bay and Waiheke Island.

① Auckland
② Gisborne
③ Hawke's Bay
④ Wairarapa
⑤ Nelson
⑥ Marlborough
⑦ Canterbury
⑧ Central Otago

Ten to try

RED

- **Martinborough Vineyard** Pinot Noir ❹
- **Vidal** Syrah ❸
- **Villa Maria** Reserve Cabernet Sauvignon-Merlot ❸

WHITE

- **Astrolabe** Sauvignon Blanc ❸
- **Framingham** Riesling ❷
- **Kumeu River** Chardonnay ❸

- **Vavasour** Sauvignon Blanc ❸
- **Waimea** Pinot Gris ❷

SPARKLING

- **Cloudy Bay** Pelorus ❸
- **Quartz Reef** ❸

NEW ZEALAND CLASSIFICATIONS

Labels guarantee geographic origin. The broadest designation is New Zealand, followed by North or South Island. Next come the 10 or so regions. Labels may also name specific localities and individual vineyards.

south africa

South Africa has been on a steep learning curve since the demise of the apartheid regime in the early 1990s and its subsequent emergence from international isolation. It is rediscovering its past as well as forging an exciting, innovative future. A new generation is taking over vineyards and wineries and the results are dramatic.

South Africa makes all possible styles of wine, from green and tangy whites, through broad-beamed, nutty whites, to rich toasty ones; and reds from light and juicy Cinsauts, through strawberry-soft Pinot Noirs and challenging, blackcurranty Cabernets to spicy, booming Shiraz and Pinotage. There are fortifieds, too, both light and dry sherry-like ones and sweet, dark versions in the style of port.

The range of grapes encompasses all the international favourites – Cabernet Sauvignon, Merlot, Chardonnay, Sauvignon Blanc – and there's Chenin Blanc as well, mostly used for everyday whites. But carefully made Chenin from old vines is good stuff and is a good-value star in the Cape. The country's speciality is the Pinotage grape, which makes both bright, juicy reds and seriously heavyweight ones. It has an unashamed toasted marshmallow and damson flavour that is unique and thrilling at its best.

The local African population have been working in the vineyards for generations. The difference now is that thanks to Fairtrade and Black empowerment schemes they are starting to share in the benefits and profits.

Quality in South Africa is still uneven compared to
Chile or Australia – countries with which it is competing
on the international market. But one thing in South
Africa's favour is that much of the progress is being led
by single-estate wines, not those of vast corporations.

Do regions matter?
Yes, very much. Many of the most exciting wines are
coming from newer vineyards in cool, maritime areas
like Elim, Cape Point, Constantia, Elgin and Walker Bay
in the south, and Tygerberg and Darling in the west.
Others are from old bush-vine plantings scattered
through the warmer regions such as inland Swartland,
Paarl and Franschhoek. Stellenbosch is the traditional
centre of South African wine and you'll see that name
on a lot of labels.

Do vintages matter?
Most whites should be drunk young. Only the most
serious red contenders will benefit from much aging.

When do I drink them?
Anytime, but most reds need food.

Can I afford them?
Almost always, yes. Very few wines are very overpriced,
although South Africa is itching to establish some super-
premium wines at super-premium prices. Chenin is
particularly well priced and there are numerous good-
value Sauvignon Blanc, Pinotage and Shiraz wines.

SOUTH AFRICA CLASSIFICATIONS

The Wine of Origin (WO) system divides wine-producing
areas into regions, districts, wards, estates and single
vineyards. Varietal, vintaged wines for both export and
the local market must be made from at least 85% of the
named grape and vintage.

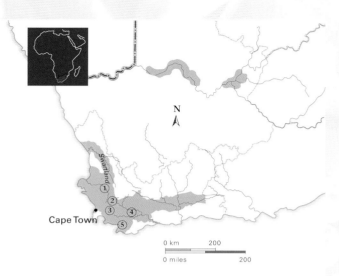

N

Swartland

Cape Town

| 0 km | 200 |
| 0 miles | 200 |

① Swartland
② Paarl
③ Stellenbosch
④ Robertson
⑤ Overberg

QUICK GUIDE ▷ *South Africa*

Location Most of the wine regions are clustered around Cape Town. Paarl and Stellenbosch, districts of the vast Coastal Region, are the best established. Robertson is good for whites. Overberg (including Walker Bay) in the far south is good for Pinot Noir. Elim, Cape Point, Tygerberg and Darling are excellent for whites. Swartland has good Syrah as well as whites.

Grapes Pinotage is South Africa's own red grape. Cabernet Sauvignon and Merlot are popular. Syrah/Shiraz and other Rhône reds, and even California's Zinfandel, are joining the repertoire. Chardonnay and Sauvignon Blanc are both widely grown whites and there's also some Riesling. Chenin Blanc is used for the simplest whites and a few high-quality ones.

Local jargon *Wine of Origin (WO)* – this official statement on the label guarantees the wine's area of origin, grape variety or varieties and vintage. *Estate wine* – wine that is grown and made on a registered estate, usually a sign of good quality.

Ten to try
RED
- **Beyerskloof** Pinotage ②
- **Bouchard Finlayson** Pinot Noir ④
- **Fairview** Shiraz ④
- **Porcupine Ridge** Syrah ②
- **Rustenberg** John X Merriman ③
- **Steenberg** Merlot ③

WHITE
- **Neil Ellis** Groenekloof Sauvignon Blanc ②
- **Ken Forrester** Chenin Blanc ①
- **Hamilton Russell** Chardonnay ③
- **Vergelegen** Sauvignon Blanc ③

other wine countries

The culture of drinking wine is catching on all over the world, especially in Asia, and more and more countries now want to produce their own wine rather than rely on imports from the well-established wine regions in Europe, North and South America and Australia.

China

China officially promotes wine (especially red, a lucky colour in China) but its potential remains unfulfilled as most Chinese are reluctant to drink it. However, demand is increasing in the cities – China recently overtook the UK in consumption – and homegrown premium wines are emerging, helped by foreign investment. Massive new plantings every year include Chardonnay and Cabernet Sauvignon, along with traditional Chinese, German and Russian varieties. China now has the fourth largest vineyard acreage in the world, with large plantings in Shandong to the east, but perhaps the best results coming from the west, especially from Ningxia and, above all, the Helan Mountains.

Cyprus

Cyprus has old vines on high sites in the cool Troodos mountains that are beginning to show real quality. The Kyperounda winery is outstanding. Modernization is slow as the vineyards are divided into so many small holdings. There are good reds from the indigenous Maratheftiko grape and whites from Xynisteri. Commandaria, a rich, sweet, amber wine, has been famous since the Crusades but is currently more of a historical footnote.

India

India's climate is generally unsuitable for wine production and only a small percentage of the vines planted are used for wine. However, wine consumption is increasing rapidly amoung the young urban professionals and the potential for growth is there. Nashik is India's largest grape-growing region. So far whites are more successful than reds, with Sula Vineyards making an attractive Sauvignon Blanc. Fratelli makes fine Chenin and good Chardonnay and Chateau Indage, east of Mumbai, produces good fizz. Grover Vineyards, based in the hills near Bangalore, use the famous and ubiquitous Frenchman Michel Rolland as a consultant.

Israel

Fine wine is being made in the cooler regions – Upper Galilee, Golan Heights and Judean Hills. Viticulture is technologically advanced and wineries tend to be up-to-date. There are good Bordeaux blends based on Cabernet Sauvignon, dessert wines and, of course, kosher wines. These last are usually suitable for vegans and vegetarians.

Right: You might think Lebanon must be a hot place for growing grapes but in fact the Bekaa Valley has long, cold winters.

Japan

The Japanese have been interested in wine for a long time but most of the wines are multi-country blends or made from indigenous varieties such as Koshu. Despite humid growing conditions, wine is produced in almost every province.

Lebanon

Lebanon's finest producers are Chateau Musar, Chateau Ksara, Chateau St Thomas and Domaine de Tourelles, making world-class spicy, chocolaty reds, but there are other promising new boutique wineries now snapping at their heels. Most wineries are in the Bekaa Valley.

North Africa

North African wine is in a transitional stage. The massive growth of the vineyards of Morocco, Tunisia and Algeria in the past was fuelled by the need of France, the colonial power, for cheap, alcoholic reds for its blending market. That market is long gone but recent European investment in Morocco and Tunisia, especially by Castel Frères, is encouraging the development of spicy reds and rosés. The Islamists' success following the Arab spring may affect progress.

Thailand

Thailand's high-altitude vineyards are beginning to produce some tasty wines, especially from Shiraz and Chenin. There are also some floating vineyards in the Mekong Delta which make pleasant rosé wines at least.

Turkey

Turkey's enormous potential is yet to be realized. It is one of the world's largest grape producers but only a tiny percentage ends up as wine because of a Muslim population and a traditional antipathy to wine. Doluca and Kavaklidere are two well-known producers but more good companies are emerging, as well as indigenous red grapes such as Bogazkere, Öküzgözü and Kalecik Karasi.

Below: Wine-drinking in China is a new phenomenon and it is still rare to see women drinking in public.

appellation decoder

The trouble with buying European wines is that many are named according to where they come from – the appellation – rather than what's in them: the grape variety or varieties. And if you have heard of a wine but aren't sure exactly which region the appellation is in, it can be a hassle to find it in a shop or on a wine list. To help you sort things out this table brings together appellations, their major styles, their regions and their key grape varieties.   KEY   ● Red   ○ White

Name	● / ○	Region	Major Grape Varieties
ALOXE-CORTON	●	Côte de Beaune, Burgundy, France	Pinot Noir
ASTI (sweet/sparkling)	○	Piedmont, North-west Italy	Muscat (called Moscato here)
BAIRRADA	●	Portugal	Baga
BANDOL	●	Provence, France	Mourvèdre/Grenache/Cinsaut
BARBARESCO	●	Piedmont, North-west Italy	Nebbiolo
BARDOLINO	●	Veneto, North-east Italy	Corvina
BAROLO	●	Piedmont, North-west Italy	Nebbiolo
BEAUJOLAIS	●	Burgundy, France	Gamay
BEAUNE	●	Côte de Beaune, Burgundy, France	Pinot Noir
BERGERAC	● / ○	South-West France	● Cabernet Sauvignon & Franc/ Merlot; ○ Sémillon/Sauvignon Blanc
BONNEZEAUX (sweet)	○	Loire Valley, France	Chenin Blanc
BOURGUEIL	●	Loire Valley, France	Cabernet Franc
BROUILLY/CÔTE DE BROUILLY	●	Beaujolais, Burgundy, France	Gamay
BRUNELLO DI MONTALCINO	●	Tuscany, Central Italy	Sangiovese
CAHORS	●	South-West France	Malbec/Merlot/Tannat
CHABLIS	○	Burgundy, France	Chardonnay
CHAMBOLLE-MUSIGNY	●	Côte de Nuits, Burgundy, France	Pinot Noir
CHAMPAGNE (sparkling)	○	Champagne, France	Chardonnay/Pinot Noir/Pinot Meunier
CHASSAGNE-MONTRACHET	● / ○	Côte de Beaune, Burgundy, France	● Pinot Noir; ○ Chardonnay
CHÂTEAUNEUF-DU-PAPE	● / ○	Southern Rhône Valley, France	● Grenache/Syrah; ○ Roussanne
CHÉNAS	●	Beaujolais, Burgundy, France	Gamay
CHIANTI	●	Tuscany, Central Italy	Sangiovese
CHIROUBLES	●	Beaujolais, Burgundy, France	Gamay
CONDRIEU	○	Northern Rhône Valley, France	Viognier
CORBIÈRES	●	Languedoc-Roussillon, France	Carignan/Grenache/Cinsaut

Name	● / ○	Region	Major Grape Varieties
CORNAS	●	Northern Rhône Valley, France	*Syrah*
COSTIÈRES DE NÎMES	●	Languedoc-Roussillon, France	*Carignan/Grenache/Mourvèdre/Syrah*
CÔTE DE NUITS-VILLAGES	●	Côte de Nuits, Burgundy, France	*Pinot Noir*
CÔTE-RÔTIE	●	Northern Rhône Valley, France	*Syrah*
COTEAUX DU LANGUEDOC	●	Languedoc-Roussillon, France	*Carignan/Grenache*
COTEAUX DU LAYON (sweet)	○	Loire Valley, France	*Chenin Blanc*
CÔTES DU ROUSSILLON	●	Languedoc-Roussillon, France	*Carignan/Cinsaut/Grenache*
CROZES-HERMITAGE	● / ○	Northern Rhône Valley, France	● *Syrah;* ○ *Marsanne/Roussanne*
DÃO	●	Portugal	*Touriga Nacional/Tinta Roriz (Tempranillo)*
DÔLE	●	Switzerland	*Pinot Noir/Gamay*
ENTRE-DEUX-MERS	○	Bordeaux, France	*Sémillon/Sauvignon Blanc*
FAUGÈRES	●	Languedoc-Roussillon, France	*Carignan/Grenache/Syrah*
FITOU	●	Languedoc-Roussillon, France	*Carignan/Cinsaut/Grenache*
FLEURIE	●	Beaujolais, Burgundy, France	*Gamay*
FRASCATI	○	Lazio, Central Italy	*Malvasia/Trebbiano*
GAVI	○	Piedmont, North-west Italy	*Cortese*
GEVREY-CHAMBERTIN	●	Côte de Nuits, Burgundy, France	*Pinot Noir*
GIGONDAS	●	Southern Rhône Valley, France	*Grenache*
GIVRY	●	Côte Chalonnaise, Burgundy, France	*Pinot Noir*
GRAVES	● / ○	Bordeaux, France	● *Cabernet Sauvignon & Franc/ Merlot;* ○ *Sémillon/Sauvignon Blanc*
HERMITAGE	● / ○	Northern Rhône Valley, France	● *Syrah;* ○ *Marsanne/Roussanne*
JULIÉNAS	●	Beaujolais, Burgundy, France	*Gamay*
LISTRAC	●	Haut-Médoc, Bordeaux, France	*Cabernet Sauvignon & Franc/Merlot*
MÂCON/MÂCON-VILLAGES	○	Mâconnais, Burgundy, France	*Chardonnay*
MARGAUX	●	Haut-Médoc, Bordeaux, France	*Cabernet Sauvignon & Franc/Merlot*
MÉDOC/HAUT-MÉDOC	●	Bordeaux, France	*Cabernet Sauvignon & Franc/Merlot*
MERCUREY	● / ○	Côte Chalonnaise, Burgundy, France	● *Pinot Noir;* ○ *Chardonnay*
MEURSAULT	○	Côte de Beaune, Burgundy, France	*Chardonnay*
MINERVOIS	●	Languedoc-Roussillon, France	*Grenache/Syrah/Mourvèdre*
MONTAGNY	○	Côte Chalonnaise, Burgundy, France	*Chardonnay*
MOREY-ST-DENIS	●	Côte de Nuits, Burgundy, France	*Pinot Noir*
MORGON	●	Beaujolais, Burgundy, France	*Gamay*
MOULIN-À-VENT	●	Beaujolais, Burgundy, France	*Gamay*
MOULIS	●	Haut-Médoc, Bordeaux, France	*Cabernet Sauvignon & Franc/Merlot*
MUSCADET	○	Loire Valley, France	*Muscadet (aka Melon de Bourgogne)*
NUITS-ST-GEORGES	●	Côte de Nuits, Burgundy, France	*Pinot Noir*
ORVIETO	○	Umbria, Central Italy	*Trebbiano*
PAUILLAC	●	Haut-Médoc, Bordeaux, France	*Cabernet Sauvignon & Franc/Merlot*
PESSAC-LÉOGNAN	● / ○	Bordeaux, France	● *Cabernet Sauvignon & Franc/ Merlot;* ○ *Sémillon/Sauvignon Blanc*

Name	● / ○	Region	Major Grape Varieties
POMEROL	●	Bordeaux, France	*Merlot/Cabernet Sauvignon & Franc*
POMMARD	●	Côte de Beaune, Burgundy, France	*Pinot Noir*
POUILLY- FUISSÉ	○	Mâconnais, Burgundy, France	*Chardonnay*
POUILLY-FUMÉ	○	Loire Valley, France	*Sauvignon Blanc*
POUILLY-SUR-LOIRE	○	Loire Valley, France	*Chasselas*
PRIORAT	●	Spain	*Garnacha (Grenache)*
PULIGNY-MONTRACHET	○	Côte de Beaune, Burgundy, France	*Chardonnay*
QUARTS DE CHAUME (sweet)	○	Loire Valley, France	*Chenin Blanc*
RÉGNIÉ	●	Beaujolais, Burgundy, France	*Gamay*
RÍAS BAIXAS	○	Spain	*Albariño*
RIBERA DEL DUERO	●	Spain	*Tempranillo (called Tinto Fino here)*
RIOJA	● / ○	Spain	● *Tempranillo/Garnacha (Grenache);* ○ *Viura*
RULLY	● / ○	Côte Chalonnaise, Burgundy, France	● *Pinot Noir;* ○ *Chardonnay*
ST-AMOUR	●	Beaujolais, Burgundy, France	*Gamay*
ST-CHINIAN	●	Languedoc-Roussillon, France	*Carignan/Cinsaut/Grenache*
ST-ÉMILION	●	Bordeaux, France	*Merlot/Cabernet Sauvignon & Franc*
ST-ESTÈPHE	●	Haut-Médoc, Bordeaux, France	*Cabernet Sauvignon & Franc/Merlot*
ST-JOSEPH	● / ○	Northern Rhône Valley, France	● *Syrah;* ○ *Marsanne/Roussanne*
ST-JULIEN	●	Haut-Médoc, Bordeaux, France	*Cabernet Sauvignon & Franc/Merlot*
ST-NICOLAS-DE-BOURGUEIL	●	Loire Valley, France	*Cabernet Franc*
ST-VÉRAN	○	Mâconnais, Burgundy, France	*Chardonnay*
SANCERRE	○ / ●	Loire Valley, France	○ *Sauvignon Blanc;* ● *Pinot Noir*
SAUMUR	○ / ●	Loire Valley, France	○ *Chenin Blanc;* ● *Cabernet Franc*
SAUTERNES (sweet)	○	Bordeaux, France	*Sémillon/Sauvignon Blanc*
SAVENNIÈRES	○	Loire Valley, France	*Chenin Blanc*
SOAVE	○	Veneto, North-east Italy	*Garganega/Trebbiano*
TORO	●	Spain	*Tempranillo (called Tinto del Toro here)*
VACQUEYRAS	●	Southern Rhône Valley, France	*Grenache/Syrah/Mourvèdre*
VALPOLICELLA	●	Veneto, North-east Italy	*Corvina*
VINO NOBILE DI MONTEPULCIANO	●	Tuscany, Central Italy	*Sangiovese*
VOLNAY	●	Côte de Beaune, Burgundy, France	*Pinot Noir*
VOSNE-ROMANÉE	●	Côte de Nuits, Burgundy, France	*Pinot Noir*
VOUGEOT	●	Côte de Nuits, Burgundy, France	*Pinot Noir*
VOUVRAY	○	Loire Valley, France	*Chenin Blanc*

the most useful words in wine

Acidity Acid, naturally present in grapes, gives wine its intense and refreshing qualities.

Appellation An officially designated place of origin. In Europe many wines have to be made from a specified grape variety or varieties to qualify for the appellation name.

Barrel aging Time spent maturing in wood, often 225-litre oak barrels called **barriques**. The wine takes on oak flavours from the wood.

Barrel-fermented Describes wine fermented in oak barrels. Like barrel aging, this process gives the wine characteristic oak flavours.

Blend Mixture of wines of different grapes, styles, origin or age. Blending is carried out to improve the balance of the wine, or to maintain a consistent style.

Botrytis or **noble rot** A fungus which sometimes attacks grapes, reducing the water content and concentrating the sugar and acidity, making the grapes ideal for making intense golden, sweet wines such as Sauternes.

Climate A critical influence on the style and quality of wine. Cool climate areas such as Germany, Champagne and Oregon are at the coolest limits for grape ripening and are good for reserved, elegant styles. In warm-climate areas vines ripen easily but often need to be irrigated. Warm-climate wines are rich and high in alcohol. Red grapes generally need a warmer climate than white grapes.

Cold fermentation Long, slow fermentation at low temperature to extract freshness and fruit flavour from the grapes. Crucial for white wines in warm climates.

Corked Term used to describe wine tainted by a contaminated cork. Corked wine has a mouldy, musty smell.

Cru French term meaning 'growth', used to refer to the wine of an individual vineyard and often in conjunction with a quality ranking, such as Premier Cru (First Growth).

Cuvée Literally the contents of a *cuve* or vat. The term refers to a particular blend, either of different grape varieties or of wine from selected barrels and is used to distinguish, for example, a producer's top Chardonnay from his everyday Chardonnay.

Domaine A wine estate, particularly in Burgundy.

Dry A wine that is not perceptibly sweet.

Enologist A wine scientist.

Estate-bottled A wine made and bottled by a single property, though this may encompass several different vineyards. Equivalent terms are **mis en bouteille au château/domaine** in French, **imbottigliato all'origine** in Italian and **Erzeugerabfüllung** or **Gutsabfüllung** in German.

Fermentation The process of transforming sugar into alcohol.

Late-harvest or **vendange tardive** (France) Wine made from super-ripe grapes picked after the normal harvest. Late-harvest wines are usually sweet.

Malolactic fermentation A natural process which turns harsh malic acid in a wine into softer-tasting lactic acid. Malolactic fermentation is prevented in many white wines to preserve the refreshing bite.

Négociant French term for a merchant or shipper who buys wine or grapes from growers, then matures, maybe blends and bottles the wine for sale.

New World The non-European wine-producing countries that have come to the world's attention since the 1970s. The United States, Australia, New Zealand, Chile, Argentina and South Africa are all New World countries. By extension, New World is also an attitude of mind that embraces new technology in the attempt to produce fresher, fruitier wines.

Noble rot *See* botrytis.

Oak The wood used almost exclusively to make barrels for fermenting and aging fine wines. Oak barrels contribute characteristic toasty vanilla flavours and a rounded taste. Oak chips dunked into the wine or even oak flavouring are cheaper alternatives.

Old vines or **vieilles vignes** (France) Mature vines producing grapes with intense flavours. There are no legal definitions of how old a vine has to be to qualify, but the term is a fairly reliable indicator of quality.

Old World The traditional wine-producing countries of Europe, home to most of the world's established wine styles and grape varieties. Old World can also refer to wines from other countries that seek to emulate these styles.

Producer The company that makes the wine and the most important consideration when choosing a wine. In the same region and the same vintage a good producer will make far better wine than a poor one, and the wine won't necessarily be any more expensive.

Reserva (Spain) and **riserva** (Italy) Legally defined terms for wines that receive extra aging either in oak barrels or in bottle (or both) before they go on sale. These terms carry quality connotations. Elsewhere 'reserve' has no legal definition and does not necessarily indicate a higher quality of wine.

Residual sugar Sugar left over in the wine after fermentation is complete. A perceptible level of residual sugar makes the wine taste sweet.

Single-vineyard Wines with real individuality tend to be made using grapes from just one vineyard.

Tannin The bitter, mouth-drying component in red wines, which is harsh when young but adds depth to the flavour and is crucial to a wine's ability to age.

Terroir A French term used to denote the combination of soil, climate and exposure to the sun – that is, the natural physical environment of the vine.

Varietal Wine made from, and named after, a single or dominant grape variety.

Vendange tardive *See* late-harvest.

Vieilles vignes *See* old vines.

Vinification The process of turning grapes into wine.

Vintage The year's grape harvest, also used to describe the wine of a particular year.

Viticulture Vine-growing and vineyard management.

Vitis vinifera The species of vine, native to Europe and Central Asia, that all the classic grape varieties belong to.

Winemaker The person responsible for controlling the vinification process.

Yield One of the most important factor in determining the quality of a wine. The lower the quantity of grapes each vine is allowed to produce, the more intense the juice in the grapes and the flavours in the wine will be.